UNDIVIDED LOYALTY

Retirement Plan Governance and How to Reduce and Manage Fiduciary Risk

Charles J. Yovino

Published by Global HR GRC LLC®
Atlanta, Georgia

Undivided Loyalty

Cover design by Vada Caldwell, Mark Bray, Cindy Prince and Phillip Yovino.

Cover photo by John Lund/Blend Images and used with permission under a license agreement.

ISBN-13: 978-1-7320385-0-9

Printed in the United States of America

"The distinguishing or overriding duty of a fiduciary is the obligation of undivided loyalty."[1]

"A trustee is held to something stricter than the morals of the marketplace. Not honesty alone but the punctilio of an honor the most sensitive is then the standard of behavior. As to this, there has developed a tradition that is unbending and inveterate. Uncompromising rigidity has been the attitude of courts of equity when petitioned to undermine **the rule of undivided loyalty** *by the 'disintegrating erosion' of particular exception."*[2]

---

[1] <u>Australian Securities and Investments Commission v. Citigroup Global Markets Australia Pty Limited (No. 4)</u>, (2007) FCA 963, paragraph 289 (2007) 62 ACSR 427, Federal Court (Australia) (Cites omitted, italics added.)

[2] From Chief Judge Benjamin Cardozo's opinion in <u>Meinhard v. Salmon</u>, 164 N.E. 545, 546 (NY 1928) (Emphasis in italics and bold added.)

This book is dedicated to my family, which has always provided me with support, encouragement, and inspiration.
They are the best of the best.

This book is also dedicated to the men and women who have unselfishly and tirelessly served on plan committees. They are largely responsible for the largest capital formation in the history of the world, which has helped to make this country great.

I hope *Undivided Loyalty* will help you and your successors continue this great achievement.

Acknowledgements

This book reflects the aggregation of almost 35 years of experience working with retirement plans. I've benefited from all of the professionals with whom I have worked, from my early days as a tax associate in a law firm, to my years with the Internal Revenue Service's Employee Plans Division, and finally my time with PwC.[3] I've been blessed to have been able to work with many exceptional individuals and teams. I hope that what I've learned from these experiences are correctly reflected within these pages. Any errors or omissions are entirely mine.

I also wish to thank my many clients with whom I worked while at PwC. Again, I have been blessed to have worked with outstanding companies and people within those companies. The quality of the people, their capacity for innovation, and their strong moral compass never ceased to amaze me. Business decisions, especially those involving employees, are never easy. While they impact employees, you (my clients) were always able to see that your decisions impacted *people and families*.

This book was originally conceived as I approached retirement. My wife, Vada, encouraged me to write it and put off "true retirement" while I wrote, researched, and rewrote. She's always been my biggest supporter and fan, a tireless proofreader, and a true partner.

Thanks also go to my family: my children Cindy Prince, Phillip Yovino, and Mark Bray; my sister Olive, and my parents. Cindy's been my proofreader from her time in middle school, and still is one of the best writers and editors I have ever known. She read and helped rewrite numerous articles and published pieces, making me look like a better writer than I am. Phillip has always been my sounding board to divine whether something made sense and was clear. If his wit didn't cut through my work, that meant it was good. Mark brought the artistic perspective, and his imprint is clearly on the cover of the

---

[3] PwC is also known as PricewaterhouseCoopers LLP, and is one of the four largest professional services firms in the world. I worked with PwC and the legacy firm of Coopers & Lybrand from 1988 until 2016.

book. My sister has always been by my side and she's been a blessing to me every day. Of course, everything I've accomplished is thanks to my parents, Genevieve and Phil Yovino.

Special thanks also go to my editor, Beverly (Bev) Barna. She's worked with me on articles for many years and has the uncanny talent of being able to improve business and technical text without diminishing the meaning. I've never worked with an editor with such skills! However, even more than being an editor, she's been a great counselor as I found my style and worked through numerous drafts. I'll never forget her advice when I was pressed to meet a self-imposed deadline and still wasn't completely happy with what I had written. She said in an email one evening, "Looking forward to seeing what ya got *when the time is right*." Thank you again, Bev, for helping me have the patience to wait until it was right.

There wouldn't be a book without my "trusted friends" who took the time to tirelessly read different portions of various drafts. They are all exceptional professionals whose input and insights were invaluable. In the aggregate, they represent over 300 years of focused experience working on governance, retirement plans or risk management. They each often served as my guide on this exciting journey during my career and in writing this book. My readers and trusted friends, with whom I felt comfortable enough to subject this book to their critical eye, are: Bill Brossman, Phil Canning, Jana Dovgan, Luan Fox, Mike Giles, Ann O'Connell, Howard Pianko, Susan Reisner, Allen Roberson, Stephanie Strecker, Wendy Vitale, and Sandy Wheeler. My friends, I am forever in your debt.

Next, I want to thank all of my colleagues from my time working at the IRS and PwC. I'm sure that I will inadvertently omit some people, and for that I apologize. I do, however, want to thank each of my colleagues who, in their own way, helped to expand my knowledge and experience and made this book possible. At the IRS, this includes Steve Levanthal, Marty Slate, Ira Cohen, Jack Riddle, Bob Architect, Gus Fields, Charles Lockwood, Bill Hulteng, Kathy Marticello, Paulette Tino, Roland Cross, Jim Holland, and Gretchen Young.

At PwC, my closest compatriots on retirement plan governance included Wendy Vitale, Kristin Moye, Caren Bianco, Isaac Buchen, Amy Bert, Terry Richardson, Anne Waidmann, Jennifer James,

Stephanie Strecker, Mike Giles, Tracey Giddings, Joe Henderson and Joe Olivieri. Although not on governance specifically, I want to acknowledge the help I've received on compliance, risk management, and just being a better advisor, from Ann O'Connell, Jeff Davis, Joe Walshe, Susan Lennon, Amy Bergner, Mike Boro, Carrie Duarte, Jack Abraham, Cindy Fraterrigo, Andy Dahle, John Griffin, Harold Dankner, Jim Freeman, David Phillips, Rick Troy, Reed Keller, Frank Raiti, John Caplan, Ted Barna, Linda Prager, Don Weber and Jerry Dubner.

Finally, I want to acknowledge individuals who served as bookends for my legal and consulting career. Jane Edmisten was my mentor after law school and for years after. No one ever drove me harder, demanded more, or expected as much. Every legal battle was one she believe in, and losing was never an option.

The other bookend for my career are George Beckwith and Felicia Robinson: two friends who took the time to read the proof of the book and provide quotes. They are both outstanding executives who are exceptionally busy, and I'm extremely grateful they fit reading Undivided Loyalty into their packed schedules. It seems the individuals who are the best at what they do always seem to find time to do more.

Charlie Yovino
March 2018

Table of Contents

Prologue

Why This Book?

There are countless books about governance. They address how to run a business, a not-for-profit, even a government. There are not, however, many books that address retirement plan governance.

Having worked with retirement plans for over 35 years, frequently working closely with retirement committees, I've seen many well-run plans. But I've also seen others where there has been room for significant improvement. Often, the difference is whether the plan committee thinks about governance, and whether they know how to apply governance to a retirement plan.

I've spent a large percentage of my last 14 years at PwC working with companies to help them develop and improve their plan governance. To a certain extent, this book is an aggregation of what worked well and what resonated with plan committees. It is, in essence, a pragmatic approach built on the application of universal governance principles.

But why a book specific to retirement plan governance? One might argue that the principles of governance are similar whether one looks at business governance, not-for-profit governance, governmental governance, or retirement plan governance. While the governance principles for these areas may be the same, I hope that an explanation of how they are applied in the unique environment of retirement plans will provide more than just an incremental benefit.

If the reader is well versed in governance, this book should build upon that foundational knowledge and provide insights into how to extend one's governance knowledge to one's retirement plans. For the governance "novice," this book should aid in the understanding of what governance is and how it can be used to improve a plan's operation and performance.

The Audience for This Book

The principal audience for this book are the members of the governing or oversight body for the retirement plan (and by extension their support team of advisors, consultants and vendors). For private sector retirement plans, the oversight or governing body is typically called the plan committee, but other names are also used. Some plans call the oversight body the "trustees," even though they do not hold the plan assets. Other plans call the oversight body by the functional area that it oversees, such as the "administrative committee" or the "investment committee." Still others use the name "fiduciary committee," "plan committee," or "plan board."

Whatever the terminology, this book is designed to assist the body that is responsible for the oversight of the retirement plan. This obviously includes the plan committee (or other oversight body), but it also includes their advisors, legal counsel, consultants and vendors that support the plan, and thereby the committee. For simplicity, the term "plan committee" is used to refer to the oversight and governing body.

This book is also tailored for more complex private sector retirement plans[4] and non-profits (such as colleges, universities and hospitals). Although many of the principles discussed in this book are applicable to governmental plans, they are intentionally not the target audience for this book. There are enough differences and unique situations applicable to governmental plans, that the topic of governmental plan governance is left for another book.

---

[4] The focus of this book is also on U.S. plans, but global plan governance is addressed at pages 156-158.

The Business Case for Great Plan Governance

"Risk comes from not knowing what you're doing."
Warren Buffett

Why Worry? (The Retirement Plan Environment)

There are around 685,000 private retirement plans in the United States, and the fiduciaries for these plans are responsible for over $8.3 *trillion* of retirement plan assets.[5] This represents about 27% of the market value of all companies listed on the New York Stock Exchange and NASDAQ *combined*.[6] It is a staggering amount of wealth—in fact, the greatest concentration of wealth in the world.[7]

---

[5] Dep't of Labor Employee Benefits Security Admin., *Private Pension Plan Bulletin. Abstract of 2014 Form 5500 Annual Reports* (2016),at 1, *available at* http://www.dol.gov/sites/default/files/ebsa/researchers/statistics/retireme nt-bulletins/private-pension-plan-bulletins-abstract-2014. Public (or governmental) retirement plans in the United States are not included in these plan and asset counts. In 2015, about 90,000 U.S. governmental entities had pension assets (*i.e.,* excluding defined contribution assets) over $3.8 trillion. Phillip Vidal, *Annual Survey of Public Pensions: State- and Locally-Administered Defined Benefit Data Summary Brief: 2015* (U.S. Census Bureau 2016), at 1 and 3, *available at* http://www.census.gov/content/dam/Census/library/publications/2016/eco n/g15-aspp-sl.pdf

[6] The NYSE and Nasdaq are the two largest stock exchanges in the world, based on the market capitalization of the stock traded on those exchanges. As of February 28, 2017, the market capitalization of the companies listed on the NYSE was $21.078 trillion. http://www.nyxdata.com/nysedata/asp/factbook/viewer_edition.asp?mode=t ables&key=333&category=5.
As of 2015, the market capitalization of the companies listed on Nasdaq was over $9.1 trillion. Nasdaq, *Nasdaq Corporate Overview* 2 (2015), *available at* http://business.nasdaq.com/media/Nasdaq%20Corporate%20Factsheet%202 015_tcm5044-11606.pdf.

[7] *Pension Markets in Focus* (OECD 2016), at 5 ("[p]rivate pension assets are worth more than USD 38 trillion...."), *available at*

It is a cornerstone of America's retirement security, and a vital component for hundreds of millions of current and future retirees.

One would think that the oversight by plan fiduciaries would be directed by clear guiding principles that can be easily understood and applied, and that there would be an established framework supporting a structured or methodical approach. Similarly, one would think that the retirement plan role for a company's management would be clear, as would knowing how management will interact and relate to the plan's fiduciaries.

Unfortunately, that is not the case.

For the vast majority of plan committee members in the United States, overseeing their retirement plan is not their primary role.[8] Indeed, the vast majority of plan fiduciaries spend less than three percent of their time on plan matters,[9] and training can be lacking.[10]

This situation is further aggravated by the fact that the standards to which fiduciaries are held are inherently unclear and difficult to interpret. A classic example is how does one select a vendor when the standard is "prudence," which is nebulous at best? Should one pick the highest quality vendor, the lowest cost vendor, or use some other criteria? In addition, the standards are often fraught with conflict when the fiduciaries also serve as

---

www.oecd.org/daf/fin/private-pensions/Pension-Markets-in-Focus-2016.pdf. The market capitalization of listed domestic companies in the world is $64.82 trillion. *Market Capitalization of Listed Domestic Companies* (The World Bank 2017), *available at* data.worldbank.org/indicators/CM.MKT.LCAP.CD. In 2016 "pension assets relative to GDP reached 62.1%...." (footnote omitted). *Global Pension Assets Study 2017* (Willis Towers Watson 2017) at 4, *available at* www.willistowerswatson.com/en/insights/2017/01/global-pensions-asset-study-2017.

[8] Essentially, all plan members are company executives or board members. *The New Governance Landscape – Implications from the 2011 Towers Watson U.S. Retirement Plan Governance Survey* (Towers Watson 2011) at 12.

[9] Calculated based on over 80% of plan committees meeting quarterly or less frequently, meeting durations lasting four hours or less, and meetings comprising ¼ of the member's time commitment (for a total of 64 hours per year). *See The New Governance Landscape supra* at 16 for meeting frequency.

[10] *See e.g., The New Governance Landscape supra* at 10.

members of the company's management team.[11] The point at which one's management role ends and one's fiduciary responsibility begins is often unclear and ill-defined, creating tensions between the two roles.

These questions, these ambiguities, and these dilemmas are, unfortunately, stacked on top of the largest pool of assets in the world. As a retirement plan committee member, you own the risks associated with the plan *personally*. Yes, you are personally liable for civil damages *and* can be criminally convicted.[12] For most individuals, these are unparalleled personal and financial risks.

As a plan committee member *and* a fiduciary, you have hundreds, even thousands of areas that can go wrong. The Internal Revenue Code and Department of Labor rules are complex, and it can take years just to gain a familiarity with them. A growing body of case law represents ever-expanding adversarial positions between certain plan committees and participants. The data and technological requirements to run the plan are staggering, and often built on a multitude of systems that can be impossible to unravel. Then there are further complexities added from business combinations and spin-offs, changes in vendors and staff, and the evolution of the plan terms. It isn't surprising that researchers have found in the US and other countries that one-third or more of retirement programs "... suffer systematic, wholesale administration errors and omissions."[13]

---

[11] The concepts of prudence and conflicts of interest are explored in detail starting at page228.

[12] As a fiduciary you can also be liable for the acts or omissions of other fiduciaries. ERISA § 405(a), 26 U.S.C. § 1105(a). The concept of co-fiduciary liability is discussed further in the chapter on Fiduciary Responsibility. *See* page 254.

[13] Bernard Marr, Jocelyn Blackwell and Kenneth Donaldson, *Restoring Confidence: Measuring and Managing Performance in Pensions* (Cranfield University School of Management December 2006) at 4, http://umbraco.ap-institute.com/media/14130/pm_in_the_pensions_industry.pdf, citing one-third of plans "... suffer systematic, wholesale administration errors and omissions." While there is no recent data on the percentage of US retirement plans that have errors, IRS Employee Plans agents have told me that the majority of plans have some plan errors. This is supported by a 401(k) compliance study the IRS

Amid this profound complexity and lofty risk, hundreds or thousands of employee retirement plan participants and their beneficiaries[14] are relying on the plan committee for their retirement security. They depend on the committee to make sure the plan is operating correctly, the plan document is being followed, they are getting the right benefit, their money is being managed well, and costs are being controlled. A study done by Towers Watson[15] in 2012 found that "[n]early two-thirds of responding employees say their company's retirement program is their primary means of saving for retirement."[16] The vast majority of the employees who work for your company have trustingly placed their retirement eggs in the basket that you are holding.

They deserve your undivided loyalty and that of the plan committee as a whole.

Moving from Chaos to Order

The plan committee can tame this potential chaos and risk by adopting strong governance. This isn't a new or novel theory. There are scores of studies showing how corporations with better corporate governance have better operating performance and market valuations.[17] Although not quite as numerous, there are also studies that show that plans with better governance achieve

---

conducted in 2000, which found 44% of the plans reviewed had compliance errors. U.S. Gov't Accountability Office, *Private Pensions – IRS Can Improve the Quality and Usefulness of Compliance Studies,* GAO-02-353(April 2002). More recently, an IRS survey of 1,200 401(k) plans found a number of patterns of errors. *Section 401(k) Compliance Check Questionnaire – Final Report,* Internal Revenue Service TE/GE Employee Plans (March 13, 2013).

[14] Throughout this book the use of "participant" is intended to encompass both plan participants and beneficiaries.

[15] Towers Watson merged with Willis Group Holdings in 2015 to become Willis Towers Watson. When a study or report was published before the merger under the Towers Watson name, that is the name that used.

[16] Steve Nyce, *Retirement Planning in a Post-Crisis Economy* (towerswatson.com/research/insider January 2012) at 14.

[17] *See e.g.,* Paul A. Gompers, Joy L. Ishii, Andrew Metrick, *Corporate Governance and Equity Prices* (The Wharton School 2003), Leora F. Klapper and Inessa Love, *Corporate Governance, Investor Protection and Performance in Emerging Markets* (Development Research Group, The World Bank April 2002).

better financial results and do a better job overseeing other areas, such as managing conflicts of interest.[18]

Despite the fact that better governance drives better results, retirement plans have historically failed to focus on improving or building good plan governance.

> In the corporate world, it has long been recognized that to get to the top, and to stay at the top, an organization needs a strong governance framework linked to a co-ordinated system of strategic performance management that together drives toward a common and clearly articulated goal. This thinking has not yet been fully embraced by the pension industry.[19]

Most executives in larger companies already understand the rules related to governance. Many may even be experts in corporate governance. Thus, having an executive serve on a plan committee, where they can leverage their governance knowledge, can be a tremendous advantage. All they need to learn is how to apply the governance principles to overseeing retirement plans.

Contrast this with what is typically asked of an executive invited to serve on the plan committee. Rather than being asked to apply familiar governance principles, they are asked to apply the standards applicable to fiduciaries and trust law. These are two areas in which most executives will not have any knowledge or experience.

---

[18] *See e.g.,* K. Ambachtsheer, R. Capelle, H. Lum, *Pension Fund Governance Today: Strengths, Weaknesses, and Opportunities for Improvement,* Financial Analysts Journal (October 2006); F. Steward and Juan Yermo, *Pension Fund Governance – Challenges and Potential Solutions* (OECD Publishing 2008); Manuel Ammann and Christian Ehmann, *Is Governance Related to Investment Performance and Asset Allocation? Empirical Evidence from Swiss Pension Funds* (March 2014) at 40 (concluding there is a "statistically significant" improvement in return for better governed plans), available at www.asip.ch/assets/Corporate-Governance/Pension-Fund-Governance-Paper-2014-03-31,

[19] Bernard Marr, Jocelyn Blackwell and Kenneth Donaldson, *Restoring Confidence: Measuring and Managing Performance in Pensions* (Cranfield University School of Management Dec. 2006) at 4.

In my work with plan committees, I've found that focusing on governance gives the committee greater confidence. They often see themselves as an expert when dealing with governance, and are more inclined to be engaged and challenge their advisors.

Once the plan committee adopts and begins to apply good governance to the plan, it will begin to do a better job as a fiduciary to the plan. This is because being a good fiduciary is already built into all facets of the overall governance architecture. Therefore, once you have a strong governance structure in place, you will be well positioned to meet your fiduciary obligations.

Fiduciary Rules Reflect the Governance Rules for a Trust

If we take a step back to understand the source of the rules of fiduciary behavior, one sees that the duties of a fiduciary are, in essence, a compilation of rules for how to run an enterprise where there is a trust relationship.[20] A beneficiary of a trust places their trust in the trustee; the heirs of an estate place their trust in the executor of the estate; the participants of the plan place their trust in the plan fiduciaries (or the plan committee).[21] In short, the fiduciary rules are, in part, the governance rules for a trust.

The solution is not a mystery for most plan committee members. As executives in their business they understand that better governance will drive better performance and financial results. The key questions are:

- *How to apply the principles of good governance to a retirement program?*

---

[20] "Because trust law follows this pattern, supplying both fiduciary governance and asset partitioning, the law of trusts is a species of organizational law." (Footnote omitted.) Robert H. Sitkoff, *Trust law as fiduciary governance plus asset partitioning* contained in <u>The World of the Trust</u>, (Lionel Smith ed., Cambridge University Press 2013), at 452.

[21] Restatement of the Law of Trust (Am. L. Inst. 1930), Introductory Note, at 11, provides: "A trust is one of several judicial devices whereby one person is enabled to deal with property for the benefit of another person."

- *How to structure, build and improve the plan's governance?*
- *How to raise the overall intelligence of the plan committee on retirement plan governance?*

How this Book will Help Build Good Plan Governance

This book will explain the 12 basic governance principles[22] and apply those principles to the oversight of retirement plans. This includes:

1. Establishing goals for the committee and others responsible for the plan
2. Understanding the risks associated with retirement plans, including the fiduciary risks, and examining effective ways to mitigate and manage those risks
3. Establishing clear roles, responsibilities and accountability
4. Improving the knowledge and skills of the committee and everyone working on the plan
5. Creating clear performance standards
6. Maintaining a compliant environment
7. Avoiding conflicts of interest
8. Being transparent and accountable to the plan participants
9. Meeting one's fiduciary duties
10. Having a succession plan, both for committee members and key vendors and plan personnel
11. Conducting periodic assessments of the plan's governance, and all the above items
12. Providing strong, continuous and effective oversight

---

[22] The number of principles used by different authors will vary because some authors will combine or divide some of the principles. In almost all cases, upon close examination, one will find the same 12 principles. *See* the table at page 41 that compares the governance principles used by CalPERS, OECD, and CAPSA.

When to Begin?

"By failing to prepare you are preparing to fail."
Benjamin Franklin

Imagine that you have just given birth to a child. When is the optimal time to begin to raise, teach, and provide the child with what he or she needs to grow and to survive? Should some time pass, perhaps a year or two, to allow things to settle?

While a plan isn't a living being, it is a legal being and it comes into existence on the day it is established. If you are a parent (committee member) who is charged with raising a child (a plan), you must engage immediately. You are responsible from day one for the growth and survival of the child.

Waiting for the "optimal" time at some point in the future isn't planning, it is neglect. Plan committee members need to recognize that on day one they have some form of governance in place. The choice is yours whether you will work to be a great committee member (parent) and have strong governance in place that will allow your plan (child) to excel.

Fortunately, plan governance isn't anywhere near as difficult as raising a child; it will rarely wake you up at 2 a.m. needing to be fed. Just as there are books on how to succeed as a new parent, this book will help you adjust to and become comfortable in your role as a plan committee member. Hopefully, it will also provide you with the tools to allow the plan to excel.

It is important to recognize, however, that implementing good governance is a process. One doesn't become great, or even good, overnight. It is a journey, and my experience suggests that establishing good governance can take from two to four years.

So, let's begin.

The Plan Committee

"Put first things first."
Stephen Covey, The Seven Habits of Highly Effective People

Introduction

The retirement plan committee is analogous to the board of directors for a corporation. It is *the* body charged with the oversight of the retirement plan on the participants behalf. Just like a ship needs a captain to begin its journey, the plan needs the plan committee to begin its governance journey.

Because there are risks for the committee members,[23] the employees, and the company for poor committee decisions, the selection of the committee members and the decision as to how the committee will be structured is of paramount importance. Despite the significance of the selection of members and development of the structure, these decisions are often made by default or with little critical thought.

For the vast majority of plans, neither the committee nor the structure for the plan's oversight body are mentioned in the plan documents.[24] These plan documents will typically identify a "plan

---

[23] ERISA imposes both civil and criminal penalties. ERISA section 409 provides, "Any person who is a fiduciary with respect to a plan who breaches any responsibilities, obligations or duties imposed upon fiduciaries by this title shall be *personally liable....*" 29 U.S.C. § 1109. (Emphasis added.) *See* ERISA §§ 411, 511, and 519 for crimes. 19 U.S.C. §§ 1111, 1141 and 1149.

[24] This is because the vast majority of plans are "boiler-plate" plan documents (called master and prototype or volume submitter plan documents), which are offered by mutual funds, insurance companies, and other investment houses to prospective clients for a nominal fee or for free. Larger plans are less likely to use a "boiler-plate" documents and are more likely to use a custom drafted plan. For example, in 2013 17.8% of 401(k) plans with 10,000 or more participants reported on Form 5500 using a master and prototype or volume submitter plan. (Calculated from Form 5500 data.)

administrator" and a "plan fiduciary" and usually name the "employer" or the "company" as the body to serve in those roles. In essence, the key fiduciary body responsible for the oversight, governance, risk management, and operation of the retirement plan is left ill-defined or undefined. [25]

A second reason why more attention isn't paid to identifying the individuals who are responsible for the plan as fiduciaries and the operating structure: the IRS simply does not care about such matters in its approval process. This isn't to say that it isn't important. It is, in fact, critically important. But the identification of the plan fiduciaries, the plan oversight architecture, and ensuring that the participants will be protected is not the primary function of the IRS. Instead, these areas fall within the purview of the Department of Labor, which is not involved in the review of the plan documents.

In short, the plan documents largely ignore the critical step of *identifying* the plan fiduciaries who are charged with protecting the plan participants and defining how they will *govern*. The role of the plan administrator and the plan fiduciary are described with a nebulous reference to the "Company" or "Employer." Unfortunately, this often means this responsibility falls upon the company's board of directors. Any board members who are told they are fiduciaries and are responsible for overseeing plan

---

[25] This terribly weak oversight comes about because most plans are based on a template document or template language that is offered to hundreds or thousands of companies. These templates by necessity must be generic enough to accommodate almost any situation. Thus, such documents fail to accommodate the naming of the actual fiduciaries or the structuring of the committee members. The formal name for these template documents used by the Internal Revenue Service are "prototype," "master and prototype," or "volume submitter" plan documents. The IRS generally encourages the use of these documents for efficiency, dedicates more resources to these plans, and extends preferential treatment to the review of these types of plans. Plans that are prepared that do not fit into one of these categories, typically called "individually designed" plans, are often based on pre-approved IRS language. The IRS pre-approved language is called the "List of Required Modifications" and is often heavily relied upon by attorneys who draft these documents; if the IRS has already approved the language, it will expedite the approval process and avoid embarrassing questions or challenges from the IRS.

investments, plan expenses, and plan administration (among other areas), would be surprised.[26]

If you haven't thought about who will be your plan fiduciaries, it is very possible that your board has unwittingly inherited this responsibility. In any case, the selection of who should be on the plan committee is an important conversation.

Who Should Be on the Plan Committee?

As noted earlier, serving on the plan committee involves significant responsibility. Upon accepting the role, one must be willing to accept personal liability for bad decisions.[27] The committee members hold the plan participants and, in many cases, the company's future in their hands. The importance of the role is probably why the majority of plan committee members are from senior management.[28] The board knows the members of senior management, and feel comfortable giving them the responsibility of overseeing a retirement plan if they've given them the responsibility of running the company.[29]

But is that the right decision? Does the fact that one can serve in a senior management position necessarily mean that same individual can or should oversee a retirement program?

Issues that arise when the default action is to appoint the most senior members of management are:

- They are appointed to the role with little preparation or training.
- They are too busy with the core company endeavors to be active and engaged in the committee actions.
- They are almost singularly focused on the success of the company, and have a difficult time not considering the

---

[26] Most companies generally attempt to shield the board from exposure.
[27] ERISA section 409 imposes personal liability on plan fiduciaries. 29 U.S.C. § 1109. Insurance is available; *see* discussion starting at page 113.
[28] *The New Governance Landscape supra at 12*, Figure 17.
[29] *The New Governance Landscape supra* at 12, Figure 16.

company priorities when serving as a committee member and a fiduciary.

- They lack the knowledge and experience to properly oversee plan operations and don't have the time to expand their knowledge.
- They consider the plan as essentially run by third-parties and their involvement is merely a formality or perfunctory.
- They don't understand the roles and responsibilities of a committee member.

What are some warning signs that the committee is not operating effectively?

- There are relatively few meetings (*e.g.*, less than four per year), or the meetings are not scheduled far enough in advance to allow the members to prepare, attend, and actively participate.
- The meeting agenda is dominated by presentations by one or two vendors, such as the plan investment advisor or the plan actuary.
- The committee does not set objectives and identify what it wants to accomplish to protect the participants, improve plan performance, and the like.
- The vendors attend the entire meeting, making it difficult for the committee to evaluate the vendors' performance and consider other areas.
- Because the vendors are essentially always in attendance, the committee can't evaluate the current vendors against the market.
- Recommendations by the vendors are almost always approved, with the committee serving as the body to rubberstamp the recommendations of the vendors, rather than establishing the path for the plan.
- There is limited or no training for new members to the committee.
- There are few or no general training sessions on an ongoing basis for the committee members to improve their knowledge.

- There is little succession planning or training for the next generation of members.

Correlation Between Meeting Frequency and Good Governance Indicators

A 2007 survey done by the Pensions Regulator,[30] the UK body responsible for regulating "pension schemes," found the following areas of correlation between how frequently the committee meets and several good governance indicators.

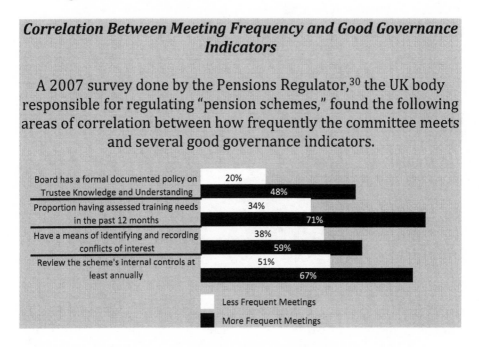

Characteristics of a Strong Committee Member

Plenty of potential problems can arise from selecting the wrong members to be on the committee. So, what should the board (or other body making the selection of the committee members) consider? The short answer is to seek out individuals who have the **availability, aptitude, and skills and knowledge** to serve on the committee.

Upon closer examination, one can see that a failure in any one of these three areas will produce a weak committee member and create risk for the entire endeavor. Let's take availability as the first characteristic to explore. If an individual appointed to the committee misses meetings, doesn't review the materials, is not prepared, or is distracted or multitasking during the meetings, the individual isn't available. Being too busy, unwilling, or

---

[30] The Pension Regulator, *Occupational pension scheme governance – A report on the 2007 scheme governance survey* (July 2007) at 18. The graph is a reproduction from the report.

uninterested makes a potential member unavailable. Individuals who are unavailable will not be performing at their highest level, and very likely will not be meeting the high standard placed on plan fiduciaries.

Aptitude reflects the fact that not every person will have the experience, demeanor, and confidence to serve as a committee member. A committee member who has the aptitude necessary to be effective in the role will be inquisitive, questioning, able to work well in a committee environment, understand the roles of the committee and others, and be able to put their personal interests aside.

For example, when evaluating a vendor, the committee member will want to know such things as: What are the appropriate criteria to use to evaluate a vendor in their area? What performance measures should they be held to? How has their past performance been? What have they charged, and have they billed properly? In addition, committee members will need to have the ability to step away from their perspective and bias as an officer or executive of the company, and be capable of focusing solely on what will be in the best interest of the plan participants.

Ideally, knowledge would mean that committee members know what is expected of them, understand the burdens of fiduciary duty, and know what must be done to govern the plan from an administrative and investment perspective. Unfortunately, few individuals have this knowledge base and can seamlessly step into the position of a plan committee member. Accordingly, knowledge is often viewed as the knowledge that the whole of the committee possesses. Individuals from the Finance area will be knowledgeable about investments, managing and governing investment advisors. Individuals from Human Resources will bring knowledge about plan administration, and potentially fiduciary duty.

A good committee will reflect upon and assess the skills and knowledge of both the individual members and the committee as a whole to determine where there may be gaps or weaknesses. This gap analysis will allow the committee to develop a plan to fill those gaps, and improve both the knowledge of the plan committee as a whole and the individual committee members.

The committee and members' skill and knowledge assessment is not intended to be a one-time event. Rather, it's part of the continual process to improve the overall skills and knowledge of the committee, by such means as performing periodic evaluations when events change, and new members join the committee.

An example of broad events that could trigger the need for additional training are the six events that will directly influence the risk exposure for the plan. (These risk events are discussed in greater detail later.) The six risk events that require an assessment of a committee's training are:

- New laws or regulations
- Changes in the plan design or terms
- Change in vendors, the type of vendors, their service, or contracts
- Change in the company or plan personnel responsible for the plan operations, controls, or compliance
- Changes (including degradation, outsourcing or automation) to processes or controls
- Changes to the company's or vendor's systems or technology involved in plan operations (such as HRIS systems, calculations, data storage or management)

Most plans will experience at least one of these six risk events every year. These six risk events are broad-based events that can cause related, specific risks to blossom. For example, hiring a new vendor can cause contract changes and monitoring, compliance, performance, and other risks to bloom. Anticipating, preparing for, and training for the risks associated with these events is an important step in managing the risk. Of course, these six risk events are only part of the spectrum of all the plan's risks, and risk is but one facet of the spectrum of responsibilities that the committee must understand.

Who Would be a Strong Committee Member?

The evaluation of any committee member must consider their availability, aptitude, and knowledge. Some roles, however, have a better likelihood of the individual meeting some of these qualities. Individuals with a senior role in Finance[31] will usually be able to understand the plan investments and plan expenses and have the aptitude to question the investment advisors and managers, and the assumptions being made. Similarly, individuals with a senior role in Human Resources will usually have a good understanding of employee needs and preferences, and plan operations and administration, and also have an aptitude to question vendors and plan administrators.[32]

At the same time, the senior Finance and Human Resources executive roles can be detriments. These individuals can be in the position of an officer and could be irreparably biased toward the company. They could also be so busy in their job that they do not have adequate time to commit to plan matters. Thus, individuals such as chief financial officers could be viewed as having the strongest financial background and a questioning, inquisitive aptitude. However, CFOs' role and perspective could render them too busy to serve or to make plan decisions without weighing the impact on the company.

In these types of cases, it is worth considering the person one level down, such as the controller instead of the CFO. The controller may have near equally strong financial knowledge and a very good aptitude, but not the biases or time constraints of the CFO. Selecting the "right" individual is a balancing act.[33]

---

[31] "Finance" in this context is used broadly to include individuals in the Accounting, Finance or Treasury functions.

[32] The use of senior Finance and Human Resources individuals is not coincidental. The most common executives (by title) serving on a retirement plan committee are the individuals over HR, Compensation, Benefits, or the CFO or treasurer. *See, The New Governance Landscape supra* at 12, figure 17.

[33] We'll soon explore whether it's better to identify the committee member by job title or have the board or other body name the individual on a case-by-case basis.

There are other possible representatives beyond those from Finance and Human Resources. Many committees will have a representative from Operations, such as the president of a division or subsidiary, that serves as the voice for the rank and file employees. While these proxies often will have a strong focus on the needs of the employees, they can lack the knowledge necessary to evaluate investments, investment advisors, vendors, compliance, and other areas essential to plan operations.

At this juncture, someone striving to select the perfect plan committee member is unquestionably frustrated. The frustration is warranted. *There is no such thing as a perfect plan committee member.* That's why it is important to assemble a committee that, in the aggregate, possesses all the skills, knowledge, and attributes for an outstanding committee.

The Imperfect Plan Committee Member

In Jim Brown's book, *The Imperfect Board Member,* he discusses corporate boards, which have similar oversight responsibilities to a plan committee. In his book he states, "... we board members are all imperfect, because no one is flawless and no one knows everything. Fortunately, this need not prevent us from having a great board, as the best boards are teams of highly talented and experienced people who bring unique strengths and complement each other's weaknesses."[34] Plan committee members will also all be "imperfect" individually, which is why building a strong committee is so important.

Should Rank and File Employees be on the Committee?

Although there are several arguments in favor of including rank and file employees on the committee, there generally are more arguments against doing so. Some of the arguments raised for including rank and file employees on a plan committee include:

- Typically, the rank and file employees make up the bulk of the workforce and the plan participants. Accordingly, their

---

[34] Jim Brown, <u>The Imperfect Board Member</u> (Jossey-Bass 2006) at xiv.

interests and perspectives are representative of the bulk of the participants.

- The rank and file employees generally won't have as significant a conflict between the interest of the company and the interest of the plan participants as members of senior management. Most participants, however, do not want to take action that could jeopardize the overall viability of the company, so some conflict will exist.
- There is a continued, lingering Enron[35] and WorldCom effect. Rank and file employees will remember the most recent scandal where retirement funds were lost and have a skeptical eye toward management. Having rank and file involvement, even if it isn't necessarily as a member on the committee, could help to alleviate some of that distrust.

The reasons why rank and file employees should not be included on the plan committee in most cases are:

- Assuming they're hourly, they would have to be paid. Usually committee members are not paid.
- They would have to be willing to take positions that may be contrary to positions held by supervisors and executives. Would they have this "independent" attribute?
- They would have to be willing to accept the potential personal financial liability, and criminal liability for their actions.
- Perhaps the most compelling argument against having rank and file employees serve on the committee is that they may not have the knowledge necessary to oversee a plan. For example, plan administrators and committees are constantly struggling with the fact that the plan participants, the rank and file employees, do not have the necessary understanding of investments to make effective investment decisions. Most of these individuals also would

---

[35] The Enron situation is particularly insidious because the executives were telling employees to continue to hold Enron stock in their 401(k) and other accounts, while the executives were selling over $1 billion of their stock. John C. Maxwell, There's No Such Things as "Business Ethics," (Warner Business Books 2003) at 1.

lack advanced degrees that provide an understanding about governance, controls, risk management, vendor management, and the like. Members of management are overseeing a business enterprise worth millions or billions of dollars, often a worth far in excess of the assets held in the plan. Experience in overseeing a like-sized enterprise is of paramount importance.

Should the Committee Members be Chosen by Title, or on a Case-by-Case Basis?

Assume one has gone through the analysis outlined earlier for identifying and selecting committee members, and considered the individual's availability, attributes, and knowledge and skills. One will find that in most instances, the attributes, knowledge, and skills[36] that are sought are also required for the individual's position (or based on job title).[37]

For example, controllers and chief financial officers will often be selected to serve on a committee for their ability to analyze issues critically, view information objectively, and for their financial acumen. These same characteristics, are also those that qualify them for their position as the controller or CFO. For this reason, it is sometimes best to identify the positions within the company that possess the requisite characteristics for a committee member and choose the committee members by title.

---

[36] Although availability is a factor for serving on the committee, it isn't generally a characteristic of most positions, so it is omitted from the following discussion. Senior executives, however, often have a strong ability to prioritize work and use a variety of resources to accomplish what needs to be done in the allotted time. Accordingly, for many organizations, "availability" is sometimes presumed of members of senior management.

[37] According to a 2011 survey by Towers Watson, 90% of organizations chose committee members based, at least in part, on the individual's level, title, or position within the organization. *The New Governance Landscape supra* at 13, figure 18.

There are a number of advantages to naming committee members by title, including:

- The ability to have a smooth succession. The business's succession plan for senior individuals can be leveraged and used so the next generation of committee members is identified and can attend some of the training and meetings to learn about their future role as a committee member.
- By defining the role of committee member as part of a position, the company can establish clarity about the role of the committee member in the job description. This allows for individuals to be able to prioritize their time and have resources available to help them fulfill all their responsibilities.
- It leverages the overlapping skills between the company position and the role on the committee.
- It allows for the building of a committee that can function smoothly, since replacement members will fill the gap left by any departing member.

There are, however, several potential problems with this approach that the selecting body needs to consider and monitor.

- If, for whatever reason, the individual holding the job title that is to serve on the committee doesn't have the time to serve (*e.g.,* because of inexperience, qualifications, or other reason).
- The individual is not interested, or performs poorly in the position. The selecting body should monitor the member's performance, and take action when performance is inadequate.
- The proposed member possesses some inherent conflict of interest that would make it difficult or impossible to act in the best interest of the plan participants.
- The position would remain unfilled for an extended period, such as when the individual becomes sick or disabled, or is on an extended leave or assignment.

Where any of these potential problems exist, the selecting body should consider selecting a different individual to serve, or consider ways to remediate the situation, such as providing additional support.

What is an Appropriate Structure for the Committee?

There is a correlation between the size and complexity of the retirement plan and the plan committee structure. Simple plans with relatively fewer assets usually have one committee. More complex plans with greater asset amounts are more likely to have more than one committee.[38]

According to a GAO survey, of 90 plan sponsors with plans with over $200 million in assets, 60 of them (or 66%) had a single committee.[39] The other 30 had more than one committee.[40] In general, the size of the committee and the number of committees will grow as the plan size and complexity grows. Small businesses will often have just the owner serving as the sole fiduciary.[41] Large governmental plans will have many committees that specialize in an array of focused functions.

A Towers Watson survey found that 47% of plans that participated in the survey had one committee, and 38% had separate committees for plan administration and plan investments.[42] In addition to administration and investments, other sub-committees include funding, communications, auditing, governance, and operations.[43]

---

[38] *See e.g., Occupational pension scheme governance – A report on the 2007 scheme governance survey supra* at 19, which provides: "The use of committees is particularly relevant for larger schemes that actively manage the scheme's operations. As committees can play an integral role in assisting the board to discharge its responsibilities, and may have an impact on the level of activity undertaken by the board, the use of sub-committees may also be a driver in raising governance standards."

[39] U.S. Gov't Accountability Office, *Private Pensions – Fulfilling Fiduciary Obligations Can Present Challenges for 401(k) Plan Sponsors*, GAO-08-774 (July 2008) at page 18.

[40] Id.

[41] Id.

[42] *The New Governance Landscape supra* at 11.

I've found that the committee structure will often imitate the company structure. Companies that are lean will tend toward a single committee (with three or five members).[44] Companies that have larger organizations and more hierarchy will have separate committees for administration and investing. I've rarely seen separate sub-committees in the private sector for auditing, governance, communications, or funding, although these would not be unusual for larger governmental plans.[45] It is common to have a separate body (not always called a committee) that handles appeals from participants.

The following are three illustrations of common committee structures:

Single Committee Structure

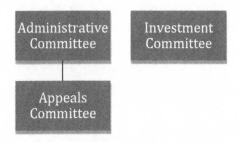

Dual Committee Structure with Appeals Sub-Committee

---

[43] *Occupational pension scheme governance – A report on the 2007 scheme governance survey supra* at 19.

[44] Companies owned by a private equity will often fall into this category.

[45] For example, CalPERs, the largest pension plan in the United States, has six committees (Board Governance; Finance & Administration; Investment; Pension & Health Benefits; Performance, Compensation, and Talent Management; and Risk & Audit), which are a proxy for where the CalPERS plan believes it should focus attention and which parallel many of the "good governance" principles espoused in this book. *See,* https://calpers.a.gov/page/about/board/board-committees

More Complex Sub-Committee Structure

What is an Appropriate Number of Committee Members?

Surveys and studies on the number of plan committee members report various ranges. They do show that the most common results are four to six members:

- A 2010 survey by Aon Hewitt of Canadian pension committees found that where a committee existed, the sizes ranged from three to 22 members, but half of the respondents reported either five or six members.[46]
- A 2011 survey by Towers-Watson reported that the range in the number of members where there was a single committee was one to nine, with the average number of members being 4.1.[47]

There is an entire field of study that evaluates the optimal number of members on a working team or a committee. One article quoted Evan Wittenberg, the director of the Wharton Graduate Leadership Program, as saying that, "while the research on [the] optimal team is 'not conclusive, it does tend to fall into the five to 12 range, though some say five to nine is best, and the number six has come up a few times.' "[48]

Selecting the optimal number for one's committee will be impacted by a number of factors. The following should be considered:

---

[46] Rosalind Gilbert and Sara L. Hakim, *Creating effective pension committees* (March 24, 2011) available at benefitscanada.com.
[47] *The New Governance Landscape supra* 13, figure 19.
[48] Knowledge.wharton.upenn.edu, *Is Your Team Too Big? Too Small? What's the Right Number?* (June 14, 2006).

- The size of the plan, both the number of participants and the amount of assets
- The complexity of the plan, both its design and features, and its investments
- The level of outsourcing, particularly if any fiduciary functions have been outsourced, thereby relieving the plan committee of some of its responsibilities
- The skills, knowledge, experience, and availability of the committee members
- The challenges confronting the plan

The larger, more complex the plan, and the less knowledgeable the members, the more members and/or committees that will be required to handle the oversight. I've found that plans with $100 million to around $1 or $2 billion, that aren't overly complex and with experienced and knowledgeable committee members, can operate well and efficiently with five to seven members on one committee. Having one committee simplifies the structure and reduces the level of coordination and time needed. Indeed, by having co-chairs (such as the HR lead chairing during administrative meetings and the Finance lead chairing during investment meetings), you can get the benefit of specialized chairs without the burden of coordinating with a second committee.

The size and composition of the plan committee also impacts the committee's ability to think creatively, critically, and independently. The use of a committee structure for decision-making raises the risks that Groupthink will influence the committee.[49] The plan committee, like any committee or group

---

[49] Groupthink was coined by Irving Janis in <u>Victims of Groupthink</u> (Houghton Mifflin 1972), and is defined as the drive for consensus that is so strong that it suppresses disagreement and critical evaluation of alternatives.
John Maxwell, the best-selling business author said in his business ethics book, "[t]he more people involved, the greater the pressure for conformity.... No matter how much pressure there is, you can't allow others to force you into making unethical decisions." <u>There's No Such Things as "Business Ethics"</u> at 60-61 (bold and heading capitalization omitted). *See also* the discussion later on Ethics at page 224.

decision-making body, should anticipate that Groupthink is a threat to good decision-making, and take actions that will reduce its influence. The following preventative measures have been suggested:

a. The leader should assign the role of critical evaluation to each member.
b. The leader should avoid stating preferences and expectations about the outcome at the beginning of any discussion.
c. Each member of the group should routinely discuss the group's deliberations with a trusted associate and report back to the group on the associate's reactions.
d. One or more experts should be invited to each meeting on a staggered basis. The outside experts should be encouraged to challenge the views of the members.
e. At least one articulate and knowledgeable member should be given the role of devil's advocate (to question assumptions and plans). The leader should make sure that a sizeable block of time is set aside to ... [assess various risks].[50]

Is it Better to Fail Conventionally than to Succeed Unconventionally?

In 2015, plan governance expert Keith Ambachtsheer noted the risks associated with committee decision-making:

"Anthropologists O'Barr and Conley ... [observed in 1992] the behavior of nine major US pension funds over a two-year period, [and] they concluded that the aim of the funds appeared to be focused more on responsibility deflection and blame management than on good governance and creating value for fund stakeholders. This observed behavior is very much in line with Keynes' 1936 remark about investment committees that 'worldly wisdom teaches that it is better for reputation to fail conventionally than to succeed unconventionally...' "[51]

---

[50] These are some of the suggested ways to avoid groupthink suggested by Janis in <u>Victims of Groupthink</u> *supra.*

How Often Should the Committee Meet?

The plan committee needs to meet as often as necessary to accomplish its goals and fulfill its fiduciary responsibilities. Surveys have found that for larger plans, that means meeting quarterly or more frequently.[52] The more participants that are in a plan, the more often it will meet.[53]

Although it is helpful for the plan committee to have regular meetings that can be planned and scheduled, the committee should periodically review its meeting frequency. It is easy to become accustomed to quarterly meetings where the investment advisor covers familiar material, little else is discussed, and there is little or no need for advance preparation.

Should the plan committee find that it is falling into such a routine, it should consider adding additional meetings to cover non-investment items.[54] The additional meetings can give the committee the opportunity to consider whether the other governance principles discussed in this book are being adequately addressed.

For new plan committees, I would often suggest that they schedule six meetings. Plan investments and other recurring items would be addressed at the meetings falling after the end of each investment quarter. The other two meetings would be reserved for establishing goals, assessing risks, developing

---

[51] Ambachtsheer, Keith and McLaughlin, John, *How Effective is Pension Fund Governance Today? And Do Pension Funds Invest for the Long-Term?* (KPA Advisory Services LTD January 2015) at 4. (Footnotes omitted.)

[52] *The New Governance Landscape supra* at 15, figure 22 (2011), reporting that 76% of plans with single committees meet quarterly. *Occupational pension scheme governance – A report on the 2007 scheme governance survey supra* at 17, reporting that 75% of DC plans with over 1,000 participants and 92% of DB plans with over 5,000 participants meet at least quarterly.

[53] *Id. at* 17.

[54] An alternative is to extend the time for the existing meetings. I prefer having separate meetings, however, so the committee is dedicated to the non-investment topics that are identified.

training, reviewing compliance items, reviewing vendor performance, establishing vendor search criteria, and so on.

Similarly, plans (and companies) that are undergoing significant changes may want to add additional meetings. Examples of events that might trigger the need for additional meetings are:

- Potential significant plan design changes
- Plan mergers or spin-offs
- Larger system or vendor changes
- Significant legislative or regulatory changes
- Major personnel changes

Committee Voting

Committee members should be independent and not vote in a way that's inconsistent with their beliefs. But the committee should avoid split votes, since the dissenters will be the witnesses testifying against the committee's decision should it reach trial.

> *"We must, indeed, all hang together*
> *or, most assuredly,*
> *we shall all hang separately."*
> Benjamin Franklin

Who Should Serve as the Committee Chairperson?

Typically, the chairperson is the highest titled company officer serving on the plan committee. Thus, if the CEO is on the committee, then the CEO is the chair. If the CFO is the top person, then the CFO would be the chair. I would like to step back and challenge this typical notion of having the highest titled person serve as the plan committee chair.

It is quite different to lead a committee of members, each with an equal say and vote, then it is to lead an organization where your decisions are final and there are individuals who provide input, but don't have a vote. When you have a plan committee, everyone is a fiduciary, and they all will have input into the decision. It isn't a situation where the chair will hang and everyone else will be left alone. *Everyone hangs together.*

Without getting into committee dynamics too much, the traits that make someone a great CEO, CFO, or other executive are not necessarily the same traits that will make for a great plan committee chair. While the chair must lead the committee, that means they must be able to establish an open and collaborative culture.[55] The chair should visibly show a passion for and an understanding of, the role and the responsibility.

The Apathetic Chair

One of the worst committees I encountered had a completely apathetic chair. The chair was an outstanding executive, but it was clear that chairing the plan committee (or even being on the plan committee) was not his interest, and probably was seen as a waste of time.

His apathetic, even negative attitude infected the other plan committee members and they would often be ill-prepared, late, or absent. They would quickly rubberstamp what was proposed by HR or the plan vendors, and spend as little time as possible on plan matters.

A new chair, and several new members, quickly changed the committee culture. The chair's enthusiasm, direction, and leadership quickly reversed the negative attitude. The transition didn't only transform the committee, but it also dramatically improved the performance of the vendors and internal staff. The new chair was a subordinate of the original chair.

---

[55] Some suggestions to engage members are:
- "Draw out the thinking of quiet members; limit the contributions of outspoken member
- Use structured activities to engage everyone in the discussion rather than simply relying on everyone speaking up at the board table"

The Imperfect Board Member *supra* at 25 (bullets in original).

Plan Governance Structure for Multiple Plans

Many companies will have multiple plans, perhaps separate 401(k) plans for different divisions, or a defined benefit plan and a 401(k) plan.[56] What should the governance structure be in that situation? Should the same plan committee oversee all of the plans? Should all of the plans be addressed at the same meetings? If there are separate plan committees and meetings, should there be any overlap between the plan members on each committee?

It is common for the same committee to cover several plans,[57] and that is potentially the most efficient use of the members' time. The question, however, is whether that is the best design for the plan participants. I would direct the reader to the beginning of this chapter where the characteristics of a good plan committee member are discussed.

Perhaps the same individuals are the best to serve both plans. That conclusion should be a reasoned answer, not a default to conserve the individual members' time.

Even if the same individuals serve as the committee for both plans, one should be careful not to lump all the issues for both plans together. The plans may have different participant populations, be different types of plans, and have different investments and vendors. Indeed, the plans may need to have different strategies that require very different goals and approaches. Keeping the focus separately on each participant group the plan committee is seeking to serve will show that the committee didn't make a decision for one plan based on the other plan's facts.

Finally, having separate meetings helps preserve the integrity of the meeting minutes. For example, if one plan is sued, the minutes for the other plan would not be part of discovery. If, however, the

---

[56] In addition to retirement plans, companies also have health and welfare plans that are similarly regulated and need a governing or oversight body.
[57] *The New Governance Landscape supra* at 11, figure 15, reporting that in companies that have both a defined benefit and defined contribution plan, 80% use a single committee to serve both plans.

minutes are combined, then the minutes for both plans will be discovered, which could lead to additional exposure.

Quick Hits

Throughout this book, at the end of most chapters, you'll find examples that illustrate how some of the ideas in each chapter can be implemented to help the plan committee work at quickly seeing improvements. Some of these examples will make sense for your plan; others may not. You should consider them judiciously.

1. Can you identify the plan committee from the plan document, board meeting minutes or delegation, or some other document that clearly creates and empowers the plan committee?
    a. Concerning the creation of the plan committee, is it clear who is on the committee, how many members the committee should have, how they are selected, and how the committee will operate?
    b. If there is no documentation or if it is ambiguous, consider having a plan committee charter developed.

2. Evaluate and consider taking action on potential committee weaknesses, such as:
    a. Meeting too infrequently to accomplish the committee's objectives
    b. Plan committee structure is not optimal because it does not correlate with the size of the plan (*i.e.*, the number of committees, subcommittees and members doesn't reflect the employee and asset size)
    c. Number of members is too lean or too cumbersome, so meetings and workload are not efficiently managed
    d. Plan committee members lack either the availability, aptitude, or knowledge to serve on the plan committee
    e. Members' attendance at the meetings is not consistent
    f. The chair is ineffective in leading a fiduciary committee, where building consensus is important (*e.g.*, does the chair state preferences and steer the conversations toward one conclusion and possibly skirt critical evaluation?)

What Is Plan Governance?

"The time is always right to do right."
Nelson Mandela

Introduction

Plan governance is the structure, system and process for successfully overseeing retirement plans. It addresses who is responsible, how they will be held accountable, manages risks, compels compliance, satisfies fiduciary duties, and strives to achieve the mission and goals of the plan.

Although it can accomplish great things, plan governance is simple in that it is built upon 12 basic principles. These governance principles are also already part of the knowledge and experience for most executives.

For many executives, most of the plan governance principles are the same or similar to principles they have studied or lived as part of corporate governance. These parallels should make it easier for members of management who will, at a minimum, have an intuitive appreciation for corporate governance, to understand plan governance. Executives who are well-versed in corporate governance should find the transition from corporate to plan governance almost effortless, as it involves the same principles, but with a different application.[58]

---

[58] Stanford has an excellent paper on the best governance practices for institutional investor funds that details a number of governance principles that could easily be adapted for retirement plan governance, showing that the governance principles are universal. Committee on Fund Governance – Best Practice Principles, Peter Chapman, Chair (The Stanford Institutional Investors' Forum May 31, 2007).

Abandon the Misperception that Governance is Compliance

Many plan committee members incorrectly see plan governance as synonymous with plan compliance. This is understandable, but incorrect.

It is understandable because in the US most of the emphasis on retirement plans has been related to plan compliance. (Tax benefits are lost if plans aren't compliant. The plan documents historically had to be submitted to the IRS for approval that they were compliant. IRS audits looked at plans for compliance. During a financial audit, the independent auditor requests a representation letter from ERISA[59] counsel that the plan is compliant.) Because of this focus on compliance, many plan committees feel that if they are compliant, the plan is operating properly and there is nothing else that needs to be addressed or overseen.

Although compliance has been a central focus for US retirement plans for many years, it is only one element of plan governance. Even the IRS, the champion and guardian of retirement plan compliance, has begun to advocate that plan governance and controls are important areas of emphasis.[60]

The 12 Plan Governance Principles

The 12 plan governance principles are:

1. Establishing a mission statement and goals
2. Clarity of roles, responsibilities, and accountability
3. Establishing and maintaining a risk management process

---

[59] ERISA stands for the Employee Retirement Income Security Act of 1974, and it and its amendments constitute the primary body of legislation addressing retirement plans.

[60] *See e.g.*, Andrea L. Ben-Yosef, *IRS Focusing More on Internal Controls*, BNA Pension & Benefits Reporter (March 5, 2013). On August 8, 2013 the IRS Employees Plans group also had a "Phone Forum" on "The Importance of Good Internal Controls." IRS plan examiners were also provided with a "System Procedures and Internal Control Questionnaire" on plan administration.

4. Acquiring the requisite knowledge and skills
5. Establishing and monitoring clear performance measures
6. Establishing and maintaining a compliance process
7. Creating an ethical culture including having a conflict of interest policy and code of conduct
8. Being transparent
9. Meeting one's fiduciary duties
10. Having a succession planning process
11. Performing periodic assessments
12. Oversight

Each of these principles will be examined separately in the chapters that follow, with extended discussion on how the principle applies to *retirement plan governance.*

Use of Principles by High-Performing Committees

Have these principles been applied by actual high-performing committees? Indeed, a plan that is consistently given high marks for its overall performance is the Ontario Teachers' Pension Plan.[61] The board for that plan, as part of it overall governance oversight, has acknowledged the following responsibilities, which are aligned with the 12 governance principles:[62]

a. "[S]atisfy itself as to the integrity of the ... [individuals operating the plan];
b. "adopting a strategic planning process and approving, on at least an annual basis, a strategic plan that takes into account ... the opportunities and risks of the plan and fund;
c. "identifying the principal risks of the plan and fund, and ensuring the implementation of appropriate systems to manage these risks;
d. "succession planning (including appointing, training and monitoring senior management);
e. "adopting a communication policy...;

---

[61] Canada has a strong plan governance framework and structure, and provides excellent models that can be applied in the United States.
[62] Ontario Teachers' Pension Plan Board available at http://www.otpp.com/documents/10179/20940/mandate0608.pdf/ad67da1 0-5de2-41e9-9700-f52ec0a9aca6.

f. "ensuring the … internal control and management information systems are adequate; and

g. "developing the … approach to corporate governance, including developing a set of corporate governance principles and guidelines that are specifically applicable to the organization."[63]

Globally Accepted Plan Governance Principles

Regardless of whether the source examining plan governance is the Canadian Association of Pension Supervisory Authorities (CAPSA), the Organization for Economic Cooperation and Development (OECD), or CalPERS (the largest US pension fund),[64] the principles used to create plan governance are very consistent. (*See* the table at page 41.) This book draws upon these near-universally accepted principles as the foundation in building a great plan governance framework.

Beyond the wide-spread applicability and consistency of the principles, the global nature of these principles is important for several reasons:

- The 12 principles provide an approach that works when applying plan governance internationally for businesses that have plans in other countries.

---

[63] Mandate of the Ontario Teachers' Pension Plan Board (OTPP), including responsibilities described in The Teachers' Pension Act and The Partners' Agreement, available at http://www.otpp.com/documents/10179/20940/mandate0608.pdf/ad67da1 0-5de2-41e9-9700-f52ec0a9aca6.

[64] CalPERS, or the California Public Employees' Retirement System, is the largest pension fund in the United States, with over $300 billion in assets and 1.6 million members and retirees. The California Public Employees' Retirement System, "Global Governance Principles" (updated March 16, 2015), at 6, available at https://www.calpers.ca.gov/docs/forms-publications/global-principles-corporate-governance.pdf. CalPERS has been in the forefront of both plan and corporate governance at least since the mid-1980s. CalPERS' "Global Governance Principles" addresses corporate governance principles, which overlap with its plan governance principles. The plan governance principles can be found at California Public Employees' Retirement System Board of Administration, "Governance Policy," (Revised December 2014), available at https://www.calpers.ca.gov/docs/board-governance-policy.pdf

- Using this structure outside the US won't be viewed as applying a US-centric approach, but an internationally recognized approach.
- By adhering to an international standard, all plans globally can follow the same approach. Local representatives that are responsible for retirement plan oversight can leverage tools, training, best practices, and methodologies that have been developed by others.

Plan Governance Definitions

There are several excellent definitions that reflect the key governance principles that are the foundation for building strong governance. One of my favorite definitions is by CAPSA:[65]

> *Pension plan* governance *is about delivering on the pension promise consistent with the pension plan document and pension legislation. ...Pension plan governance refers to the structure and process for overseeing, managing and administering a pension plan to ensure the fiduciary and other obligations of the plan are met.*[66]

Like CAPSA, the OECD[67] also focuses on oversight and following the law and plan document, but also emphasizes the need to have clear roles and responsibilities:

---

[65] The Canadian Association of Pension Supervisory Authorities (CAPSA) is an association of the pension regulators in Canada "whose mission is to facilitate an efficient and effective pension regulatory system in Canada." As part of its mission, it has developed pension governance guidelines and checklists. Available at http://www.capsa-acor.org/en/.

[66] Guideline No. 4, Pension Plan Governance Guidelines and Self-Assessment Questionnaire, Canadian Association of Pension Supervisory Authorities (CAPSA) (October 2004), at 3, available at http://www.capsa-acor.org/en/init/governance_guidelines/Guideline_Self-asses_Questionnaire.pdf

[67] OECD, or the Organization for Economic Cooperation and Development, is an organization comprised of 34 democracies that work together with 70 non-member countries to promote economic growth. "OECD member countries account for 63 percent of world GDP, three-quarters of world trade, 95 percent of world official development assistance, over half of the world's energy consumption, and 18 percent of the world's population." Available at http://usoecd.usmission.gov/mission/overview.html.

Good governance calls for a clear identification and separation of the operational and oversight responsibilities of a pension fund. To the extent that a pension entity is established that owns the pension fund on behalf of plan/fund members and beneficiaries, the assignment of these responsibilities needs to be clearly stated in the pension entity's statutes, by-laws, contract, or trust instrument, or in documents associated with any of these. These documents also need to state the legal form of the pension entity, its internal governance structure, and its main objectives.[68]

Finally, the US Government Accountability Office's definition incorporates concepts of transparency and improving knowledge and skills:

Plan governance generally refers to the systems and processes that plans use to manage the administration of benefits for the plan beneficiaries and manage the investment of retirement assets, with the objective of maximizing investment returns at an acceptable level of risk and reducing potential conflicts of interest. These systems and processes cover areas such as organizational transparency; having clear, documented, and accessible policies; and commitment to knowledge and skill enhancement.[69]

All these definitions are built on the 12 governance principles.

---

[68] OECD Guidelines for Pension Fund Governance (June 2009) Annotations to Guidelines for Pension Fund Governance, I.1, available at http://www.oecd.org/pensions/private-pensions/34799965.pdf.
[69] U.S. Gov't Accountability Office, *State and Local Government Pension Plans – Governance Practices and Long-term Investment Strategies Have Evolved Gradually as Plans Take on Increased Investment Risk*, Report to the Ranking Member, Committee on Finance, U.S. Senate, GAO-10-754 (August 2010) at 8, available at http://www.gao.gov/assets/310/308867.pdf.

Perspectives for the Journey Ahead

Plan governance encompasses the oversight of all things related to the plan. However, when listening to an investment manager, it can sound as if governance involves only investments. Similarly, when speaking with an attorney, it can sound as if it involves only compliance.

As a member of the plan committee, you will need to take a broader view of governance and its foundational principles. For example, when considering succession, your focus should be broader than just the succession of plan committee members. You should also be focused succession for critical staff and vendors. Similarly, when considering risks, you will want to consider risks broadly ranging from investment risks, risks related to the diminution of value from administrative and investment fees and expenses, and transactional risks.

The next stage of this journey is to apply one's general governance knowledge to retirement plans in a pragmatic and efficacious way.

"For what you see and hear depends a good deal on where you are standing; it also depends on what sort of person you are."
C.S. Lewis, The Magician's Nephew

Similarity in Plan Governance Principles

The following table demonstrates that the preeminent sources on plan governance all largely rely upon the same governance principles, which are the basis for the governance principles in this book.

GOVERNANCE PRINCIPLES	CAPSA	OECD*	CALPERS˅
Plan mission and goals	√†	√	√
Defined roles, responsibilities, and accountability	√°	√	√
Oversight	√∞	√	√
Risk Management	√	√	√
Transparency and disclosure	√	√	√
Clear performance measures	√	√	√
Adequate knowledge and skills	√	√	√
Compliance	√	√	√
Ethics: Conflicts of interest and code of conduct	√	√	√
Meeting fiduciary duties	√		√
Succession planning			
Periodic assessments	√Δ	√	√

Notes on Next Page

Notes From Preceding Table

* The OECD Guidelines for Pension Fund Governance bundle several principles together under a single heading. For example, under the heading "identification of responsibilities," it discusses the following principles: separation of operational and oversight responsibilities, stating plan objectives, and risk management. (*See* page 7, Section I.1.)

ˇ In some cases, CalPERS' list of governance principles do not explicitly include the governance principles we've identified. For example, there is not a principle related to "defined roles, responsibilities, and accountability." However, CalPERS' governance policy provides extensive detail on the roles and responsibilities of the board and other members. Similarly, although it does not have a separate principle related to "performance measures," the guidelines emphasize overseeing and assessing both the board's and others' activities throughout.

† CAPSA uses the term, "governance objectives," which it defines as follows: "The plan administrator should establish governance objectives for the oversight, management, and administration of the plan." Page 5 of CAPSA Guideline No. 4.
Later, it provides that "[t]he objectives, which should be clearly documented, should build on any of the plan sponsor's objectives for the pension plan, as well as on the plan terms and regulatory requirements. Pension plan governance objectives help develop effective governance practices leading to the efficient and successful operation of the pension plan." (*See* page 6.)

° CAPSA includes accountability with transparency. While transparency does help provide accountability, we believe that a critical part of the governance structure is to define roles and responsibilities, and include as a component of the roles and responsibilities oversight and reporting to help ensure accountability.

∞ CAPSA combines oversight and compliance. We treat these as separate components because the oversight can and should cover more than just compliance areas.

Δ CAPSA has as its principle "governance review" or to "conduct a regular review of its plan governance." We believe this should be done, but the periodic review should be broader and include periodic reviews of compliance, controls, vendor performance, and the like.

Establishing a Mission Statement and Goals

"[L]eadership is not about getting things done; it is providing a mission worth doing in the first place."
August Turak[70]

"Strategy without tactics is the slowest route to victory. Tactics without strategy is the noise before defeat."
Sun Tzu, The Art of War

Introduction

In the private sector, very few retirement plans have an established vision, and therefore lack a mission statement clarifying the vision.[71] Perhaps related to the lack of a mission statement is that many committees fail to set explicit goals at the beginning of the year for the plan and the committee. However, plans that have "clarity of mission" perform better than plans that don't.[72]

This isn't to suggest that plans without goals don't accomplish things during the year; they do. But they are not accomplishing everything that needs to be done. It might be an overstatement to suggest that the achievements are random, but it isn't too strong a statement to say that these accomplishments are not strategic.[73]

---

[70] August Turak, <u>Business Secrets of the Trappist Monks</u> (Columbia Business School 2013) at 35.

[71] Ambachtsheer noted that when senior US pension fund executives were "... asked to identify the sources of excellence shortfall, respondents most frequently cited ... a lack of focus and clarity of mission." (Footnote omitted.) Keith Ambachtsheer and John McLaughlin, *How Effective is Pension Fund Governance Today? And Do Pension Funds Invest for the Long-Term?* (KPA Advisory Services LTD January 2015) at 4.

[72] G. Clark and R. Urwin, *Best-Practice Pension Fund Governance*, Journal of Asset Management (2008).

Flying on Autopilot

What does a plan without a mission or strategic goals look like?

About once a quarter, a meeting is called and an agenda is circulated. The agenda is developed by a consultant with some input from someone in the Human Resources Department or Benefits area. The topics are familiar, because they are generally the same items discussed at every meeting.

The bulk of the agenda and time is dedicated to the outside investment advisor who walks the committee through a report on the investment results of the plan. The advisor discusses the investments and how they're performing; perhaps they discuss a money manager that needs to be monitored. Usually, what is discussed is informational and there are few or no changes to the investment policy, the asset managers, or the actual investments. If the advisor makes a recommendation, it is almost always approved by the plan committee.

At the end of the meeting, the committee feels like it has done its job. The meeting is couched with all the formality of a parliamentary proceeding: the minutes read, a motion made to approve them and seconded, and so on. Committee members even pose a handful of questions.

The meetings continue like this each quarter, and seem familiar and comfortable to the committee members and other attendees. Perhaps events like these have played out at your plan committee meetings? But amid that feeling of familiarity, do you also have a sense that things are on autopilot? If so, instead of acting as the captain, the committee is just along for the ride as a passenger.

---

[73] The OECD identifies as one of the four "governing body's main strategic and oversight responsibilities…" the "setting out of the pension fund's **key goals or mission,** identifying the main risks, and laying out the main policies…." (Emphasis added.) OECD Guidelines for Pension Fund Governance (June 2009), Annotations to Guidelines for Pension Fund Governance, section I.2, available at http://www.oecd.org/pensions/private-pensions/34799965.pdf.

The problem with this scenario is that the plan committee isn't setting the direction for the plan, and doesn't have goals that *it* needs to accomplish. Instead what the committee needs is a governance framework to guide it, and a mission statement and specific goals that will place the plan committee in control.

When a plan committee has this strong plan governance structure in place (and it applies the 12 governance principles introduced earlier), the meetings tend to look very different. This is because the plan committee *proactively* looks at all the areas, such as compliance, risk management (or controls), performance measures (or vendor management), conflicts of interest, and so on. The list of areas to oversee is, without a doubt, lengthy. Accordingly, having a mission statement helps guide the plan direction and decisions, and it becomes vital to use clearly established goals to prioritize efforts.

The problem for most plan committee members isn't that the company executives don't understand how to establish a mission or goals. To the contrary, executives understand goals and mission statements: they establish them for their business unit or company effortlessly.[74] However, establishing goals or creating a mission statement for a retirement plan is not as intuitive for executives who spend just a small portion of their time overseeing these programs.

I've encountered many situations in which an executive, who will often manage against goals in the business, expresses frustration because the plan's management isn't goal oriented. Because they don't have the level of knowledge of the individuals in the Benefits Department or of the outside consultants, they would sometimes feel like they could not challenge these experts. The governance framework detailed in this book provides the committee members with the knowledge and ability to proactively oversee the plan.

---

[74] Indeed, in a recent survey of CEO's, 92% agreed or strongly agreed that it is, "important to have a strong corporate purpose, that's reflected in our values, culture and behaviours". *20 years inside the mind of the CEO... What's next?*, 20th PwC CEO Survey, 2017 at 22.

As we work through each of the principles, the goals for the plan will become clearer and more concrete. Since it is recognized that, at least in the beginning, it may not be natural for members of the committee to create goals for the governance of the plan, this book provides examples of goals to help the committee in each chapter and in "Quick Hits" at the end of each chapter.

What do Meetings for a Goal-Oriented Plan Look Like?

When a plan has a mission and goals, the meetings are dramatically different from the one described previously. Let's consider a committee that is highly engaged, and it is the first meeting of the year. The meeting has been on the calendar for almost a year, so all the members are able to attend. The focus of the meeting is two-fold: to review progress against the goals that were established the prior year (a periodic assessment), and to establish goals for the year ahead.

In anticipation of developing goals for the upcoming year, the plan committee made several requests for information from several of its vendors and internal partners. Because one of the issues that had arisen during the prior year had to do with risk management, the committee directed stakeholders (HR, the investment advisor, the plan trustee, the recordkeeper, and legal counsel) to provide a risk assessment in their respective areas ahead of the next meeting. Specifically, the committee directed each of these players to assess the potential risk in the following areas: performance of vendors and staff (performance measurement),[75] effectiveness of controls (risk management), plan operations (performance measurement and compliance), operational continuity (succession), status of any reviews performed on operations, compliance, expenses, controls, and other areas (periodic assessments).

Based on what was accomplished during the prior year, and the reporting from the various groups, the plan committee proceeds to develop goals for the year to come. The goals are designed to manage risk and drive the plan's mission (*e.g.,* manage expenses

---

[75] The governance principles that the activity support are in parentheses.

and improve investment performance), based on available time and resources at the committee's disposal. Not all potential risks necessarily rise to the level of being a goal for the current year because of time or resource constraints. The committee will need to prioritize the areas to address, and which ones must be postponed. Prioritizing goals is a critical function of the committee and one of its key fiduciary roles.

The agendas for the remainder of the year are then laced with updates and decision-making that will help further the achievement of the plan goals.

The Evolution of a Goal Over a Year

The following is an example of how a specific goal might evolve over the course of a year.

Let's assume that legal counsel has identified compliance with ERISA section 404(c)[76] as a risk because of a change in investments available to plan participants. If this was added to the list of goals for the year, the committee would request that legal counsel review the plan and provide an opinion on whether the plan satisfies ERISA section 404(c) by the second meeting.[77] Thus, the risk is identified and prioritized; a goal is established; responsibility is clearly assigned; and a specific deadline is associated with its completion.

---

[76] ERISA requires that plan fiduciaries diversify plan investments. When participants select their investments, as is the case in most 401(k) plans, the plan fiduciary remains responsible for the investment selection and diversification, unless the requirements of ERISA section 404(c) are satisfied.

Fred Reish, a well recognized attorney in the area of ERISA section 404(c), has noted that, in his experience, most plans do not satisfy 404(c). Fred Reish, *404(c): Myth or Magic – What you think you see may not be what you get*, Plansponsor magazine (May 2006), Available at http://www.plansponsor.com/magazine/404c-myth-or-magic/. *See also* David Loeper, The Four Pillars of Retirement Plans (John Wiley & Sons, Inc. 2009) at 173. 404(c) compliance "will be a lightning rod for lawsuits against fiduciaries." Id.

[77] It would have been ideal to have Legal assess the investment change before it was implemented. This example illustrates that risks can be managed on recurring occasions.

At the second meeting, legal counsel would present its opinion and discuss whether the plan is in compliance with ERISA section 404(c) or if there are potential compliance problems. At that time, if it is determined that the plan is not meeting ERISA section 404(c), the goal would change to correcting or evaluating the compliance problem and potentially outlining options. In either case, individuals would be identified to address or manage the issue, responsibility clearly assigned, and targeted completion or status dates identified and pursued.

Goals Should Be Established for Four Groups

A number of parties interact with the plan, and it can be helpful for all of them to have goals. Indeed, one way for the plan committee to accomplish more with its limited resources is to have goals assigned to these other parties.

The four groups of that can, and should, establish goals are:

- The plan (established by the committee)
- The committee (as an oversight body)
- Individual committee members
- Vendors and staff (which can be set or guided by the plan committee or self-established)

For simplicity (and uniformity), the goals can be structured around the 12 governance principles. For example, goals can be related to compliance, ethics and conflicts, risk management, and so on. Each of the four groups may place emphasis on different areas, but building off of the 12 governance principles guarantees that all the necessary areas will, at a minimum, be considered. Also, not everything that needs to be accomplished will be a current goal. As noted (and discussed in detail shortly), goals will need to be prioritized based on importance and available resources.

For example, every year the plan will need to file a Form 5500. That is a recurring task (that should be assigned and monitored), but it isn't necessarily a goal. A good way to differentiate between tasks that need to be accomplished and items that are goals is to recognize that goals will *potentially change or improve* the situation (*i.e.,* the plan, the committee, the member, or the vendor or staff). The following are a few illustrations of ways to potentially change or improve:

- The plan, by performing a compliance, controls, or vendor review
- The plan committee, by structuring training on governance or committee effectiveness
- New members, by supplying them with on-boarding material and training on ERISA and governance
- Staff, by having them create controls for transactions, test them for effectiveness, and document the controls

What Should the Goals Be?

Most companies maintain a retirement plan to meet some larger company objectives, whether specifically articulated or not. These objectives possibly include providing competitive benefits, attracting and retaining talented employees, or reducing the financial stress on employees so they can be more focused at work. The company also has as unspoken expectations that the plan will be compliant, risks managed, and there will be good governance and oversight.

The plan committee has to take these general objectives and translate them into specific goals that can be monitored, measured and managed. The 12 governance principles can help in building these goals. Thus, there will be goals related to compliance, risk, avoiding conflicts, and so on. Recognizing that organizations and plan committees can have preferences about how to set goals, they may prefer to use a method that has worked for them in the past. Regardless of the approach, however, all 12 governance principles should be considered when establishing your goals. This will help the committee in meeting its fiduciary duty and avoid inadvertent breaches.

Goal-Building Approaches

Other ways to categorize, synthesize and compartmentalize goals that committees have used are:

- *Transactional* – Goals related to investments, administration, and data transfers
- *Organizational* – Goals related to parts of the organization, such as IT, HR, and specific vendors
- *Opportunistic* – Goals that leverage other activities in the company, such as reviewing controls related to 401(k) deductions when Internal Audit is performing a payroll audit
- *Recommendation Driven* – Goals that are initiated by recommendations by the plan's advisors, such as legal counsel, HR, consultants, the recordkeeper, or the investment advisor

Because the plan committee will need to establish goals based on its specific needs, there isn't a comprehensive list of goals that are completely applicable to every plan. However, at the end of each chapter on the 12 governance principles, you'll find "quick hits" that include illustrative goals that may prove useful for the committee.

The following is a hypothetical that suggests goals that the plan committee might consider:

> At the plan committee meeting, the members receive a report from the company's Internal Audit Director. The Director informs the committee that they just completed an audit of several areas within the company that may impact the plan. The Internal Audit Director details the findings related to the 401(k) plan:
>
> > Over the past five years, the company added a number of new compensation codes[78] into the

---

[78] A compensation code is a data field in the payroll system that tracks a specific type of pay. For example, Payroll will typically have separate compensation codes for base pay, overtime pay, shift differential, bonus pay, incentive pay, commissions, and more. Companies will typically have 50-100 compensation codes, but can have over 400.

payroll system. No one in Payroll notified Benefits about the new codes and these codes may not be properly structured for the plan. It is possible that employee elective deferrals, the company match, and the company profit-sharing contributions are not being calculated using the correct compensation amounts. It is also possible that the plan may not be transmitting the correct compensation to the recordkeeper for discrimination testing, which could result in incorrect test results.

The targeted goals established by the plan committee will depend on a few factors: the sophistication and experience of the plan committee members, whether some of the key advisors for the committee were present and able to provide input during the meeting, and whether the plan committee thought it had all the necessary information or if additional fact-finding was required. Different goals will be appropriate for different committees. In all situations, however, the plan committee should conduct a thorough evaluation based on its sophistication and experience, and by using the 12 governance principles.

Building on the above hypothetical, the plan committee evaluates the Internal Audit Director's comments, and takes the following response:

The plan committee is concerned by the Internal Audit Director's findings, and thanks the Director for identifying these issues. The committee discusses the Internal Audit findings using the 12 governance principles to help establish goals (or other action items). As none of the plan committee's key advisors attended the presentation by the Internal Audit Director, the committee decides on the following goals:

- Request that Internal Audit, Legal, HR/Benefits, and Payroll meet within the next 21 days to review the issues and develop a plan that will:

o Identify whether any participants were affected by the issues (or what action will be required to make this determination)

o Develop a plan to correct any compliance issues that occurred and address whether any notification or submission is required to the IRS or DOL

o Modify company and plan procedures to avoid these issues going forward (*e.g.*, new compensation codes should not be established without consideration of the impact on the plan; manual pay adjustments have a step that also adjusts plan contribution amounts; elective deferrals are contributed on a timely basis)

o Institute controls related to the creation of new compensation codes, such as requiring in-system sign-offs by HR before new codes can be activated

o Have the procedures and controls clearly identify individuals or groups that have responsibility, to whom they are accountable, and how they will periodically report when any exceptions or actions/testing/reconciliations are taken

o Recommend training for staff to improve knowledge and skills and help avoid these issues in the future

- Request that Internal Audit, Legal, HR/Benefits, and Payroll meet within the next 30 days to review the issues and, extrapolating from these issues, propose other areas where the plan committee should consider having a deeper review conducted to help manage risk, improve compliance, clarify roles and responsibilities, or heighten oversight.

- Request that the findings of the group and the approach for addressing these items be presented to the plan committee within 60 days for review or approval by the committee. Each item should include a list of alternatives, time and cost projections, and the possibility that the company will bear the cost of the action.

The course of action taken by the plan committee considers all 12 principles, and directly addresses seven of the governance principles:

- The committee is fulfilling its *fiduciary duty* by protecting plan participants and moving to correct any errors that may have impacted them.
- The committee is looking to identify and correct any *compliance* issues.
- The committee is *managing risk* by asking that new procedures and controls be added. As part of this, it emphasized that *roles, responsibilities, and accountability* be clearly defined.
- By asking that staff training programs be recommended, the committee is focusing on the staff's *knowledge and skills*.
- In taking a prospective approach, the committee is seeking to improve its *oversight* and also expand the areas where *assessments* can be performed.

In this example, the issue presented was rather technical, but nevertheless, the goals that were developed were focused on the plan, the committee, and company staff (HR/Benefits and Payroll). In other situations, the goals may also touch on individual plan committee members or vendors.

Establishing SMART Goals

Plan, committee members, vendors and staff goals should be "SMART" or:
    Specific
    Measurable
    Achievable
    Relevant
    Time bound

There is a wealth of excellent writing on SMART goals, and most executives are familiar with the concept. Accordingly, detail on SMART goals aren't repeated or summarized here. [79]

While most of the SMART components are self-evident, there is one that committees often misapply: goals that are time bound (or have a target date for when they will be accomplished). Thus, some goals will have a short duration (a month or a quarter), some will be for a longer period (a year), and some can even have a longer horizon, such as two or more years.

Some plan committees try to have all goals completed within a single plan year. That is not always necessary and can even be counter-productive. Allot enough time for goals to be completed properly; in other words, the amount of time that a prudent fiduciary would recommend.

Prioritizing Goals

For most plans, the number of potential goals will outstrip the available resources; for some plans, the potential goals may be overwhelming. Thus, the question is how to prioritize goals when the committee won't be able to achieve all of them immediately.

Let's pause for a moment, since the thought of not *immediately* addressing all of the goals is often distressing for some plan committee members. There may be a concern that if a goal is identified, it should be handled right away. Isn't it a potential fiduciary breach to fail to act promptly?

It's simply not feasible to accomplish all goals immediately. Thus, the committee needs to prioritize goals and address the most significant ones first. Prioritizing goals does not mean ignoring the other goals, especially if doing so could have catastrophic consequences. The plan committee needs to manage the goal-

---

[79] The first known use of the term occurs in the November 1981 issue of *Management Review* by George T. Doran.

setting process, recognizing that there are three variables to consider:

- Available resources
- Number of goals
- Amount of time needed to achieve each goal

When a committee is confronted with a significant number of goals which, if not accomplished, could have catastrophic consequences for the plan and the plan committee, it needs to look at the three variables and try to change some of the variables. For example, the committee could secure additional resources (from internal or external sources) to help accomplish some of the goals. Internally, using Payroll, HR, Finance, IT, or Internal Audit representatives can help increase the resources available.[80] External resources can be secured by using temporary staffing services and individual actuaries (who are often also very knowledgeable about DC plans), or by hiring a vendor[81] that can source an entire team.[82]

It is important to remember that not all of the goals will draw upon all of the resources at the same time. Often, some goals will require some research or work be done by other individuals or groups before the project can begin. For example, a committee confronted with three major goals might schedule and prioritize them as follows:

- *Goal One* – Begin correction process (requires intense work immediately).

---

[80] Often, a plan issue will have a mirror issue for the company. The plan committee can sometimes leverage the work being done by the company to address that issue's impact on the plan.

[81] Existing and potential vendors will sometimes agree to help the committee meet some of its goals at a reduced or no cost to further develop its relationship with the committee, or simply to gain insight into the goals the committee is pursuing.

[82] For defined contribution plans, the plan committee needs to be aware of the cost of hiring third-parties, since that will impact the potential return received by participants.

- *Goal Two* – Collect data for correction process (may be able to be delegated to junior staff or temporary employees).
- *Goal Three* – Use a vendor to perform a study on possible correction methods.

The plan committee can also look at the list of goals under consideration and reduce the number it will attempt to accomplish. A useful guide to prioritizing goals is to categorize them and rank them according to the following criteria:

- *Goals for Avoiding Disqualification and Fiduciary Breaches* – These are goals that relate to potential plan disqualification and fiduciary breaches that should always be addressed first. The potential disqualification and fiduciary breach covered by this category are imminent issues or problems that have already occurred and need to be corrected.
- *Goals for Improving Investments and Reducing Costs* – These are goals related to improving investments and reducing costs, which are ongoing duties of the fiduciaries. They should be constantly considered and a top priority following the avoidance of imminent plan disqualification or a fiduciary breach. Examples include vendor evaluations or searches or periodic assessments such as compliance or controls reviews.
- *Goals for Improving Governance* – This category includes goals which would all relate to improving the plan's governance (following the 12 principles). It would include goals related to improving the identification of conflicts, risk management, training, and the like.

Over time, the number of goals that fall into the first category (a form of crisis management) will decline, and most of the goals will fall into the second and third categories. The migration from crisis management to strategy and planning reflects improved governance and plan oversight.

Goals Related to Information, Studies, and Benchmarking

Plan committees often overlook the need to establish goals related to gathering information that might help the plan committee make better decisions. This includes participating in studies or obtaining surveys, benchmarking data, or other information. Numerous studies and surveys are performed each year,[83] and the groups performing the study or survey are often seeking plans to participate. Participating in one of these gives plans an opportunity to get free or reduced cost benchmarking or other information that may help the plan committee better shape its mission and goals.

Note that not all surveys, benchmarks, and studies are created equally, and the plan committee should be judicious in considering those in which it would be relevant and desirable to participate. Some will not address plans with a similar population, asset size, industry, or other perspective. Others will be new and not able to provide historical context, while still others will just not be of a high quality.

Also, the plan committee may not need to incur significant or any costs to get good survey data. For example, the Bureau of Labor Statistics provides a wealth of information on retirement plan topics ranging from access, participation, contributions, and plan features.[84]

The Mission Statement

When Should You Develop a Plan Mission Statement?

One would presume that the logical time to create the plan's mission statement is when the plan is created or when the process begins to improve the plan's governance. In theory, this is true. However, experience has shown that allowing some time to pass (and experience to grow), is a better approach.

---

[83] Studies and survey are performed by HR consulting firms, accounting and business advisory firms, law firms, investment advisors, mutual funds, non-profits and governmental agencies.
[84] *See* bls.gov.

As the plan committee gains experience in truly governing the plan, the mission will become clear. What is the primary driver for the plan: Cost? Participant education? Electronic access? Personal assistance? Familiar investment options?[85] As the committee learns more about the participants' needs, preferences and desires, and as the committee develops its own philosophies on what will generate the most benefit for participants, the mission will begin to develop and become clearer.

Practically speaking, it can take from one to three years for the committee to gather enough experience to be capable of clearly articulating the plan's mission statement. During this time, the committee should begin to think about developing straw models of possible mission statements, which can then be challenged by decisions the committee makes or actions taken by individuals involved in the operation of the plan.

Why Should You Develop a Plan Mission Statement?

A committee that is establishing goals and working to achieve those goals within the overall governance framework will be running the plan well (or at least much better than a plan with no goal setting process or governance structure). What then, does having a mission statement contribute?

The mission statement serves as the guiding framework, or North Star, that can be used by the plan committee, the vendors, the staff, and others involved in administering and operating the plan to help guide and direct their actions. It will guide them and help put the plan committee instructions into context.

Let's look at two examples of mission statements to see how they can help guide all the groups involved with the plan. The first mission statement provides that the plan is intended to deliver benefits in a cost-effective manner, reducing plan expenses and

---

[85] These are just an illustration of some of the considerations that will go into the development of a plan's mission statement and isn't intended to be all-encompassing.

thereby increase the participants' ultimate benefit. The second mission statement provides that the plan will provide participants with tools and assistance that will increase their investment intelligence and allow them to invest wisely. The first hopes to benefit participants by minimizing costs, and the second pays more for technology, tools, and assistance to maximize participants' benefits. Both have a common goal, but they seek to achieve this goal in different ways.

If, in these two situations the plan committees request a review of the services available in the market, the individuals that will do the market study can be guided by the mission statement. The mission statement will provide guidance to the team performing the evaluation as to where they should focus. The team evaluating the plan with the first mission statement would focus on cost. The team with the second mission statement would focus on participant tools. Simply put, the mission statement points everyone working on the plan in the same direction—serving as their North Star.

Mission Statement Examples

It is relatively easy to find mission statements for *public* retirement programs, and relatively difficult to find mission statements for *private* retirement programs.[86] Accordingly, the sampling of mission statements that are reproduced are overwhelmingly for public retirement programs.

CalPERS, which is one of the largest pension funds in the world, has one of the simplest mission statements. It provides:

> Mission – Provide responsible and efficient stewardship of the System to deliver promised retirement and health benefits, while promoting wellness and retirement security for members and beneficiaries.[87]

---

[86] A public retirement program is one run by a state, city, or municipality. A private retirement program is one run by a non-governmental entity, such as a corporation.

[87] CalPERS' website, https://www.calpers.ca.gov/page/about/organization/strategic-business-

CalPERS expands on its mission statement by identifying core values[88] and guiding principles,[89] and by identifying strategic plans, which are longer-term goals. For 2012-2017, some of the objectives of the strategic plan that supported its broadly stated mission were:

- Fund the System through an integrated view of pension assets and liabilities
- Educate employers and other stakeholders to make informed decisions about retirement security and health care
- Deliver target risk-adjusted investment returns
- Deliver superior, end-to-end customer service that is adaptive to customer needs
- Actively manage business risks with an enterprise-wide view[90]

In the mission statement for the State Retirement and Pension System of Maryland (System), the board of trustees[91] noted that it "is charged with the fiduciary responsibility for administering the . . . retirement benefits of the System's participants, and to ensure that sufficient assets are available to fund the benefits when due."[92]

---

plans.

[88] The core values are quality, respect, accountability, integrity, openness, and balance. Available at https://www.calpers.ca.gov/page/about/organization/strategic-business-plans.

[89] The guiding principles include items such as: obtaining and retaining a quality, motivated workforce; accuracy; security; quality; ethics; cost-effectiveness; prudence; and timeliness. Available at https://www.calpers.ca.gov/page/about/organization/strategic-business-plans.

[90] CalPERS 2012-17 Strategic Plan (July 1, 2013 edition), available at https://www.calpers.ca.gov/docs/forms-publications/2012-17-strategic-plan.pdf.

[91] Governmental plans often have a board of trustees rather than a plan committee, but the roles are similar.

[92] Comprehensive Annual Financial Report for the Retirement and Pension System of Maryland for the year ended June 30, 2000, cover page. Available at http://www.sra.state.md.us/agency/downloads/cafr/CAFR-2000-Intro.pdf.

The board goes on to state that to accomplish this overarching mission, it must focus on the following elements:[93]

- To **prudently invest** System assets in a **well-diversified** manner to optimize long-term returns, while **controlling risk** through excellence in execution of the investment objectives and strategies of the System.
- To **effectively communicate** with all retirement plan participants to inform them about the benefits provided by the System, and to **educate** them about planning and preparing for all aspects of their future retirement.
- To **accurately and timely** pay retirement allowances provided by State pension law to the System's retirees and their beneficiaries.
- To implement an **automated, comprehensive and integrated pension administration** and electronic document management system.
- To efficiently collect the required employer and member contributions necessary to fund the System.[94]

The Ontario Teachers' Pension Plan, which is often recognized for its good plan governance, has one of the most streamlined mission statements. It simply provides, "Outstanding service and retirement security for our members – today and tomorrow."

Mission statements can be simple, such as the Ontario Teachers' Pension Plan, or detailed like CalPERS. The key is that they reflect the vision and mission behind having the plan, and what the company and plan committee are attempting to accomplished through the plan.

---

[93] While the mission statement actually identifies the following bulleted items as "key goals," the use of "goal" in this context is a little confusing, since they are intended to serve as key elements to the overall mission of the System.
[94] Comprehensive Annual Financial Report for the Retirement and Pension System of Maryland *supra* cover page. Emphasis added.

Quick Hits

1. Have the plan committee develop several reasonable goals that address the most pressing needs, based on the governance areas that need improvement, the plan's mission, or where there is a need to support plan participants. (Many of the "Quick Hits" in the following chapters can potentially become goals, and the committee can consider them as a starting point in developing plan goals.)

2. Based on the governance areas that need improvement, have the following individuals and entities develop goals that address their most pressing needs:
   a. Individual plan committee members
   b. Vendors
   c. Company staff who work with the plan
   For example, each of these stakeholders should develop goals related to improving quality, identifying and reducing risks, improving participant service and experience, and compliance. Initial goals might relate to collecting data (or in the case of the plan members, improving knowledge and skills). Have the goals be "SMART."

3. Set an agenda for each meeting and have the agenda items correspond to the goals established for the upcoming year.

4. Begin the process of creating a mission statement.

Clarity: Roles, Responsibility, and Accountability

"I always wanted to be somebody, but I should have been more specific."
Lily Tomlin

"High fees, poor performance, lack of disclosure, and a system devoid of accountability characterize the financial industry."
Tim Hatton[95]

Introduction

A core concept of governance is knowing and understanding *what* needs to be done (the role), *who* must do it (responsibility), and *how* they will be held accountable (accountability). Indeed, after establishing goals, the most important principle is the need to have clarity about the roles, responsibilities, and accountability of all of the individuals and entities interacting with the plan.

There are four separate parts to this principle: clarity, roles, responsibilities, and accountability. Unfortunately, the concept is often misconstrued as the need to align specific individuals to responsibility for specific areas, based on function. For example, the investment advisor is responsible for the investments, or the recordkeeper is responsible for the day-to-day administration. But when the approach is to shift responsibility without having clarity concerning the role or without outlining accountability for the area, one is *not governing, but rather abdicating responsibility*.

---

[95] Tim Hatton, <u>The New Fiduciary Standard. Princeton</u> (NJ, Bloomberg Press, 2005) at xv.

This chapter defines what it means to have clarity about roles, responsibilities, and accountability, and provides illustrations on how to achieve it.

Like a Cascading Waterfall

Sometimes descriptions of defining roles, responsibilities, and accountability sound like a painful HR exercise—a gruesome task that no one embraces, and one that exists only to torture employees who are otherwise engaged in productive endeavors. From that perspective, I can appreciate why most plan committees have neither mapped out nor documented their plan's roles, responsibilities, and accountability. At best, it's made to sound like it's not fun, and at worst potentially pointless.

Let me paint a different picture that more accurately portrays how defining roles, responsibilities, and accountability should be viewed. I see it as a tall waterfall, one that is cascading from some great height, funneling down to various levels below. At each level, there are pools, where some of the water rests, while still more water cascades down to the next level. Everything starts at the top. The falls below would not exist without the water descending from the falls above.

The plan and the plan committee are created by someone or something. For many companies, it is the board of directors or members of the company's executive team. What powers do board members retain and what powers (or roles and responsibilities) do they delegate? If they delegate powers, roles, or responsibilities, to whom are they delegated? What reporting does the delegating body expect to receive? Or what oversight does it expect to provide? Like a waterfall, the powers either rest in a pool at the current level, or cascade down.

At a high level, the structure of the roles, responsibilities, and accountability for a plan may look like this:

Each party (represented by a level or box) should have a parallel description of its roles, responsibilities, and accountability that describes the powers that are held by that party, what the party's roles are, who is responsible for carrying out those roles, and how they are to be held accountable. It will also describe what roles are being delegated, who is responsible for the delegated roles, and how they, in turn, will be held accountable. The process continues cascading down until all that needs to be done for the plan is clearly owned by a specific party.

Defining Clarity of Roles, Responsibilities, and Accountability

What is meant by clarity, roles, responsibility, and accountability? In general, the terms can be defined as follows:

> **Clarity** – The delegation of roles, responsibilities, and accountability must be clear and specific, with the scope of authority identified and limitations detailed. This also means that as areas are delegated, it is clear how the party executing the role will report back and be held accountable. And it means that all 12 of the governance principles are addressed. It is *clear*:

- Who is responsible
- What each party will contribute to the area
- How each party will report back (be held accountable)

As these bullets suggest, multiple parties may be responsible for an area. For example, although it might be intuitive to state that ERISA counsel is responsible for plan compliance, this would likely be an over- simplification.[96] The investment advisor may be responsible for compliance with ERISA section 404(c) (requirements to shift fiduciary responsibility for investment decisions from the committee to participants), or with obtaining a Form ADV (registering investment advisors with the Security Exchange Commission), and other items. But the recordkeeper will also own areas of compliance, such as following the terms of the plan, adhering to the Internal Revenue Code testing requirements for discrimination, and ensuring that notices are done properly to allow the plan to qualify for safe-harbors.

Just as multiple parties can have responsibility for one area, such as compliance, a single party can have responsibility related to multiple areas. For example, a single party can have roles and responsibilities in areas such as risk management, ethics (*e.g.,* avoiding conflicts), transparency, succession (*e.g.,* for staff transition), and knowledge and skills (*e.g.,* for changes in plan terms, laws, systems, and the like).

Clarity also encompasses clearly communicating the roles, responsibilities, and accountability *to* the parties. The preference is to clearly document each parties' roles, responsibilities, and accountability. By having it documented, the delegating and receiving party can review and retain the document, which can be updated as

---

[96] It could also be completely erroneous, as discussed in the upcoming sidebar, "Who's on First?"

vendors, personnel, and systems change. This documentation also provides a guide for assessing performance, as the details related to what is expected are delineated and can be reviewed.

> ### *Who's on First?*
>
> When interviewing plan committee members and personnel supporting plan committees, I would typically ask, "Who is responsible for compliance?" On several occasions, the response would be that their attorney was responsible for plan compliance. When counsel was later asked the same question, they would say the plan committee was responsible for compliance, and that they served only as a legal advisor.[97] This lack of clarity regarding something as basic as compliance, which can jeopardize a plan's tax qualified status and have a significant potential impact on the plan, participants, and the employer, shows the importance of having clarity about who is responsible for all areas and clearly communicating those designations.

Roles – A description of a party's role must answer the following four questions:

- *What must be done?*
- *What are the expectations?*
- *What is the timing?*
- *What standards or criteria are to be used, if applicable?*

The roles can be described at a high level, such as an overall objective or goal for a party, or they can be more granular and detail the jobs or the tasks that must be performed. For example, the plan committee might

---

[97] Typically, I was conducting the interview because there had been a compliance problem. The fact that no one actually had responsibility for compliance explains why the problem arose.

describe the Payroll Department's role for the plan at a high level as *maintaining a controlled environment for transmitting accurate payroll data to the recordkeeper each pay period.*

Within the Payroll Department, however, this role might be defined in greater detail to ensure that the staff in Payroll understands what is encompassed by the role (or goal) described by the plan committee. Payroll might define its role in greater detail as follows:

> *Payroll's role in relation to the accurate and compliant operation of the retirement plan is to transmit accurate data to the recordkeeper. This role requires the following of Payroll:*
>
> - *Compensation and service must be captured accurately, requiring that: compensation and service codes will be accurately maintained to agree with the plan terms; compensation amounts and service will be captured accurately (pulling from the correct codes/fields); deferral election feeds from the recordkeeper are timely loaded and validated so they agree with the number of active participants and any limitations in the plan; the recordkeeper is quickly informed of changes or adjustments to compensation or service.*
> - *Caps or limitations on pay are taken into account (as well as any tables used to track such caps or limits) and are accurate and validated at least annually.*
> - *Every data transmittal to the recordkeeper is validated for completeness and accuracy, with reconciliations performed to: check individuals that have stopped participating and new participants that have entered the plan; reconciliations will also be done for contribution and loan amounts.*

- *Transmittals to the recordkeeper are done timely (pursuant to DOL regulations).*
- *Controls are in place for all manual and automated processing, and controls are tested quarterly, with any exceptions reported to the plan committee.*
- *Personnel are trained regularly on system, IT, and plan provisions that may impact processing.*
- *At least annually, Payroll will report to the plan committee about its processes and any changes that have been made that could impact the plan; any exceptions or errors that occur will be reported to the plan committee immediately.*

In the high-level description, the following items are clear:

- *What must be done* - transmitting accurate payroll data to the recordkeeper
- *What are the expectations* – maintaining a controlled payroll environment
- *What is the timing* – each pay period
- *What standards or criteria are to be used, if applicable* - Not addressed in the high-level description, but in the detailed version (*e.g.*, data transmittal to the recordkeeper is validated for completeness and accuracy)

In the granular description prepared by the Payroll Department, each of these elements is further developed.

It is helpful if, in addition to a description of what must be done, there is also a description of how the job or task relates to the overall responsibilities or other parties.

Responsibility - The party (which can be an individual, vendor, or group) that is charged with completing the job or task is the one responsible, and thus is charged with accomplishing the job or task. Where a description of the roles answers the "what" question, a description of the responsibility answers the "who" question.

Where one party is responsible, identifying the responsible party is simple. However, there are situations where an area will have multiple parties responsible for the success of the activity or goal, or where there will be reliance on others.

In these situations, the fact that there are multiple parties responsible must be recognized by a description of how they should coordinate and interact. Ideally, one party should be the primary owner and have ultimate responsibility (if that is possible). Similarly, where one party is primarily responsible for the success of the goal or task but they are dependent on others, the dependency, interactions, and hierarchy should be described.

Let's build on the Payroll example used earlier. Let's assume that Payroll is responsible for the accurate calculation of participant elective deferrals to the plan. However, one of the steps in the process is the correct application of limits and caps. HR is the party charged with providing the limits and caps to Payroll so it can update the tables in the payroll system.

In this situation, Payroll would be primarily responsible, but would be dependent on HR for key information related to the limits and caps. The dependency should be noted, and it should be made clear that HR is *required* to provide updates on limits and caps before the first payroll run of the year, or whenever there is a change in any limit or cap related to the plan.

Accountability – The inclusion of accountability is what changes this from an activity that will complete a task into one that is built upon a governance framework. The addition of accountability creates the oversight structure by incorporating reporting, standards, and feedback.

In our Payroll example, the Payroll Department's description of its role included a statement about accountability:

> *At least annually, Payroll **will report to the plan committee** about its processes and any changes that have been made that could impact the plan; **any exceptions or errors that occur will be reported to the plan committee immediately.***

This statement above is relatively broad: "any exceptions or errors" will be reported to the plan committee. Over time, the plan committee will be able to refine or limit when it will receive exception reports. For example, payroll runs will often have differences due to rounding, or timing differences when hours worked were not correctly captured but that are corrected in the next payroll run. If the plan committee decides that de minimis differences or minor timing differences are not significant, it can note that these are not exceptions that should be reported.

Using the "RACI" Framework[98]

If you're looking for a framework to build your plan's clarity of roles, responsibility and accountability, then a good option is the "RACI" framework (or the responsibility assignment matrix). RACI is a method of identifying the party in any process that is:

Responsible – the doer of the job or task
Accountable[99] – the person ultimately responsible and answerable for the activity, and the decision-maker

---

[98] *See e.g.,* Michael L. Smith and James Erwin, *Role & Responsibility Charting (RACI)*, and Balaji Viswanathan, *Understanding Responsibility Assignment Matrix (RACI Matrix)* (April 8, 2015) at Project-Management.com, available at http://project-management.com/understanding-responsibility-assignment-matrix-raci-matrix/.
[99] Depending on how the RACI matrix is structured and how it is being used, the "A" in RACI could also stand for Approve or Approver. There are also slight variations on what the "C" and "I" can mean.

> Consulted   – individuals who have valuable input (such as subject matter experts and stakeholders)
>
> Informed   – individuals who need to be informed after the job or task is completed, or following a decision

The RACI technique supports the governance principle to have clarity for roles, responsibilities, and accountability. By ensuring that one similarly identifies the parties who must be consulted and informed, you clearly enhance the communication that is critical to this principle.[100] When identifying jobs, tasks, or decisions, the RACI framework provides excellent suggestions for promoting clarity. For example, it suggests that the activities that make up the job, task, or decision be prefaced with strong action verbs, such as:

- Calculate
- Review
- Evaluate
- Approve
- Recommend
- Document

How to Begin Structuring Clear Roles, Responsibilities, and Accountability

It starts at the top.

For private retirement plans, the company's board of directors or senior members of the executive team create the retirement plan, and all power flows from them. What they don't delegate to others, they retain. Therefore, the place to begin in defining roles, responsibilities, and accountability is at the top, with the board of directors or the senior members of the executive team.

---

[100] In the RACI framework, the "Roles" description is typically addressed in the part of the matrix that covers the tasks. The description of the tasks in the RACI matrix is often a summary, and may not be in adequate detail to have *clarity* related to the description of the *role.*

Let's begin by recognizing that, theoretically, anything is possible. The board could retain all the power or delegate all of it. The board could delegate all power to the plan committee or to an individual. Rather than chasing theories, however, let's view the delegation process through the governance lens, and sharpen its focus with a pragmatic perspective.

In most situations, the board or executive team will not want to be involved in the oversight of the plan and will delegate all (or practically all) power to the plan committee and specific members of management. To understand the delegation from the board or executive team, one also needs to understand:

- What powers might the board or executive team want to retain, and why?
- Why are the duties delegated potentially split between the plan committee and specific members of management?
- What duties are typically delegated to the plan committee or specific members of management?

Powers Retained by the Board or Executive Team

It is common for the board or executive team to relinquish all or almost all of their powers with respect to the plan. Any powers retained are usually for the most significant plan events or activities, such as terminating or merging the plan, removing plan committee members, or changing the person or entity to whom they've delegated power. In some cases, the board or executive team will also retain the authority to make plan changes that will have a significant cost to the company. Examples are increasing the plan benefit, increasing the level of the company contribution, or expanding the level of plan participation.

Why Split Duties Between the Plan Committee and Members of Management?

The short and simple answer is *clarity.*

The duties being delegated from the board or the executive team fall into two categories: those that are fiduciary duties and those that are not fiduciary duties (sometimes called "settlor functions" in trust law). I've found that when the fiduciary duties are placed solely with the plan committee, the members know that when they are meeting, they are acting as fiduciaries and must act in the best interest of the plan participants.

Similarly, when only non-fiduciary duties (or settlor functions) are placed solely with members of management, they don't need to worry about the fiduciary standards, and can act solely in the interest of the company and the shareholders (or other owners). This division provides clarity for the members of management and the plan committee about the standards they need to use when approaching a decision.

Dumping all Duties with the Plan Committee

Unfortunately, it is common for the plan committee to have all duties delegated to it.[101] The committee thereby becomes the owner of both fiduciary decisions and management (non-fiduciary) decisions related to the plan.

When this happens, the committee members can become unsure about whether they are acting in their role as a fiduciary or a member of management when making a decision. I've seen committee members discuss in interviews and in meeting minutes their uncertainty about what role they were playing when making a decision. In some cases, they clearly applied the wrong standard.

Placing non-fiduciary decision-making outside the committee, and having the plan committee focus on fiduciary matters is a very

---

[101] *The New Governance Landscape supra* at 14.

> simple approach to helping ensure that plan committee members apply the correct standard. It is a way to build a control into the decision-making process.

Placing all the fiduciary duties with the plan committee also has the benefit of removing all fiduciary duties from the board (except their duty to pick the plan committee members). This helps to insulate the board from potential fiduciary liability, and alleviates the board of the burden of understanding the ERISA fiduciary rules. If we look back to the description on page 73 of the possible duties or powers that might be retained by the board, none of them are fiduciary duties; they are all "settlor functions" or powers or duties that don't carry the weight of the role of a fiduciary.

What Duties are Delegated to Management versus the Plan Committee?

If the goal is to isolate the fiduciary decisions with the plan committee, the question then becomes, what are the fiduciary versus the non-fiduciary areas of decision-making? The Department of Labor has provided detailed guidance on what constitutes the non-fiduciary or employer functions (or "settlor" functions). While some of its guidance is summarized here, note that when structuring these delegations and approaching these decisions, the ultimate determination of whether an activity is a fiduciary act is a legal decision that should be made on the advice of counsel.

Employer Functions (Not Fiduciary Functions)[102]

- Designing, creating, or establishing the plan
- Design activities in advance of the adoption of a plan amendment, such as plan design studies or cost projections. (Studies and design activity could be for

---

[102] *See e.g.,* DOL Advisory Opinion 97-03A (Jan. 23, 1997); DOL Advisory Opinion 2001-01A (January 18, 2001); letter to Kirk Maldonado from Elliot I. Daniel (March 2, 1987); letter to John Erlenborn from Dennis M. Kass (March 13, 1986).

early retirement windows, participant loan programs, or plan spin-offs.)

- The decision to terminate the plan (but "...activities undertaken to implement the plan termination decision are generally fiduciary in nature...."[103])
- The decision to merge the plan
- Increasing benefits under the plan
- Increasing employer contributions under the plan
- Changing eligibility criteria for participation in the plan

Mapping the delegation from the board to the management team and the plan committee is, however, only the beginning. The heavy lifting, and where plans often fail, involves documenting clear roles, responsibilities and accountability.

How to Build and Document Clear Roles, Responsibilities, and Accountability

The operation of most large retirement plans are complex endeavors involving a multitude of tasks carried out by an array of parties. Building and documenting roles, responsibilities, and accountability will take some time, and will require modifications over time.

A somewhat organic approach is to begin at the top with the board and the plan committee, and then have the plan committee request that each of parties involved in the plan's operation document and describe their roles, responsibilities, and accountability. The plan committee does not need to build these descriptions; it just needs to request that they be done by all the parties and then critically evaluate what has been prepared.

When requesting these descriptions from the parties, the plan committee should provide at the outset a specific framework indicating how the descriptions should be prepared. For example, the description can use a RACI framework, a format similar to the Payroll Department example (see pages 68-69), or another approach that is familiar and used company-wide. Any approach,

---

[103] DOL Advisory Opinion 97-03A at 3.

however, should clearly define who has the role, what is the responsibility, and how they will be held accountable.

Since so much of the success of a plan's governance depends on the clarity of the roles, responsibilities, and accountability, it is helpful if their description and documentation is kept visible. A way to keep these descriptions central to the operation of the plan is to include them in the plan committee's charter. This consolidates the descriptions of all the parties and incorporates the descriptions into the plan committee's central operating document.

Customizing RRA Descriptions

The descriptions of the parties' roles, responsibilities, and accountability should reflect the mission, goals, and challenges the plan and plan committee face. For example, if the plan committee has delegated to other parties certain fiduciary functions (investment advice, or certain plan interpretations), and if issues have arisen over who is serving in a fiduciary role, the committee can use the description of roles and responsibilities to identify the fiduciary functions that are being performed by the various parties. Similarly, if issues have emerged concerning the escalation of certain plan challenges or problems, the roles and responsibilities description may identify when escalation is required.

As issues arise and the plan committee grows in experience, the descriptions of the roles, responsibilities, and accountability will also grow.

The Relationship Between Transparency and Accountability

Transparency, one of the principles of good governance, is closely related to accountability; the two clearly support one another. On the one hand, when establishing roles, responsibilities, and accountability, clarity and completeness related to the roles is critical. The person or entity that is accountable needs to know what is expected of them, and how they should be reporting to their supervisor. In other words, the supervisor needs to be transparent about their expectations.

Similarly, the person or entity that is accountable needs to be clear about their performance, their accomplishments, and the challenges they are encountering. They need to be transparent about how they are fulfilling their roles and responsibilities.

Perhaps the most fundamental example is the relationship between the plan committee and the plan participants. Clearly, the plan committee is accountable to the plan participants. But what does this "accountability" look like?

Shortly after the turn of the 20th century, Associate Supreme Court Justice Louis Brandeis coined the now famous saying, "[s]unlight is said to be the best of disinfectants...."[104] Transparency serves to keep the players honest, dissuade individuals from conflicts of interest, and hold individuals accountable.

Let's take two plan committees. Both plan committees set goals at the beginning of the year, identify performance measures, and specify the timeframe. However, only the first plan committee is transparent with the plan participants by communicating this information to them in some way. What is the likelihood that the first committee will strive to accomplish its goals and meet the performance measures within the prescribed timeframe,

---

[104] Louis D. Brandeis, *Other People's Money and How the Bankers Use It.* (Frederick A. Stokes Company: New York 1914) at 92. Originally published in Harper's Weekly. Also http://www.law.louisville.edu/library/collections/brandeis/node/196. The phrase was coined before Associate Justice Brandeis was appointed to the Supreme Court.

compared to the second committee, which hasn't communicated with its plan participants? Transparency will unquestionably help to hold the plan committee accountable to the plan participants.

Risks Related to Transparency

There is a school of thought that the plan committee should not be completely transparent. By detailing its goals, performance measures, and timeframes, it leaves itself open to lawsuits if it doesn't meet these expectations. Indeed, I've seen and heard this argument raised several times by counsel for the plan committee.

The opposing argument is that the plan committee's duty is to the plan participants, and that nothing should be hidden from them.

There is validity to both arguments, and it is one of the areas where the plan committee will need take a pragmatic approach and balance its duty to the plan participants with managing the risk of potentially frivolous lawsuits. The plan committee's duty to the participants will need to assess how much transparency and disclosure is appropriate so that the plan committee is holding itself accountable to the plan participants. The plan committee's duty to manage risk will require it to evaluate how the potential risks from a frivolous lawsuit can distract the plan committee from its focus on the plan participants.

Quick Hits

1. Gather any current descriptions of roles, responsibilities, and accountability and assess what exists and what is missing.

2. Starting with the Board of Directors, identify their roles, responsibilities, and accountability. What have they delegated, and to whom (*e.g.*, the plan committee, or members of management)? What, if anything, has the board retained? If there is ambiguity, look into clarifying the delegation.

3. Next, begin to prepare (and document) the roles, responsibilities, and accountability of the plan committee, members of senior management, or others to whom the board delegated any responsibility. How is the committee (or other entity receiving a delegation) accountable to the board? What reporting must be done for informational purposes, and when does the plan committee need to seek the board's approval? What has the committee delegated to other entities, individuals, or parties? (Of the areas delegated, which ones have been documented, which ones need documentation prepared, and which ones need the delegation clarified?) For example, how will the following areas be handled?
   a. Appeals
   b. Day-to-day plan administration (recordkeeping, benefit calculation, claims processing)
   c. Plan funding, assumptions, and investing

4. Recognize that the plan committee will ultimately be responsible for the plan's governance. Thus, describe as part of the plan committee's responsibilities that it will be responsible for all 12 of the governance areas.

5. Ask each party involved in the plan operations under the plan committee to provide to the plan committee (for its consideration) the party's description of these relevant details:

   a. The party's roles. The party should explicitly note if any of its roles have any fiduciary duties.

   b. The identity of other individuals or entities with overlapping responsibility with the party, and which entity has primary responsibility.

   c. Who the party is accountable to, and how they will be held accountable (*e.g.*, periodic reporting, audit, and the like.). Similarly, if there are individuals or entities that are accountable to them, who are they and how will they hold them accountable?

6. Looking "down" from the plan committee and what it is overseeing, and looking up from the staff, vendors, and other parties performing services for the plan, gaps will be identified where there is ambiguity related to certain roles and responsibilities. Identify as a goal of the committee the achievement of clarity in these areas.

7. Use a standardized framework, such as RACI, to achieve consistency.

8. Identify any entities that have responsibility but that have avoided being accountable. For example, if your recordkeeper is responsible for tracking the contributions and earnings going into the plan, are they accountable for errors made and required to disclose the errors? Do performance measures place the recordkeeper's fees at risk?

Risk Management

"The first principle [of risk management] is that you must not fool yourself, and you are the easiest person to fool."
Richard P. Feynman, Nobel Prize-winning physicist

"What we learn from history is that people don't learn from history."
Warren Buffet

Understanding Plan Risks

One of the greatest challenges for plan fiduciaries is their lack of understanding of the plan risks, and without understanding the risks, the risks cannot be managed. This isn't unexpected. Typically, plan fiduciaries are not professional fiduciaries, and most committee members do not have experience in all facets of plan investing, ERISA, plan administration, and vendor management.

This chapter will help plan committee members understand who is at risk, what the risks are, and how to manage the risks. Plan fiduciaries also must identify potential risks from a number of perspectives. Some of these perspectives, which reflect a variety of risk themes, are:

- Asset and investment risks
- Resource risks
- Personnel risks
- Economic risks
- Transactional risks
- Vendor risks
- Compliance risks
- Litigation risks
- Reputational risks
- Governance risks

- Administrative risks

Risk Concerns from Towers Watson Retirement Plan Governance Survey[105]

Many of the risks listed above were concerns identified by respondents to Towers Watson's 2011 Governance Survey. The table below represents the percentage of respondents to the Towers' survey that had risk concerns.

	DC plan only	DC plan plus active DB plan	DC plan plus inactive DB plan
Regulatory compliance	86%	89%	82%
Investment volatility	82%	88%	85%
Vendor service quality	70%	67%	63%
Administrative failures	16%	17%	27%
Participant lawsuits	9%	8%	7%
Negative media attention	0%	7%	2%
IRS fines	0%	1%	5%
Other	7%	6%	6%

By exploring risks both broadly and then very specifically, we hope to bridge the knowledge gap that many fiduciaries may have related to the plan risks. The process for bridging this gap is three-fold. First, it helps to understand **who is at risk**. (Remember, it isn't just the fiduciary.) Second, it's critical to identify **what the risks are** that will impact the parties who are at risk. Note that the risks are much broader than most fiduciaries realize; often they recognize only investment and compliance risks, and "manage" these through the use of experts such as investment advisors and attorneys. Finally, the ultimate goal is to have a plan as to **how the risks will be managed**.

---

[105] *The New Governance Landscape supra* at 7, figure 4.

What, Exactly, Constitutes Risk?

Risks are those things that can prevent the plan or the plan committee from accomplishing their objectives.[106] Regardless of how the objectives are defined for your plan, the plan committee will need to manage numerous risks to increase the likelihood that the objectives will be achieved.

It is worth emphasizing that the focus is on **managing risk, not necessarily avoiding or eliminating risk.** As business people know, taking risk is what will give them a competitive advantage, present them with larger gains, or generate other positive outcomes. Just as unmitigated risk can be dangerous, risk that is understood and managed can be a positive force.

COSO's Definition of Enterprise Risk Management

"Enterprise risk management is a *process*, effected by the entity's board of directors, management and other personnel, applied in strategy-setting and across the enterprise, designed to identify potential events that may affect the entity and manage risk to be within its risk appetite, to provide reasonable assurance regarding the achievement of entity objectives."[107] (Emphasis added.)

Who is at Risk?

If you serve as a plan fiduciary, you are probably initially concerned about your risk. Can you be held personally liable for your decisions related to the plan? Can you be held liable for the decisions of other fiduciaries? Could decisions made by members of management or staff who work on plan matters create personal liability for you?

---

[106] COSO's ERM definition is, "[r]isk is the possibility that an event will occur and adversely affect the achievement of objectives." The Committee of Sponsoring Organizations of the Treadway Commission, Enterprise Risk Management – Integrated Framework – Executive Summary Framework (COSO September 2004) at 16.
[107] Enterprise Risk Management – Integrated Framework – Executive Summary Framework *supra* at 4.

If you are a member of the business's management team, you may wonder if the company can be held liable for fiduciary (or non-fiduciary) decisions. Can inactivity, inability, or ignorance by the plan fiduciaries or vendors create risk for the company or even the board of directors?

Although it is natural to focus on one's personal risk as a fiduciary, or the company's risk as a member of management, there is another very important perspective on plan risk. Plan participants and beneficiaries are the groups with the greatest risk in a retirement plan. The participants have entrusted their retirement savings and benefits to a group of individuals - the plan fiduciaries. The fiduciaries generally control the selection of the vendors, the management of expenses, and the oversight of investments. The fiduciaries are often members of the company's management team, and they are typically appointed by the board or a member of the company's management team.

Thus, there are three groups that have risk in relation to the retirement plan: the plan participants and beneficiaries, the company and members of management, and the plan fiduciaries. Although the risks for these groups are interrelated and often overlap, there is an inherent tension between them.

The participants must rely on the plan fiduciaries to oversee their savings and benefits, but the plan participants have no input in selecting the fiduciaries.[108] In addition, the participants are typically not able to oversee the plan committee's work or even have insight into the process used by the plan fiduciaries to oversee the plan. In addition, the expectations for the fiduciaries are often set by the management team for the company, who are the same individuals that have appoint them.

---

[108] In the United States, private (or corporate) sponsored retirement plan participants rarely have input in selecting plan fiduciaries or committee members. In other countries (Australia, Germany, the Netherlands, and the UK) participants are included in the committee or the selection of committee members.

There is, however, a significant potential conflict. While the fiduciaries are inherently concerned about minimizing their personal risk, they are also charged with protecting the participants from risk. In addition, these same individuals, in their company or management roles, will be charged with protecting the company from risk.

The relationship between these groups and an exploration of the risks is explored in greater detail in the chapter on ethics and conflicts of interest starting at page 224.

Identifying the Risks

If you are a plan fiduciary, you need to identify what the potential risks are from a variety of perspectives. What are the plan participant and beneficiary risks that you need to manage as a plan fiduciary? What are the risks that you personally have as a plan fiduciary (*e.g.*, from plan participants, the Department of Labor, or the IRS)? If you are a member of the company's management team and you also serve as a fiduciary, what risks are there to the company, and what additional risks do you have due to potential conflicts of interest? It's essential to understand these risks before you can attempt to effectively reduce or manage them.

When trying to identify risks from a *governance perspective*, it's critical that the plan committee have a process for periodically identifying potential risks. Examples of a risk assessment process include:

- *Have risk assessments as a goal for the plan committee each year.* A risk assessment goal can include broad goals to look at higher-level risk across all plan areas, or focused assessments that look at more discrete areas. There are numerous ways to evaluate risk:

    o *Topically* – Risk can be evaluated based on areas or topics such as compliance or investments. Many plan committees will periodically undertake compliance reviews or investment reviews to assess the risks they have in those areas.

- o *Functionally* – The evaluation of risk can focus on specific functional areas, such as HR, Payroll, Finance, or specific vendors (such as the recordkeeper, actuary, or trustee/custodian). These can be particularly useful if there is a question about the performance of a specific area or vendor. It allows the risk assessment to be focused and yet limited in scope. It also can be an efficient way to perform an assessment if the employer (*e.g.,* its Internal Audit group) is going to perform an assessment and the plan committee can leverage that work.

- o *Transactionally* – A review can be done to assess in detail the risks related to specific transactions, such as plan distributions. The review would look at compliance, process, systems, vendors, internal operations, and so forth. Similarly, an assessment could look at how a business transaction, such as a merger, might create risks for the plan.

- *Dedicate time at a meeting or a retreat to identify and assess potential risks.* Reserving a block of time that is focused on risk identification and assessment will allow the committee to explore the possible areas of risk.

- *Give the committee structured ways to consider risks.* Experienced plan committees and seasoned executives can often make significant progress by dedicating some time to brainstorming in a given area, such as identifying potential risks. Because of this, I would never suggest that the committee avoid brainstorming risk as a group. However, if the plan committee brainstorming gets stalled, or the committee members don't have the experience to generate meaningful ideas, it can be helpful to have structured ways to help the committee navigate the various risks. Some ways to help the committee identify risks are:

o *Based on the plan's history or experience.* The plan will have a history of activities that have created risks or problems (*e.g.*, cost overruns). Looking at the history or experience, the plan committee can plan for a course of action. If a vendor transition caused problems, they could evaluate any recent or planned transitions. If a system implementation created cost overruns, recent or upcoming system changes could be explored. If staffing changes create inconsistent operation, the assessment could examine staffing changes or the training process for new staff. The plan committee can get this historical information through interviews or feedback from individuals who have been involved in the plan over time.

o *Based on others' history or experience.* In addition, the plan can use the experience of other plans to help identify potential problems. The plan's vendors will be working with numerous plans and can be a source of problems encountered by similar plans. There are also surveys published each year that address problems plans have encountered during the year. The surveys can show the plan committee the areas where other plans have had problems (*e.g.*, compliance, investments, administration, and the like). The IRS and the Department of Labor also publish studies that show compliance and fiduciary challenges with which employers are struggling.[109] The plan committee can request presentations from its vendors on studies done in the market, or ask its legal counsel for studies published by the IRS or DOL.

---

[109] *See e.g.*, IRS TE/GE Employee Plans EPCU, *Section 401(k) Compliance Check Questionnaire – Final Report* (March 2013), available at https://www.irs.gov/pub/irs-tege/401k_final_report.pdf; Dep't of Labor Employee Benefits Security Administration, Office of the Chief Accountant, *Assessing the Quality of Employee Benefit Plan Audits*, (May 2015), available at https://www.dol.gov/sites/default/files/ebsa/about-ebsa/our-activities/resource-center/publications/assessing-the-quaity-of-employee-benefit-plan-audits-report.pdf.

- o *Functional risks.* Another way the plan committee can assess risk is to consider it functionally. Very often, members of the plan committee will be able to personally relate to risk that can arise from a functional area. For example, risks in Payroll will be well understood by the officer who oversees Payroll. Is the time correctly captured? Is it correctly captured for the right periods? Is the pay correctly categorized as includible or not includible based on the plan's definition of compensation? Are there issues with the transmission of pay information from Payroll to the third-party vendor (or the internal calculation of benefits)? How do system changes, process changes, people changes, operational changes, controls changes, and regulatory changes impact each functional area, including not only Payroll, but also IT, Operations, Vendor Management, and HR?

- *Seek the feedback of experts[110] who encounter risks in the industry or from other retirement plans, and who are aware of risks that can arise from:*

  - o Regulatory agencies
  - o Plan participants and beneficiaries
  - o Incidents that arise with vendors
  - o Investment risks that aren't raised by one's investment advisor
  - o Data aggregation, transfer, and transmission
  - o IT or HRIS system risks in relation to the retirement plan

---

[110] Experts can be external experts, or individuals you have internally that have experience in these areas. There will typically be different experts who can talk to these different areas. For example, at a risk retreat or risk-focused meeting, legal counsel might speak to the regulatory and compliance risks, while a consultant that focuses on retirement plan risk assessments might discuss vendor and system risks.

- *Identify risk activities.* Identify activities and events that can create new risks or increase existing risks, and assessing whether any have occurred, such as:

  o Updates to systems (such as payroll, IT, or HRIS)
  o Changes in vendors (such as plan administrators, payment processors, investment managers or funds, or payroll)
  o Acquisitions or divestitures of entities or larger employee groups
  o Shifts in personnel in a key department or among those who handle key functions, or at a vendor
  o Alterations in plan terms, plan design, or plan processes
  o Increases in the number of errors identified or participant complaints
  o Deviation from industry benchmarks
  o Changes in the law, regulations, the enforcement environment, or the litigation environment

Plans with a Process in Place to Identify Risks

In a 2007 survey in the UK, only 46% of DC plans had "a process in place to identify risks that could affect the [plan] and its members."[111]

Managing the Risks: Prioritization

When a structured, systemic approach to identifying risks is taken, such as the one described earlier, the plan committee can find that it is confronted with numerous risks, perhaps more than the committee can address based on available resources. Like any other situation where the resources don't match the need, the plan committee will need to evaluate the risks, prioritize them, and develop a plan that considers what risks to address now versus what risks will be addressed later (or potentially not addressed).

---

[111] *Occupational pension scheme governance – A report on the 2007 scheme governance survey supra* at 43.

When prioritizing the risks and developing a plan, some factors the plan committee may want to consider are:

- The level of the potential risk – If the risk is very large (or it has the potential of having a greater impact on the finances, operations, or reputation of the plan or company), it will need to be a higher priority.
- Remoteness of risk – If there is a high likelihood that the risk will occur, it needs to be a higher priority; risks that occur only if there is the convergence of a number of unlikely events should be a lower priority.
- Level of effort to manage or mitigate the risk – Sometimes the level of effort to manage or mitigate the risk outweighs the level of the risk.
- The efficiency of addressing risks together – If there are multiple risk areas that can be managed or mitigated in the time it would take to manage a single, equal risk area, then it is more important to manage the multiple risks.
- Availability of staff and vendors (compared to competing needs) – In some situations, the staff or vendors do not have time to assist, and the work cannot be accommodated.
- Potential for creating risks – Unfortunately, there will be cases when pulling resources away from other endeavors will create risks. If staff or vendors are already stretched, having them focus on managing a potential risk may cause errors in some of their recurring activities.

In all likelihood, the committee will often find that it initially lacks adequate information and data to estimate the size and probability of the risk, or fail to appreciate the resources that might be required. That's to be expected. Request the individuals who have responsibility for the areas to conduct a more detailed assessment, and to come back with realistic estimates and options.

I've seen situations where a problem was identified and without understanding the scope of the problem, the recommendation to the committee was to drive forward at full speed with an expensive and time-consuming correction program. However, after more detailed analysis, it was realized that the problem did not actually affect any participants. Take the time to get credible information and evaluate the options.

Errors without Impact

On occasion, I've encountered situations where I discovered an operational error, only to realize upon further review that the error actually didn't have any impact. One situation involved compensation codes that should have, but were not being used to determine plan earnings. Those codes, however, were all used for highly paid individuals whose pay had been capped, so the extra pay was irrelevant.

Errors with Enormous Impact

Typically, in my experience, the errors with the greatest impact on an organization are systemic errors—those errors that are built into a system and automatically have a wide-spread effect. These are often very easy to correct prospectively by adjusting the programming or table used in the system, but very difficult to correct retroactively because many, even all participants can be effected.

Some examples of systemic errors are:
- Matching rates in 401(k) plans
- Benefit percentages or offsets in defined benefit plans
- Compensation codes being incorrectly mapped to the plan terms

Using Quantitative Data to Help Prioritize Risks

When attempting to prioritize the risk and develop a plan to manage those risk, it is tremendously helpful if the plan committee has quantitative data to use in its analysis. When performing the initial risk assessment, several of the approaches described previously can lend themselves to producing some degree of quantitative data. How many times in the past did an error or issue arise? What do industry surveys show is the incident rate for a particular issue? How often has manual intervention led to a higher error rate?

Not all quantitative data is created equal. Merely counting the rate of an in incident may not be relevant. For example, if a plan is evaluating transactional risk, knowing that a plan has 10,000 errors out of 1 million transactions (or 1% of all transactions have errors) is relevant, but the quantitative data would be more meaningful if you also knew whether each error resulted in a deviance of one penny, or $10,000.

When working to prioritize risk, it is also helpful to understand the cost of managing the risk. How much will it cost to help mitigate the risk in dollars and hours? Also, are there other potential costs associated with the risk, such as reputational risk, that can't be quantified easily in dollars or hours? If, in addition to information on frequency and cost, the plan committee is provided with information illustrating the time cost, financial cost, reputation cost, and other potential costs it deems significant, it will be better able to prioritize the risk.

Managing the Risks: Evaluating the Options

After the risks have been identified and prioritized, the plan committee will need to identify its options for managing the risk. In general, there are four basic options: avoid the risk, modify the environment, shift the risk, [112] or own the risk.

Let's take an example of a potential risk and see how a plan committee might evaluate these options. Assume that the plan committee is considering adding a new loan feature to its plan. It has evaluated the potential risks of having loans in the plan and understands that loan repayments can be problematic in a number of ways. It also sees that based on data from the IRS and DOL, plans commonly have problems with loan administration. The plan committee considers its options:

---

[112] The shifting of risk typically does not eliminate the oversight duty for the plan committee. It is, however, a growing trend and is discussed in more detail at pages 123-126.

- The first option is to avoid this risk by not adding a loan feature to the plan. Thus, the risk is avoided.
- The second option is to modify the environment to reduce the risk level. This can be done by limiting the number of loans (*e.g.,* only one loan per participant can be outstanding at a time, or only authorize loans for limited purposes), or adding controls to the management of loans.
- The third option is to shift the risk to a third party. This can be done by having a third party both administer the loans and agree to correct any errors at its cost and indemnify the plan for any cost or losses.
- The fourth option is to own the risk, or decide that the risk of loan errors occurring is manageable and the plan will take on that risk (possibly by limiting loans to one per participant, adding controls, using experienced third-parties, and so on).

In real-life situations, plan committees may combine these approaches.

As the plan committee evaluates its options, the objective isn't to avoid all risk at all cost, but to evaluate ways to manage risks that exist as the plan committee works toward achieving its mission and goals. For example, in the prior example, the plan committee might have as part of its mission to increase plan participation and the level of contribution by participants. It has determined that participants not being able to access their funds in certain situations depresses the level of participation and contribution. Accordingly, the plan committee is considering adding a loan feature to the plan to help achieve its mission.

However, adding a loan feature is not without risk. The plan committee evaluates the risks and considers its options. Knowing the potential risks and understanding the options will help the committee design a strategy to implement a loan program that will mitigate the risks.

Managing the Risks: Establishing and Evaluating Controls

Except in cases where the plan committee is avoiding or shifting the risk, establishing and evaluating controls will be an important step in managing risks. The key elements are:

- Understanding the magnitude of the risk so appropriate controls can be implemented[113]
- Establishing controls to mitigate or manage the risks
- Periodically evaluating both the risks and the effectiveness of the controls in managing the risks (or have third-party assessments of your *identification of risks* and the *effectiveness of your managing that risk)*[114]

Because the use of controls is central to the concept of managing risks, let's take a moment to discuss what constitutes controls. COSO, which is perhaps the leading authority on internal controls, describes internal control as "... a process ... designed to provide reasonable assurance regarding the achievement of objectives relating to operations, reporting, and compliance."[115] Part of the process involves the establishment of control activities (which are often viewed as the actual controls). Examples of control activities are:

- Segregation of duties – For example, the person who calculates a benefit under a plan would not be the person approving that the participant is entitled to the benefit, and different from the person who authorizes the payment from the trust.

---

[113] If a risk is relatively small, an appropriate control would not consume a large amount of time or resources. The control needs to be the "right size" for the level of risk.

[114] *See* The Committee of Sponsoring Organizations of the Treadway Commission, "Internal Control – Integrated Framework" (COSO May 2013) at 5 and 130-131.

[115] The Committee of Sponsoring Organizations of the Treadway Commission, "Internal Control – Integrated Framework (COSO May 2013) at 1. COSO Internal Control Framework can also be found at http://www.coso.org/documents/internal%20control-integrated%20framework.pdf.

- Reviews, approvals and authorizations – An example would be that the work done by the person calculating the benefit would be reviewed and approved by a senior, more experienced person.
- Physical safeguards – Keeping the plan assets safe would be one type of physical safeguard, but so would keeping the plan data and records secure and confidential.
- Reconciliations – This is typically a check to test that calculations or transactions agree with separate sources of information. For example, in a defined contribution plan, the sum of all the participants' account balances should equal the value of the assets in the trust.[116]
- IT controls, such as edits, validation checks, etc. – Within the software and systems that help run the plan, there are often controls or checks built in to help ensure the accuracy of the data. For example, the system might require that Social Security numbers have nine digits, or that dates of birth fall within certain parameters (*e.g.,* not before 1900), or employee deferrals cannot exceed the annual limit or the employees total pay.
- Change Management – Because of the numerous parties, systems and rules involved, change is often a constant with retirement plans. Many of the risks relate to changes (such as changes in vendors, systems, laws, design, and personnel), and an effective changes management process can minimize these risks.

It is important to note that controls help to *mitigate or manage risks. Controls do not necessarily eliminate risk.* The expectation is that a control will be effective, meaning that it will work most of the time. There are, however, numerous situations that can cause a control to become ineffective. A few illustrations include changes in the IT system programming, changes in the law or plan document, and changes in the procedures related to the plan.

---

[116] This is a very simple example, and the individuals responsible for reconciling these amounts will attest that the reconciliation of the account balance to the assets is not quite as simple as suggested.

Plans with Appropriate Internal Controls

The following graph from the 2007 UK Pensions Regulator survey shows the "[p]roportion of all schemes [or plans] that are 'very confident' that they have appropriate internal controls in place to monitor and mitigate risks arising from ..."[117] the following items:

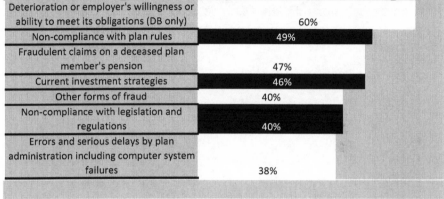

Deterioration or employer's willingness or ability to meet its obligations (DB only)	60%
Non-compliance with plan rules	49%
Fraudulent claims on a deceased plan member's pension	47%
Current investment strategies	46%
Other forms of fraud	40%
Non-compliance with legislation and regulations	40%
Errors and serious delays by plan administration including computer system failures	38%

Because controls are neither perfect nor eternal, a critical component of having a strong control environment is that the control must be monitored. This means that periodically, the control must be reviewed or tested to determine if it is working properly. Building off of the examples of control activities we've covered, testing could involve looking to see if:

- Any individuals receive benefits who were not entitled to those benefits
- Any benefit amounts paid were incorrect
- There is documentation of reconciliations being performed and performed correctly
- There are no missing or erroneous Social Security numbers or individuals who deferred an excessive amount

Although it is appropriate for the plan committee to have employees of the company test or assess controls periodically, or have the vendor self-test, it is also important to have a third party periodically perform this monitoring or testing for two reasons.

---

[117] *Occupational pension scheme governance – A report on the 2007 scheme governance survey supra* at 45. The graph is a reproduction from the report with the exception that "plan" was used instead of "scheme."

First, a third party such as the company's Internal Audit group or an outside auditor will often have greater expertise in testing controls and will be able to bring additional insight to how the control environment can be improved. Second, using a third party recognizes that the self-testing by the plan staff or by the vendor involves a potential conflict of interest. Knowing that a third party will periodically test the effectiveness of the controls will help keep the self-testing more accurate and honest.

Frequency of Testing Internal Controls

The 2007 UK Pensions Regulator survey found that 64% of boards reviewed internal controls annually, 21% every two or three years, and 13% less frequently. The Regulator commented that they were nevertheless concerned because only 60% of the plans had "a process in place to identify risks."[118] Clearly the first step in the risk management process must be risk identification.

Managing Vendor and Risks Related to Outsourcing

Almost all companies, regardless of size, outsource some facets of their retirement plan's administrative, investment, and professional services,[119] and the trend toward outsourcing is expected to continue.[120] For example, almost all 401(k) plans outsource their recordkeeping to a third party.[121] According to a

---

[118] *Occupational pension scheme governance – A report on the 2007 scheme governance survey supra* at 46. The graph is a reproduction from the report.
[119] Some services, like plan audits, have to be outsourced. Other services, like investment funds and use of custodians or trustees, are almost always outsourced, except by financial institutions. *See also,* Advisory Council on Employee Welfare and Pension Benefit Plans, *Outsourcing Employee Benefit Plan Service* (November 2014) available at
http://www.dol.gov/ebsa/publications/2014ACreport3.html.
While private sector employers outsource almost all of their recordkeeping and much of the other services required by the plan, it isn't uncommon to find multiemployer (or union) plans and government sponsored plans that are administered in-house.
[120] *See, 20 years inside the mind of the CEO... What's next?,* 20th PwC CEO Survey, 2017, at 16, which reports that between 61% and 77% of CEOs find it is either somewhat difficult of very difficult to find talent with creativity and innovation, leadership, emotional intelligence, adaptability, or problem solving skills.
[121] The BrightScope/ICI Defined Contribution Plan Profile: A Close Look at

report prepared by The BrightScope/ICI, the following percentages of plans in their database serve as the plans' recordkeeper:

Asset Manager	31.2%
Insurance Company	41.2%
Brokerage Firm	6.4%
Bank	7.9%
Pure Recordkeeper	13.3%

A report by the ERISA Advisory Council[122] states that traditionally outsourced plan services include:

> ***Investment Services:*** Examples include investment strategy, asset allocation, underlying investment management, manager selection and monitoring, and proxy voting.

> ***Administrative Services:*** Examples include record-keeping, processing claims for benefits, distribution of participant notices and other plan communications, preparation of necessary government forms (Form 5500, 1099-R, for example), contribution processing, execution of investment instructions, and processing plan distributions.

> ***Professional Services:*** Examples include actuarial, legal, and accounting services.[123]

401(k) Plans (December 2014), page 36, available at https://www.ici.org/pdf/ppr_14_dcplan_profile_401k.pdf
Insurance companies, brokerage firms, banks, and pure recordkeepers will often use their own recordkeeping service. Companies that do not provide recordkeeping service almost universally outsource this service.
[122] The Advisory Council on Employee Welfare and Pension Benefit Plans (the ERISA Advisory Council), consists of representatives from the public who are appointed by the Secretary of Labor and advise the Secretary. *See* description at https://www.dol.gov/agencies/ebsa/about-ebsa/about-us/erisa-advisory-council
[123] *Outsourcing Employee Benefit Plan Services supra* at 4, available at https://www.dol.gov/sites/default/files/ebsa/about-ebsa/about-us/erisa-

There are tremendous advantages to outsourcing that can't be ignored: corporate staff not being distracted by additional duties; work performed by individuals specializing in retirement plan administration and investments; availability of compliance and other experts, greater efficiency; dedicated technology (such as web-based election, modeling, and investment platforms); potentially shifting the risk for administrative, investment, and compliance failures to a third party; and potentially reduced cost. Why run a pension or a 401(k) plan when that isn't your core business?

Outsourcing retirement plan administration and investing is so common now that one can expect that every plan will have some degree of outsourcing. Because plan committees place a high degree of reliance on outsourced vendors, they need to be careful not to fall into some common traps.

> *Abdication* – After the outsourcing, the plan committee essentially abdicates all responsibility in the area(s) of outsourcing. Any recommendations made by the outsourcing vendor are followed or approved. Indeed, the outsourcer is often the group that sets the agenda for the plan committee and they "attend" all committee meetings and lead the meeting discussions. The plan committee very heavily relies on the outsourcing vendor and rarely questions anything the vendor proposes.

> *Lack of Oversight* – The agreement with the outsourcing vendor has details related to performance and responsibilities, but the plan committee neither requests nor reviews any reports on the outsourcer's performance or checks that all agreed-upon services are being performed. Indeed, the plan committee rarely reviews anything done by the vendor; the work done by the vendor isn't put out to bid; and there hasn't been a change in the vendor for a significant period.

***Lack of Clarity on Roles and Fiduciary Duty* –** There is ambiguity in the contract related to the vendor's duties and whether any fiduciary responsibility shifts. Similarly, there's a lack of clarity on whether the outsource provider needs to avoid conflicts (or disclose conflicts), or adhere to any code of conduct.

***Stimulating Dialogue followed by Absolute Deference* –** The outsourced vendor comes with stimulating presentations that evoke provocative discussions. The plan committee members become engaged and often debate amongst themselves what is being presented. At the end of the day, however, the recommendation of the vendor is always followed (perhaps with a minor tweak around the edges).[124] This is very common when the outsourced vendor is an investment advisor, and the discussion can traverse across macro-economics, politics, and rapidly changing investment trends.

If your plan outsources services, you must ask, what are the potential risks related to outsourcing, and how can those risks be managed? A major problem with outsourcing, as these examples suggest, is handing over responsibilities related to the plan and not monitoring, overseeing, or managing what is being done by the third-party vendor.

Without getting into a lengthy description of the ERISA rules, a key and universal principle is that the plan fiduciaries and the plan committee can delegate roles and responsibilities, *but generally they can't delegate away their fiduciary responsibility.*[125] Thus, they must continue to be diligent in overseeing the vendors

---

[124] "Boards do not ask for or accept recommendations – a recommendation is a decision in disguise." The Imperfect Board Member *supra* at 70. Instead, the board, or plan committee, seeks options that are evaluated with pros and cons. *Id.*

[125] The fiduciaries' and plan committee's inability to delegate away most of their fiduciary duties is two-fold. First, at a minimum, they will retain the duty to oversee the vendor to whom they've delegated the role, so some fiduciary responsibility will always exist. Second, many vendors will not accept a full delegation of fiduciary responsibility, or will do so only after charging a significantly greater amount for the same service.

and third-parties to whom they've delegated some responsibilities. In the investment arena, Tim Hatton, the author of *The New Fiduciary Standard*, notes, *"While fiduciaries can reduce their liability in certain situations, they cannot ever abdicate their duty to monitor the overall investment process for which they are always responsible."*[126] (Emphasis in original.)

The paradox, however, is that the plan committee often is delegating to a more capable, specialized third party a role or responsibility that neither it nor the company is equipped to perform. The plan committee, however, is charged under ERISA with overseeing the expert. An interesting dilemma, indeed.

If the plan committee or fiduciary needs to oversee the expert, what exactly does that entail? According to the Department of Labor it means: "A fiduciary's primary function in outsourcing activities to a third-party is the selection and monitoring of the service provider."[127]

Exactly what needs to be done will, of course, depend on the facts and circumstances. However, some standards can be gleaned from various Department of Labor guidance:[128]

- Periodically review the vendor to determine if their performance meets the contract, plan, and statutory standards.[129]

---

[126] The New Fiduciary Standard *supra* at 75.

[127] *Outsourcing Employee Benefit Plan Services supra* at 14.

[128] This list is not intended to be exhaustive, but a starting point upon which the plan committee and plan fiduciary can build. The reader may also wish to refer to the DOL publication, *Tips for Selecting and Monitoring Service Providers for Your Employee Benefit Plan* available at
https://www.dol.gov/sites/default/files/ebsa/about-ebsa/our-activities/resource-center/fact-sheet/fs052505.pdf.

[129] 29 C.F.R. 2509.75-8, FR-17.
ERISA § 411(a) prohibits individuals who have been convicted of certain crimes from serving as either a fiduciary or a consultant to an ERISA plan, and violating this is a crime. At a minimum, the plan should require that all consultants annually verify that none of its vendors have committed any of the crimes listed in section 411. 29 U.S.C. 1111(a).

- Consideration is given to the vendor's experience and qualifications, the quality of their work, and their fees.[130]
- The vendor should employ a process that avoids self-dealing and conflicts of interest.[131]
- The information that served as a basis for the selection of the vendor should be reviewed periodically to see if it has changed.[132]
- Participant complaints about the quality of the service should be evaluated.[133]

Available Tools for Managing Outsourcing Vendors: SSAE 16 (Old SAS 70) Reports and User Controls

In many cases, a risk assessment is done by an auditor for the third-party outsourcing vendor, and a report is provided to the third party. That report is then made available to the plan committee or administrator. For example, most 401(k) recordkeepers will secure on an annual or more frequent basis an SSAE 16 report (previously known as a SAS 70 report). In general, the SSAE 16 report provides a third party's assessment of the internal control environment for the vendor.

This report, which is prepared by an independent third party, looks at various functional areas and possibly also process areas, and provides an assessment about the level of risks associated with those areas. For example, a typical report will discuss the physical security of the provider's business (in case of fire or natural disaster), and the IT security (from hacking and data breaches).

The plan committee should ensure that the individuals responsible for overseeing the vendors secures and reviews these reports. They can be extremely valuable since they provide a significant review by an independent third party at no cost to the

---

[130] DOL Advisory Opinion 2002-08A (August 20, 2002).
[131] *Id.*
[132] DOL Field Assistance Bulletin 2007-01.
[133] *Id.*

plan, and can save the plan a significant amount of time in performing a separate review.

These reports, however, do come with a number of limitations. First, the scope of the review done by the independent third party is typically defined by the entity being assessed. Thus, not all reports cover the same areas, and if an entity knows it has weaknesses in a certain area, it can avoid having these highlighted by excluding that area from its report. Therefore, it is critical that the plan committee carefully review the scope description of the SSAE 16 to see what areas are covered, and potentially more importantly, what areas are omitted. For example, is compliance covered, recordkeeping, data transmission, participant entry, distributions, and the like?

The second limitation of these reports relates to whether testing was performed. In many cases, the report is based on a review of the processes and controls to see if they are *theoretically* adequate for the processes to be performed correctly. Not all of the reports involve testing the processes and controls to see if, in fact, they are operating correctly. Clearly, a report where the processes and controls were not actually tested will be less reliable than one where testing was performed.

A third major limitation relates to the listing in the report of "complimentary end-user controls," or "user controls." In general, the reports will describe controls that the user (*i.e.*, the plan or the employer) must have in place and that must be operating accurately for the vendor's processes and systems to work properly. A common example of a user control is that the data provided by the plan or employer is complete and accurate. If the data is not complete or accurate, the output provided by the vendor may be flawed. Thus, it is critical that the person responsible for overseeing the vendor knows what user controls are listed in the SSAE 16, and confirms that the plan or employer has controls over these areas.

Lack of Familiarity with User Controls

Often, when asked about the oversight of user controls, members
of the plan committee or the plan administration
team are unaware of the existence of user controls in the SSAE 16
report. For example, if the outsourcing vendor has user controls
that assume the employer is providing clean and accurate data,
but the employer has been assuming that the outsourcing vendor
has been editing and checking the data to ascertain its accuracy,
the result is that no one has been checking the data for accuracy—
and the data has been wrong.

Doing a "Risk Retreat" to Identify Potential Risks

Over time, the plan committee will develop lists of risk areas that
will need to be overseen and monitored. Such lists can provide
some security and structure to the risk management of the plan. It
is, however, the risks that the plan committee hasn't
contemplated that can pose the greatest threat.

One way to try to identify these latent threats is through a risk
retreat, or a focused gathering where potential risks related to the
plan can be detected. This doesn't need to be a multi-day retreat
at a secluded location; a meeting for several hours before or after
the typical workday in a private conference room can work well.
The key is to carve out the time and allow for a focused discussion
without distractions.

Clearly, the attendees should involve the plan committee
members, but depending on the areas of focus, others can and
should attend. For example, if your business is in an acquisitive
posture, you might want to have a retreat focused on plan
mergers and integrations. Will the influx of new members stress
your systems, personnel, or procedures? Have you considered the
potential compliance issues in advance? What preparation can be
done to minimize the risk and smooth the process? What lead
time does your vendor require to make system or other changes?
How will you assess and harmonize the investments?

Using planned or potential business changes as a catalyst for risk retreats and the basis for the topics can be very effective. Here are some possible drivers and topics:

- Payroll or HRIS changes or modifications
- Acquisitions or divestitures
- Legislative or regulatory changes
- Investment philosophy changes
- Outsourcing and outsourced vendor changes
- Plan terminations, mergers, or freezes

Although managing risks for known changes will help reduce risks from known events, it is worth dedicating some time to the realm of unexpected events. Some ideas are:

- Vendor collapses
- Vendor systems become corrupted and all data lost
- Stock markets decline by 25%-50% or more
- War (traditional or cyber)
- Business system collapse

Leveraging the Business's Risk Manager

Many businesses have an individual whose focus is on risk. The individual might be as clearly designated as being the Chief Risk Officer or Risk Manager, to someone whose duties incorporate risk identification and management. Indeed, there can be several individuals whose roles touch on risk, such as individuals charged with Operations, Finance, Controls, Insurance, IT, Legal, Procurement, and other areas.

The plan committee can leverage the experience and knowledge of these individuals to identify the plan risks, especially in relation to risks that might arise from the business. These risk experts can be included periodically in meetings where risk is evaluated to help facilitate "risk retreats," or they can even serve as a subcommittee whose focus is risk identification and management.

In the latter case, the establishment of a risk subcommittee, the plan committee should be clear in identifying the goals of the subcommittee, including its roles and responsibilities, describe how it will be accountable to the plan committee, and establish its own governance structure (so performance can be measured, conflicts avoided, and so on).

The risk subcommittee does not need to be permanent. The plan committee can establish it to do periodic deep risk assessments or address potential risks that might arise from operational changes (mergers, IT system changes, vendor changes, for example). This can allow the committee to select the most appropriate members for the risk subcommittee, depending on the circumstances.

Recognizing the Different Risks for Different Plans, Employers, Demographics, Systems, Vendors, and More

Although it can be helpful to have a "checklist of plan risks" as a starting point for identifying risks, these should be used with caution. This is because different types of plans carry different risks.

A defined benefit plan, where the employer retains all the investment risk, has different risks than a defined contribution plan where participants direct their investments. Employers that are undergoing rapid expansion or acquisitions have different risks than a mature, slower-growth enterprise. Workforce demographics will also affect the types of risk. For example, a younger, technologically-savvy population may want and use technology more frequently and widely than a less technologically sophisticated group. (Not using technology and using "manual" systems such as paper forms creates other risks.)

Managing a Mismatch Between the Risks and the Committee Members

Let's assume you've done a thorough risk assessment. You've held a risk retreat. You've brought in experts to help you excavate the hidden risks associated with your plan.

As you look over the more significant risks for the plan, you realize that none of your plan committee members have the experience, knowledge, or skills in managing any of those risk areas. There is, very simply, a mismatch between the experience, knowledge, and skills of the members of the committee and the risks that are jeopardizing the plan.

This revelation can be sobering. But the most important steps have been taken: you have identified the major risks for the plan, and you have identified the gaps in your ability to prevent those risks. That is the beginning of the process.

There are a variety of ways that the plan committee can close the gap, including the following, but the key is that you are working to close those gaps.

- Training for the committee members to improve their knowledge and skills
- Supplementing or replacing members to add the needed knowledge or skills
- Having vendors or staff add additional or different controls and processes to help mitigate the risks
- Hiring experts to help advise the plan committee on the area where it lacks the appropriate knowledge and skill
- Outsourcing the activity or area to a third party that has the expertise to oversee or perform the activities that contain the risk
- Shifting the risk to a third-party (vendor or insurer) so the risk is shifted from participants and the plan to the third party

Plan Committee Risks

The plan committee will naturally focus on risks to the plan when exploring potential plan risks. However, there are specific risks related to the plan committee, and the committee should periodically take an introspective look at its own risk profile. The plan committee should consider its potential risks broadly, just as it would evaluate any other risks. It should also consider having its risks assessed by a third party or from outside the committee. (Two ways to have an external look at the plan committee is by having former committee members or potential future committee members assist with the review.)

The following are several recurring areas that should be included in any plan committee risk assessment:

- *Is the committee comprised of the right members?* Do all the members dedicate adequate time to the performance of their duties as plan committee members? This is more than just attending meetings, but becoming prepared for the role by undertaking necessary training, and coming prepared to the meetings by reviewing the materials, and taking any additional steps that might be required to be fully conversant in the topic. Members who don't attend meetings, take time to learn the necessary skills, and become familiar with the plan and the committee charter may not be the right individuals to serve as plan committee members.

- *Do the members embrace the concept of avoiding conflicts of interest?* I've found that plan committees that are more focused on avoiding conflicts of interest identify more conflicts than committees that are not focused on conflicts. Members that are focused on conflicts will probe new vendors over their relationships and look at their own familiar relationships and investments to see if there is even the potential for a conflict. Conflicts, like land mines, are always buried. If left undiscovered, they will cause an unexpected level of damage at a most inopportune time.

- *Are there clear expectations and performance measurements for the committee and the members?* Performance expectations should be established for the committee and the members so there are no ambiguities about the expectations. Performance expectations could relate to areas such as attendance at meetings, preparation, training, proactive questions, questioning staff, avoidance and identification of conflicts, and expecting high-quality work products from staff and vendors.

- *Does the committee establish and managing toward goals?* Is the committee setting goals each year, and managing toward the achievement of those goals?
- *Does the committee as a whole, and members individually, identify areas of skill and knowledge gaps and proactively seek training?* How many training sessions were held for the committee, and how many members have taken steps to improve their own knowledge and skills?
- *Is the committee following sound governance principles?* Does the committee consider all 12 governance areas (*e.g.,* compliance, risk management, and so on) during the year and provide sound oversight across all of these areas?

At a very practical level, the committee needs to be aware of situations where individual members become distracted by other events (business, family, personal crises), precluding them from focusing on plan committee member duties. Although committees will often think they can carry the load of one member who is not performing at 100%, there are duties owned by each individual member that the committee cannot replicate. For example, how can the other committee members know of the distracted member's conflicts? How can the other committee members help fulfill the fiduciary duties of the distracted member? When a committee member becomes distracted by other events, the committee should consider asking the distracted member to take a leave until they can focus fully on their duties as a plan committee member.

Another practical consideration is for the committee to determine if any members too passive. An example is a committee member who is quiet in meetings, does not ask questions, and does not challenge presenters. This does not add value to the committee or help it fulfill its fiduciary duties.

Understanding and Managing Participant Expectation Risks

New plan committee members will often comment that the operation of the retirement plan is much more complex than they ever envisioned. They would add that, before joining the committee, when they looked at the plan as a participant, it seemed reasonable to expect the plan processing to be perfect. Similar to the expectation many have for Payroll,[134] they expected zero errors; perfection is not exceeding expectations, it is just *meeting* expectations.

The plan committee may want to strive for perfection, but having perfection as the expectation for participants is a standard that will surely result in disappointment. How then, can the plan committee manage these lofty expectations into ones that are more reasonable? How can they change the expectation from one expecting perfection to one that minimizes errors, promptly corrects errors, and is open to concerns and problems raised by the participants?

This risk is managed best through transparency. The participants shouldn't be led to believe that the plan committee, the vendors, the staff, the systems, the data, the advisors, or any other groups or activities are perfect. Rather, the plan committee should work at letting the participants know that, while the plan committee's goal is to strive for perfection, it recognizes that changes in any number of areas[135] can cause errors or problems.

That is why, in my opinion, the plan committee should let participants know that the plan has controls in place, that testing occurs, that outside advisors are used to review the plan operation, that a rigid due diligence process is used to select vendors, that vendors are periodically evaluated, that plan operations and costs are regularly benchmarked, and so on. How is this communicated? A simple, understated way of communicating all of this to the participants is by sharing the plan committee meeting agendas and goals for the year.

But won't sharing information get the plan and committee in trouble? It depends. Sharing information by a plan and committee

---

[134] Payroll is the only other area that I've encountered where achieving perfection is meeting expectations.

[135] As discussed elsewhere in this book, any number of changes can result in problems with the plan. The changes typically mentioned are changes in: the law, the plan terms or design, the systems, the vendors, the personnel involved in the plan operation, and the controls.

with poor governance will very likely highlight the plan problems. However, sharing information by a plan and committee with strong governance will highlight the fact that the plan is run well, and that the committee is constantly striving to improve.

Transparency: The Catch-22

A very good attorney and I were both advising a large retirement plan. She constantly resisted publishing anything about the committee, even such innocuous items as who was on the committee or when they would meet. In her mind, it was unthinkable to let the participants know the plan committee had annual goals (What if they weren't met?), or that the committee tested systems, vendors, and the like to verify that the plan was operating correctly (What if the participants asked about problems that might be found?). Accordingly, the goals and testing were only for the committee's consumption. Because this information wasn't provided to the participants, the committee often didn't strive to meet its goals during the year, or test as aggressively as it could have.

Since the goals weren't being met and the testing often wasn't performed, it "proved" the point of the attorney working on the plan. Publishing the committee's failures might create a lawsuit.

I looked at the situation differently, however. The risk of being sued existed because the goals were not being met and the testing was not being performed. This meant, for example, that controls, systems, and vendors were not being reviewed and potential problems were being left undiscovered. Being transparent with the participants would make the failure apparent more quickly.

If, instead of burying information about the plan committee, the plan committee strove to be more transparent, would the goals have been met and the testing performed? If one believes that transparency is the way for the participants to hold the plan committee accountable, then arguably this accountability would have gotten the committee to achieve its goals and testing.

This is, without a doubt, a delicate situation. Plan committees need to evaluate it based on their specific circumstances. While there isn't one size that will fit every plan, I would suggest that *as governance grows and matures, the level of transparency should grow and mature*. The ultimate goal, however, is to have the plan committee be accountability through transparency to the participants.

Insuring Against Risks

Two types of insurance exist for retirement plans. The first is a fidelity bond, which ERISA requires for all plans.[136]

Under a fidelity bond, every person[137] who handles funds must be bonded with a fidelity bond equal to 10% of the plan assets up to a maximum of $500,000.[138] The bond is to protect the plan against loss through fraud or dishonesty by a plan official. The policy should cover not only the trustee or plan committee members, but also anyone handling the assets.

The second type of insurance is fiduciary insurance, which covers the plan for liabilities or losses caused by an act or omission by a plan fiduciary. The committee is a fiduciary. (Others may be a fiduciary, depending on what they do. These individuals or entities can be identified based on the roles and responsibilities that are detailed during the governance process and in consultation with counsel.) Fiduciary insurance isn't required under ERISA,[139] but it is highly recommended.

Fiduciary insurance can be purchased by the plan, the company, or the fiduciaries. The issue of who purchases it will make a difference on whether the fiduciaries can be sued by the plan participants. If the plan purchases the insurance, the fiduciary insurance will provide that the insurance company has recourse

---

[136] ERISA section 412. 29 U.S.C. § 1112.

[137] There are exceptions for third-parties that are otherwise regulated and have substantial assets, such as banks and insurance companies.

[138] The $500,000 maximum has not been updated since ERISA was enacted in 1974, and clearly would not be adequate coverage for a loss by a larger plan.

[139] ERISA section 410(a). 29 U.S.C. § 1110(a).

against the fiduciary. In that case, it is again highly recommended that a rider be purchased that provides that the insurance company waives its right to proceed against the fiduciary. The rider should not be purchased by the plan or with plan assets. (If the company purchases the insurance, it doesn't need to provide that the insurer can proceed against the fiduciary, and you don't need the rider.)

It is not uncommon to bundle the fidelity bond and the fiduciary insurance into one type of coverage. The fiduciary insurance may also be bundled with other insurance. However, the fiduciary needs to be sure that it has: 1) the fidelity bond covering people who touch the assets or can get access to them, and 2) fiduciary insurance that protects the plan from breaches and covers the fiduciaries.

When evaluating policies, be careful how the policy defines fiduciary; sometimes it is narrow and may not cover everyone that is serving in the role of a fiduciary. Often, directors' and officers' insurance does *not* cover fiduciary violations under ERISA. It is certainly worth being careful here.

If creating a new committee as a result of a spin-off or purchase by a private equity firm, the committee may want to see what level of coverage was in place by the prior parent or seller. Typically, the insurance isn't on the full value of assets in the plan. Since recent lawsuits have had larger awards, the trend has been to increase coverage over historical levels, but that is an area where your broker should be able to provide guidance.

The ERISA Advisory Council also suggested purchasing insurance coverage for the acts of service providers:

> Plan sponsors should consider not only coverage for themselves but coverage for the acts of their service providers. Plan sponsors may want to consider a service provider's own coverage as an aspect of assessing the financial viability of the service provider. In addition, the fact that a service provider has insurance coverage in place can provide some measure of comfort that the insurance

carrier has performed due diligence on the service provider that will support the underwriting of the service provider's activities.[140]

Having fiduciary insurance does not necessarily mean that any fiduciary breach will be covered. If the plan or committee's "procedures are viewed as knowingly contributing to the impairment of a[t] least some participants' assets, your fiduciary liability insurance will not protect you from the liability...."[141]

Avoiding the Ostrich Effect

The litigious environment enveloping plans and plan committees has created a situation that I call "the Ostrich effect." The Ostrich effect is a situation where the plan committee does not want to find or hear about potential plan errors, problems, or risks. If they don't know about the risk, then they will not be charged with acting to protect the plan and the participants from those errors or risks. If something is discovered later on, then they will just need to react to that one-off occurrence, and can then return to business as usual.

I've seen the Ostrich effect even with well-run plans that have sophisticated committees comprised of outstanding executives. When asked why they don't conduct risk assessments, they've responded:

> Our concern isn't doing a risk assessment and identifying **one risk** or problem that needs to be corrected or require changes in processes to avoid the problem from occurring in the future. Our concern is doing a risk assessment and finding **so many** problems that we can't address them all quickly. The risks or problems that we know about that are left unaddressed will be an Achilles' heel for us. If one of these problems occurs, we'll be sued because it can be shown we knew about it and did nothing. That's why we

---

[140] *Outsourcing Employee Benefit Plan Services supra* at 23.
[141] The Four Pillars of Retirement Plans *supra* at 5.

feel it is better not to do a risk assessment and let sleeping dogs lie.

That committee member's concerns were not unfounded. I've seen a plan drive into broad and comprehensive risk assessments, uncovering scores of problems and issues. The committee struggled with how to address and prioritize them, and was constantly concerned about the ones that had to be left unaddressed. In that case, no lawsuit was filed, and despite the worrying, after several years the issues were all addressed and the plan was subsequently on much better footing. Nevertheless, the concern felt by the committee was real.

It is, indeed, an unfortunate environment that puts plan committees in this situation. What do you do when performing a risk assessment creates potential grievous risk? Or when doing a risk assessment illustrates that the plan committee has been lax in managing risk, or was not fully engaged? In the real world, there are many supports for inertia and just as many obstacles to action. Ignoring the risks, however, do not make them disappear or make their cost any less significant when they arise.

A solution is to start the process of performing risk assessments in a measured, focused way. For example, the committee can begin in an area where, if problems are identified they can be fixed relatively quickly and efficiently. Here are a few examples:

- Perform risk assessments for new offerings (such as the earlier example where the plan considered offering loans to participants). In these situations, if the potential risks are too great or complex to manage, the new offering can be abandoned, or the committee can consider shifting the risk to a third party.
- Have the risk assessment build off of risks or problems that have already been identified and where the plan committee is presumably already on notice. In many cases, the plan's financial audit will identify issues or risks (sometimes in a separate management letter and not in the body of the audit). Similarly, individuals involved in the plan's administration may raise issues or be aware of risks

that they may or may not have escalated to the plan committee.

- Another way is to construct the assessment so that its boundaries are narrowly defined. For example, rather than conduct a compliance review of every conceivable compliance requirement the plan must satisfy, conduct a review of the plan's compliance with the distribution requirements, or discrimination requirements, or eligibility requirements, or vesting/service requirement, and so on. Smaller initial bites will ultimately be easier to swallow.

Quick Hits

1. To begin getting a broad-based perspective on the plan's risk, the committee can schedule a risk retreat or dedicate a segment of each of the meetings for the next one or two years to risk (less frequently after the first one or two years). At the retreat or the meeting segments, the committee can hear from individuals handling risks for the company's different functional areas (*e.g.,* Payroll, IT, Employee Benefits, HR, Legal, among others), and its vendors. The individual presenting would discuss potential plan risks that may affect the plan.[142]
   a. Where possible, the presenters should provide input to the committee on the size of the risk (*e.g.,* how much it could cost the plan or participants), and the likelihood of it occurring.
   b. The presenter should also discuss the controls that are in place to manage or mitigate the risks, and explain whether the controls have been tested recently and the results of the test to see if they are working effectively.
   c. As the committee gathers risk information, it can begin to ascertain where it needs additional information, or what risk areas have a higher priority.

2. Building on the information gathered from item 1, the plan committee should evaluate how to avoid, reduce, shift, or ensure against the identified risks. If the risk is retained, the committee should request input on how to manage the risk (such as through controls).

3. After identifying the larger risks, have the controls in those areas tested for effectiveness (or if none, have controls developed).

4. Have any user controls identified in the SSAE 16 tested.

---

[142] It can help to have someone with some expertise at the meeting to help facilitate the discussion. Also, having a competitor of your vendors give a presentation on risk can provide insight into potential risk areas.

5. As part of the knowledge and skills assessment of the plan committee members, identify potential gaps in their knowledge and skills related to risks and develop a training program that will help close the gaps.

The Application of Risk Management

"If you don't invest in risk management, it doesn't matter what business you're in, it's a risky business."
Gary Cohn, President Goldman Sachs[143]

"Smart risk management is never putting yourself in a position where you can't live to fight another day."
Richard "Dick" Fuld, Jr., CEO of Lehman Brothers[144]

Introduction

For most executives, addressing risk management for a retirement plan is very different than it is for a business. In the business, there is property to protect, both tangible and intangible. There are reputational risks that can impact the value of the business or future revenue streams. There are risks related to losing qualified employees, or being unable to attract the right talent at the right time. There are, of course, competitive risks, product development risks, manufacturing risks, logistics and weather risks, and many others that don't exist with retirement plans. (There are also some similar risks, such as compliance risk, vendor risks, and investment/finance risks.)

As the executives running the business look at the retirement plan for risks, the landscape will appear dramatically different. In most situations, the executives will see that the retirement plan doesn't own any tangible property or many of the intangible types of

---

[143] Panel discussion in Washington, DC sponsored by the Institute of International Finance (2011). Mr. Cohn was President of Goldman Sachs at the time of this quote.

[144] "Fuld of Experience," The Economist (April 24, 2008), *available at* www.economist.com/node/11088839. Fuld was the CEO when Lehman Brothers filed for bankruptcy.

property like licenses, patents, or copyrights. They also see that the retirement plan does not have any employees, create any products, or have customers in the traditional sense. The existence and type of risk differs from what executives would see in their business.

It behooves the executives serving on the plan committee to familiarize themselves with the distinct risk profile associated with a retirement plan. This chapter describes the following risks that constitute the risk environment for retirement plans:

- Asset and investment risks
- Resource risks
- Personnel risks
- Economic risks
- Transactional risks
- Vendor and outsourcing risks
- Compliance risks
- Litigation risks
- Reputational risks
- Governance risks
- Administrative risks
- Multiple plan enterprise-wide risk

Asset and Investment Risks

For defined contribution plans,[145] investment and asset risks probably pose the largest potential risk. The risk from class action lawsuits alone can be intimidating. In 2015, the top seven DC plan settlement accounted for $449 million in damages.[146] These class action lawsuits generally fall into four categories:

---

[145] The focus is on defined contribution plans because in a defined benefit plan, the asset and investment risk is borne by the company and investment losses aren't the source of lawsuits and claims by plan participants. The risks to the company are, however, very real, as any CFO of a company with defined benefit plans that have experienced volatility in its asset levels will attest. Because the risk for defined benefit plans are different, they are discussed separately at page 127.

[146] Calculated from Nick Thornton, *Top 10 ERISA settlements of 2015*, (BenefitsPRO Jan. 25, 2016) available at

- Overcharging for the investments (such as when the investment advisory fee, investment management fee, 12b-1 fee, or other fund fee are considered too high)
- Not properly managing plan costs (such as when the plan is overpaying for recordkeeping, trustee, communication, legal, accounting, or other services)
- Losses caused by lack of diversification or poor investments (including "stock drop"[147] cases)
- Fiduciary breaches related to the plan's administration (such as when benefits are miscalculated, investment changes are not properly or timely executed, contributions are not made timely, or plan eligibility is not tracked correctly)

For most defined contribution plans, the plan committee spends the bulk of its time on plan assets and investments.[148] It is good that the committee dedicates time to the plan's assets because of the large potential risk. What is bad is that often the focus on the plan's assets is to the exclusion of other potential risk areas.

In some cases, the other important areas of oversight for the plan (compliance, risk management, recordkeeper/vendor management, training in non-investment areas, succession planning, and the like) suffer. They are either ignored or allocated whatever time is left at the end of the investment advisors' presentations.

---

www.benefitspro.com/2016/01/25/top-10-erisa-settlements-of-2015.
[147] In a stock drop case, the fiduciaries are accused of not acting prudently in relation to company stock held by the plan. Typically, the company stock has fallen dramatically and the plaintiffs claim the fiduciaries should have sold it earlier.
[148] *See e.g.,* Willis Towers Watson, *Unlocking Value from Effective Retirement Plan Governance – The 2016 Willis Towers Watson U.S. Retirement Plan Governance Survey* (2016) at 12: "DC plan sponsors monitor investment managers more than other aspects of their plan."

Why the Focus on Plan Assets to the Exclusion of Other Areas?

There are two significant reasons why the plan committee will invest most of its limited time on plan assets and investments.

The first is that the discussion with investment advisors of managing assets, macro-economic issues, financial trends, and politics is often captivating, intriguing, and even sexy for the typical committee member. The presentation by a good investment advisor isn't a PowerPoint journey through graphs about index funds. Instead, it consists of personal revelations available only to someone who went to prep school and college with the hottest fund managers and investment sages.

The second reason the plan committee spends a significant amount of its time on assets and investments is that the investment advisors often schedule the meetings, set the agenda, and work closely with the plan committee. The investment advisors wisely take ownership of ensuring that the committee will meet quarterly to review the most recent investment performance for the plan. These advisors often get paid a premium, and to demonstrate their worth, they will work to keep in constant contact with the committee, provide updates (often by phone) to discuss significant market developments, and work to develop a close working relationship with committee members.

The area of asset and investment risk management is a very interesting one for another reason. This is, as noted, an area of high risk but also one where most plan committees have very limited knowledge. With very few exceptions, plan committee members have not been involved in investing hundreds of millions—or even billions—of dollars.

Granted, the plan committees will hire experts. However, in most situations, the plan committee retains the right to make the final decision on investments and investment managers. If you're wondering why the plan committee doesn't try to shift the investment decision-making to the expert, you're not alone and seeing part of a larger trend.

More and more plan committees are recognizing that they don't have the knowledge or expertise to make many of the investment decisions required by their investment advisor.[149] (They also see that it can take them too long to meet and react to quickly changing events.) Accordingly, we're seeing a developing trend where plan committees are beginning to outsource the actual investment decisions related to the plan.

Although shifting risk is a valid risk management technique, the plan committee still has some responsibilities and some risks in this situation. For example, the plan committee should evaluate:

- Whether the advisor has the experience and skills in serving as a fiduciary
- Whether the advisor has any conflicts and how it monitors and manages for potential conflicts
- Whether the advisor will accept financial liability if it is found to have breached any fiduciary responsibility
- Whether the advisor has the financial resources (or adequate insurance) to pay for any losses suffered by the plan

Is the Plan Committee Accepting Active Management if the Committee Outsources Investment Decision-Making?

When the plan committee decides to outsource its investment making decisions, is it agreeing by default to have the plan investment strategy use actively managed funds? Although most advisors will say that is not necessarily the case, it seems that it is hard to justify the larger fees paid to investment advisors who are selecting the investments if they are selecting only indexed funds. (It can be hard to justify higher fees in such a case.)

---

[149] Mark P. Cussen, *The Fiduciary Rule: How and Why to Outsource Your Risk*, (Investopedia April 5, 2016) available at www.investopedia.com/articles/financial-advisors/040516/fieuciary-rule-how-and-why-outsource-your-risk.asp.

When looking at using an investment advisor who will be responsible for selecting the funds and owning the fiduciary duty for such decisions, the plan committee should ascertain two things: does the advisor have experience in such situations? And does the advisor exclusively or predominantly have actively managed funds in such plans?

Another common trend and common design related to asset and investment risk management is using lifestyle or target date funds. (One survey found that 83% of plans offer lifestyle or target date funds.)[150] These funds essentially build a series of investment portfolios that are considered reasonable or appropriate for individuals at certain ages. A young individual with retirement in the distant future will have a portfolio that is more heavily weighted toward equities. An older individual with retirement rapidly approaching will have a portfolio that is more balanced between equities and fixed income investments.

In general, most of these lifestyle or target date funds are built by combining funds that already exist. Thus, it would include the combination of several equity funds and several bond or fixed income funds.

Because the lifestyle or target funds are an aggregation of equity and bond funds, it is important for the plan committee to look behind these lifestyle or target date funds at the underlying funds. The committee should consider whether the underlying equity and bond funds are acceptable on their own. If they are poorly managed, have novice managers, high costs, or other potential issues, the lifestyle or target date fund of which they are a part might not be acceptable.[151] A wise plan committee member once

---

[150] Deloitte Consulting and International Foundation of Employee Benefit Plans, *Annual Defined Contribution Benchmarking Survey*, (2015) at 31, available at https://www2.deloitte.com/content/dam/Deloitte/us/Documents/human-capital/us-hc-annual-defined-benchmarking-survey-2015.pdf.

[151] Some fund families will use their less popular funds to build their lifestyle or target date funds. These funds can be their newer funds, costlier funds, or poorer-performing funds.

said when looking at such funds, "Trash with a pretty wrapper is still trash, and we don't need that in our plan."

Another asset or investment risk relates to compliance with ERISA section 404(c). In general, ERISA section 404(c) allows the plan committee to shift the fiduciary risk of selecting investments from the plan committee to the plan participant. However, a number of requirements need to be satisfied to get the protection of section 404(c). If these requirements aren't met, then the plan committee essentially retains the fiduciary risk of the investment decisions made by the plan participants.[152]

In some cases, the plan committee will have a false sense of security. It will think it has shifted its investment decision risk to the participants, when in fact the committee hasn't met the technical requirements of section 404(c), and still owns that risk. Rather than avoiding a risk, the committee has a significant amount of hidden risk. This is an area where periodic monitoring by the committee and regular review by legal counsel are important.

Assets and investments carry numerous other risks. To begin to build an understanding of all of your specific risks, ask your current investment advisor to provide a personal view of potential risks, and then ask a prospective investment advisor to do the same. Also ask this of your ERISA counsel, your company treasurer, and your Internal Audit Director. A few risks that may come up might include:

- The risks associated with managing your investment advisor
- The risks associated with selecting the "right" investment theory
- The risks associated with understanding and managing hidden payment, soft dollars, and revenue recapture

---

[152] *See also* discussion at footnote 76.

Asset and Investment Risks for Defined Benefit Plans

Because plan participants do not bear the investment risk in defined benefit plans, those plan investments pose less risk for them. Investment losses are borne by the company and will have to be made up by the company with additional contributions or higher investment returns in the future. Thus, the risk of investment losses in defined benefit plans rests with the company, and investment performance will be a concern for the company, its executives, and the plan committee of defined benefit plans.

Ultimately, however, if the defined benefit plan is inadequately funded because of lower than expected investment performance and the company goes bankrupt, the participants will lose at least some of their benefit[153] and the plan committee could be sued for a fiduciary breach.

Resource Risks

Most plans rely heavily on resources provided by the sponsoring employer. Compensation information comes from the employer's payroll system. Service data comes from its HRIS or hours-tracking system. Employee indicative data also resides in the employer's HRIS system. The plan relies heavily on systems, hardware, and information that is part of the employer's property.

The plan has a number of risks from relying on these resources from the employer:

- Catastrophic system failures
- Loss or corruption of data (due to system destruction, hacking, or other cause)
- Inaccurate programming that doesn't reflect the correct plan rules or isn't updated to stay current with the plan rules

---

[153] Benefits in a defined benefit plan are guaranteed to a limited amount by the Pension Benefit Guaranty Corporation, which is a U.S. Government agency.

- Access risks where individuals may have inappropriate or inadvertent access to edit data

It is reasonable for the plan to use the employer's systems and resources, but that doesn't mean that such reliance needs to be blind to potential risks. It is also reasonable that the plan committee will want to validate that the employer has backup systems and contingency plans, appropriate data security and firewalls, and proper testing and controls in place for updates and changes.

For example, a common weakness relates to employers' time tracking systems, and how those systems interface with the employers' payroll system. Having the correct hours earned by an employee can be critical for the plan for a variety of reasons: determining eligibility to be in the plan, earning adequate service to enter the plan, earning service to become vested, and tracking hours for breaks in service. However, the hours tracking system for many employers are neither designed nor programmed for the intricacies of retirement plan administration. They do not properly credit hours for computing service and breaks in service, the manual overriding of the hours, or editing the hours, nor do they capture the historical data needed that is often lost during system conversions. In addition, what counts as "hours" for plan purposes may not coincide with hours that are tracked in the hours tracking system for payroll purposes.

The plan committee shouldn't assume that just because the employer believes a resource or system is operating correctly for its business that it is operating correctly for plan purposes. The committee needs to see that there are different entities, different objectives, different uses of the system, and different masters that must be served.

Personnel Risks

Just as the plan uses the sponsoring employer's resources, it also uses the employer's personnel. Staff from HR, Finance, Payroll, Treasury, Procurement, and IT will likely help support the plan's operations.[154] The plan committee should consider the risks associated with using the employer's personnel, by asking:

- Do the personnel working on plan matters have adequate knowledge and skills to meet the plan's objectives?
- Do the personnel have adequate time and resources to perform the responsibilities assigned to them by the plan?
- Do the personnel have conflicts between expectations or incentives from the employer and the plan that could result in inadequate time or attention being dedicated to plan matters?
- Is there adequate backup in personnel so that the absence, departure, or loss of any one individual will not adversely affect plan operations or create undue risk?
- Is there sufficient clarity in personnel roles and responsibilities for the plan so they understand what needs to be accomplished, and the timeframes in which it needs to be accomplished?

A trap for the plan committee is to rely on the employer's personnel resources because they come at no cost to the plan. But the personnel may not be doing the entire job; they may be hurried, have conflicts, or be inexperienced or ill-trained. The committee needs to evaluate whether it would be better to pay for the services to overcome these risks.

Economic Risks

I am confident in saying that every plan committee is aware of the economic risks that can arise and impact the value of their plan's investments. There are additional economic risks that are envisioned here, however, that are less obvious. These additional

---

[154] In some cases, the plan may reimburse the employer for the time spent by the employer's personnel on plan matters. In those cases, the plan has a right and a duty to ensure that the personnel are performing the job for which they are being paid. For a discussion of the analysis the plan should undertake before reimbursing the company for services provided by its employees, *see* Ilene H. Ferenczy and Andrew R. McCorkle, *Reimbursing the employer for plan expenses: are the rewards worth the risk?* (CCH June 1998).

economic risks include those that can occur as a result of a general downturn in the economy—one that can put vendors out of business and potentially impact the employer's business significantly. What happens if there is such a catastrophic event?

The analysis of how significant economic events will impact the plan will vary business-by-business and plan-by-plan. Some businesses and vendors will fare less well in a volatile environment. The committee will need to understand how susceptible the business and plan are to these events, and how to mitigate these risks.

For example, if the plan has engaged a high-quality but low-cost vendor that is relatively new in the market, the plan committee may decide that this vendor lacks the customer base, lines of credit, or access to financing that would allow it to withstand a major economic downturn where it loses clients and potentially has an increase in its receivables. If this vendor plays only a small role in the overall administration of the plan (such as only processing qualified domestic relations orders, which occur infrequently), the plan committee may decide that the unanticipated loss of this vendor is manageable. However, if this vendor is serving as the plan's fiduciary for all investment decisions, the loss of this entity at a time when the investment markets are being disrupted and potentially changing by the hour may not be a risk the plan committee is willing to take.

Transactional Risks

Transactions can be very disruptive to a business, and can also wreak havoc on retirement plans. Transactions involve activities like mergers, acquisitions, divestitures, closing divisions, outsourcing, and off-shoring. Several common risks arise from these types of transactions:

- Plan committee members' focus shifts to the issues created for the **business** by the transaction.
- There is a new influx or outflow of participants, who potentially need to be accounted for and tracked separately.

- Transactions can also increase the volume of other transactions, such as a high volume of participants terminating employment or shifting participation into another plan.
- Transactions can often require the harmonization of plans or plan features, or the disaggregation of business units and the corresponding plan participants.
- Similarly, transactions can require the harmonization of systems, or the adaptation of plan operations to enable the use of multiple legacy systems for a period of time.
- Staff can be stretched because of added responsibility during the transaction, or downsizing that occurred in their department.

Because transactions are typically planned and known, as long as the plan committee is aware of the possibility of an upcoming transaction, it can plan for the event. For those situations where a transaction is being kept secret, it is helpful if the plan committee can be provided with as much information as possible so it can begin to plan and minimize risk related to the plan.[155]

Another action the plan committee can take to minimize risk is to check with plan staff, vendors, counsel, and others on whether they have experience with these transactions, and whether they would have the capacity to assist with the activity that such a transaction would require. Unfortunately, having capability but not capacity (or vice versa) is about as helpful as a politician's promise.

Finally, transactions seem to be the event that cause some of the largest disruptions to a plan's data. By making plan or system changes, outsourcing, changing vendors, or merging plans, the plan's historical data is often lost or corrupted. Accordingly, it is helpful to have a plan in place to capture historical data and also

---

[155] The retirement plan risk for a target company can also be material enough to kill a deal. I've been involved in the due diligence of a number of acquisitions where funding, compliance, or other issues have caused the buyer to walk away from the transaction.

take a snapshot of the plan and participant data on the date of the transaction to prevent the loss of potentially relevant data.

Vendor and Outsourcing Risks

Most retirement plans use a variety of vendors and have outsourced much of the day-to-day administration of the plan. The use of outsourcing and vendors bring with them a variety of risks:

- Making a minor mistake involving one participant or a significant mistake that impacts a large number of participants. These can range from a minor manual error, to errors in programming the plan terms, to accessing and using outdated or inaccurate data.
- Failing to perform in accordance with the contract, delivering what was promised, or meeting deadlines.
- Overcharging for services, padding or overstating services on bills, or charging exorbitant prices for services that were not priced in the original contract.
- Having changes in key personnel that work on the plan.
- Making changes to key controls, or to policies or processes that supported the decision to use the vendor or outsource provider.
- Having staff that embezzled funds from the plan.
- Suffering financial setbacks that introduce the risk of going out of business.

One of the advantages of using vendors or outsourcing providers is that the plan committee can strive to shift some of the risk to them, or have them agree to indemnify the plan for losses caused by the vendor's errors. In general, most vendors will resist both risk shifting and being held liable without caps for damages caused by their errors.[156] It is, however, an avenue that the plan committee can pursue, and the trend is toward a greater willingness to accept some level of risk shifting or responsibility for errors. This is an area where Procurement can provide both

---

[156] One exception is that vendors and outsource providers will agree to unlimited liability in the case of gross negligence.

experience and an independent perspective from which the plan committee can benefit.

Leveraging Procurement

I don't think anyone *loves* working with Procurement. They attach a litany of requirements and structure to the process of selecting a vendor. They often slow down the process and increase the amount of time required. While they may know procurement, they don't know the specific vendors or the goals the plan committee is trying to meet. In general, where possible, I've seen vendor searches for retirement plan services conducted without the help of Procurement much more often than I've seen Procurement used.

However, from a governance perspective, using Procurement *may* bring a number of advantages.[157] They are an independent set of eyes. They bring objective criteria to the evaluation. They stress the existence of performance measures and guarantees. And they clearly emphasize cost and quality.

Procurement can bring an added dimension to vendor searches or renegotiations. They can be the proverbial bad cop beating up on the vendor to improve cost, quality, reporting, and guarantees.

Another area that is often overlooked when assessing risks associated with vendors relates to the "user controls" that are typically listed in their SSAE 16 reports (formerly SAS 70 reports).[158] Typically, the section of the SSAE 16 report that addresses "user controls" essentially says that all the work, calculations, and output by the vendor *may be wrong* if the employer or the plan doesn't have in place the controls listed in this section (such as the transmittal of accurate data and the timely correction of information).

---

[157] The advantages of using Procurement should be balance with the potential disadvantages, such as slowing down the process, overly complicating the process, or adding an extra layer of bureaucracy.
[158] SSAE 16 risks are also discussed in detail in the text following footnote 133.

The SSAE 16 and the listing of user controls are very important and need to be reviewed carefully when a new SSAE is issued.[159] Changes in the scope of the SSAE and a listing of user controls need to be identified and the plan committee needs to assess whether these changes have created any new risks.

A Two-Question Fix

When reviewing a retirement plan's operation, I would often ask the individual charged with managing the plan vendor, "Have you reviewed the SSAE 16 (the old SAS 70) from your vendor?" Often, I would get a blank stare. If they knew what it was, I would ask, "Have you reviewed the user controls and confirmed that they are operating effectively?" If I didn't get a blank stare for the first question, I usually got a look of bewilderment for this one. This is an area that is often overlooked and can be rectified by posing those two simple questions.

Finally, an area that is fraught with risk involves plan expenses. Many of the larger participant class action suits involve situations where the plan did not properly manage plan expenses: typically, these are expenses related to the cost of an investment vehicle. This is an area that needs to be *regularly* monitored because what is a reasonable expense can, and has, changed over time.

How Often is "Regularly Monitored"?

Some commentators suggest that plan services should be put "up for bid annually."[160] Having plan services rebid annually would clearly subject the pricing and service level to annual monitoring. However, rebidding annually may neither be practical nor possible.[161] For example, some vendor contracts are entered into

---

[159] SSAEs are not necessarily issued once a year. I've seen them issued semi-annually, annually, bi-annually, and on an irregular basis.

[160] The Four Pillars of Retirement Plans *supra* at 57.

[161] Rebidding plan investments and potentially changing the investment line-up annually could be very confusing to many participants. However, investment expenses (including trading fees, advisor fees, fund fees, administrative fees, money manager fees, and other fees) should be monitored and reported quarterly.

for several years and the relationship does not anticipate annual re-proposing. Similarly, after a thorough search and evaluation process, which can take a significant amount of time (in both hours and elapsed time) it may not be practical to repeat the process. This is especially true when the plan committee needs to also address other competing goals and objectives—a frequent occurrence.

Rebidding annually is also more than is required to "regularly monitor." Regular monitoring looks at performance against the contract and predetermined performance measures. Monitoring these areas, which requires much less effort than a re-proposal process, will often occur monthly, quarterly, or annually.

When considering how often to put a service out for proposal, I find that most services should be rebid somewhere between three and seven years, *unless* there are events that would accelerate the reassessment. Events that could accelerate the reassessment include:

- Poor service by the vendor or plan participant negative feedback
- Failing to meet contract standards or deadlines
- Overcharges or additional billing beyond what was anticipated
- Major system or personnel changes
- Acquisition of the vendor by a third party, or the merging of the vendor with another entity
- Changes in documentation related to controls (such as SSAE 16 reports)
- Changes in the processes followed by the vendor (*e.g.*, work being outsourced to a third party, rather than done by the vendor)
- Weakening financial viability of the entity
- Negative trends, such as increasing litigation or governmental audits of clients of the vendor
- Changes in the industry that have resulted in lower costs, improved quality, or the growing availability of services

Compliance Risks

Retirement plans are very highly regulated, and the compliance risks can seem endless. Indeed, there are numerous books, treatises, seminars, and publications dedicated exclusively to retirement plan compliance. This book is not intended to make the plan committee member a compliance expert, but instead seeks to give the plan committee member guidance on how to improve compliance, without being an ERISA expert.

Let's start with a little background. The compliance rules can generally be found in a law called the Employee Retirement Income Security Act, or ERISA. The rules in ERISA are generally enforced by either the IRS, Department of Labor, or the Pension Benefit Guaranty Corporation. Many of these rules are required to be incorporated into the plan document, but all of them must be satisfied in operation. Accordingly, compliance is sometime divided into two branches: form compliance (is the plan document in compliance with ERISA), and operational compliance (is the plan operating in compliance with ERISA).

The form requirement generally provides that the omission or incorrect statement of a rule required to be in the plan document can result in the plan document not being "qualified" or not meeting the documentation requirements. When the plan document has the required language, it is sometimes referred to as being "qualified in form."

Historically,[162] a plan sponsor could submit its plan document to the IRS and the IRS would rule on whether the plan document was qualified in form. If the IRS ruled favorably, the plan sponsor could then rely on the document. If the document was later found to be wrong (because the IRS made a mistake), the IRS could not *retroactively* disqualify the plan. This was, in essence, an

---

[162] The IRS has announced that it will be issuing rulings that a plan document meets the form requirements only in limited situations. Rev. Proc 2016-37, 2016-29 I.R.B. 136. Thus, this insurance policy from the IRS, which is extremely valuable, will be less available. Plan sponsors will thus need to address an additional risk related to whether the plan document meets the form requirements prescribed by ERISA.

insurance policy from the IRS that the plan did not have any form defects.

While an employer could get a type of insurance from the IRS that the form of the plan is qualified, there is no such option available to eliminate risk[163] for operational compliance. Thus, it is paramount that the plan operates in compliance with the rules in the plan and ERISA.

Impact of an Operational Compliance Problem

If a qualified retirement plan has an operational compliance problem, the IRS can "disqualify" the plan. This means that the plan, employer, and participants lose the tax benefits afforded to the plan. The tax benefits are that the employees do not have to include the employer contributions and trust earnings currently in income, the employer can take a deduction even if the participants are not currently vested in the contributions, and the trust does not have to pay taxes on trust income. Thus, if the IRS disqualifies the plan, all the vested contributions and earnings would be accelerated into income for the employees, the employer would lose some of its deductions (those not vested), and the trust would have to pay taxes on the trust income. The taxes add-up quickly and can be draconian. Indeed, because of the severity of the result, this is often called the "nuclear option."

More frequently, the IRS will negotiate with the company to have the operational compliance problems corrected and penalties will be extracted from the employer. Although these correction programs are much less costly in dollars for the employer, the correction process can be very time-consuming and also expensive.

---

[163] The IRS and DOL have created certain "amnesty" programs where, for a fee, certain operational errors can be corrected by the employer and the plan's qualified status is not jeopardized. These programs can be extremely beneficial for the plan and participants, but the cost to correct errors can be high both in time and dollars. *See* Rev. Proc. 2016-51, 2016-42 I.R.B. 465 (the IRS Employee Plans Compliance Resolution System or EPCRS), and Federal Register Volume 71, Number 75, Pages 20135-20139, April 19, 2006 (the DOL voluntary fiduciary correction program, or VFCP).

Because of the high cost caused by plan errors, it is important to try to keep the plan in compliance.

While it is expected that the plan committee will become familiar with ERISA and the compliance requirements, it is unlikely that the committee members will become experts. Acknowledging that, there are several principles that I've found plan committees can use to reduce operational compliance risks:

- *Simplify (or at least avoid complexity)* – The application of the compliance rules in operation for a retirement plan is very complicated, but the committee can minimize the complexity by not adding features or making the plan's operation more complex than necessary. (Remember, avoidance is one of the ways to manage risk. Avoid plan designs or features that add to operational complexity.) Here are three quick examples.

  o *Round Peg, Square Hole* – When plans are drafted, legal counsel may show their sophistication by defining terms, such as compensation and hours of service, in long, labored, rambling definitions. Unfortunately, these legalese definitions crafted by legal counsel complicate the plan's operation if counsel didn't meet with the Payroll Department before drafting the plan to see what definition the payroll system can process. The result is that the defined term (*e.g.*, either compensation or hours) will be captured incorrectly, or Payroll will go through numerous adjustments each pay period to capture the correct definitions.

  o *Don't Opt for the Space Shuttle When All You Need is a Bike* – As things change for the plan, whether it be the law, the participant demographics, or the features available from the vendors, the plan committee will have the opportunity to consider new options. These may be investment features, changes in how contributions are made, or loan availability. For example, plan committees often decide to allow participants to access some of their account balance through loans to improve participation and contribution levels. When they add a loan feature, however, plan committees will often not restrict the loan size or number, making the administration more complicated. Keep it simple. Be sure the systems used in plan administration will easily accommodate what you're hoping to do.

- o *Don't Get Ahead of Your Vendors* – Vendors generally have created a limited, pre-structured set of services, features, and functions. If you are seeking something that isn't in your vendor's pre-built box and they will need to customize a solution for you, refrain from asking. They are process experts, not customization experts. If you need that solution, you may need to find a new vendor that offers it as part of its standard offering.

- *Have Processes, Supported by Tested Controls* – Most compliance risks are associated with compliance activities that will occur over and over. Every employee hired will be tracked or evaluated for eligibility to participate in the plan, employees will enter the plan, they will accrue benefits, they will become vested, and they will receive a distribution. The plan committee can insist that the employer's staff or the vendor handling these activities have clear (and documented) processes in place that are supported by controls that can be tested.

Can Compliance Have Controls?[164]

If you're an executive, you may think of compliance as something that your Legal Department or chief compliance officer handles. It may not have as much of an impact on your day-to-day activities. However, many of the compliance requirements associated with retirement plans are intertwined with the plan's actual operation and *processes*. Almost every facet of the how the plan operates is regulated, from who should enter to how distributions occur. Because these rules can be built into plan processes (and very often into operating systems like payroll and HRIS), controls can be built into the processes. From an oversight perspective, the plan committee will be more comfortable knowing that the compliance requirements related to the plan's operation are built into plan processes that have associated controls, which are periodically tested to show that they are effective. Indeed, one IRS employee plans audit program (called the EP Team Audit) focuses on reviewing internal controls of what they view as large employers (plans with over 2,500 plan participants).[165]

There are, however, other areas that are not recurring. Many of the activities are discretionary decisions made by the plan committee, from selecting investments and vendors to interpreting the plan document. These areas of fiduciary decision-making are not as easily controlled as strictly operational areas, but they can have controls. For example, having ERISA counsel available for advice, or to provide the legal framework can help. Also, using the governance framework detailed in this book will help

---

[164] The IRS has also emphasized that controls are important to a plan's compliance posture. *See e.g.,* Andrea L. Ben-Yosef, *IRS Focusing More on Internal Controls,* BNA Pension & Benefits Reporter (March 5, 2013). On August 8, 2013 the IRS Employees Plans group also had a "Phone Forum" on "The Importance of Good Internal Controls." IRS plan examiners were also provided with a "System Procedures and Internal Control Questionnaire" on plan administration.

[165] *Retirement Plan FAQs regarding the EP Team Audit (EPTA) Program,* at https://www.irs.gov/retirement-plans-faws-regarding-the-ep-team-audit-epta-program

provide a structured, methodical approach that will help the plan committee meet its fiduciary obligations.

- *Periodically Test* – Even assuming you have simplified the plan and have the compliance requirements incorporated in controlled plan processes, it is helpful to periodically test the plan's compliance to identify weaknesses or issues that may have arisen. For example, a simple, controlled process that seems to be working well might have flaws that could have arisen because of changes in the law, systems, vendors, personnel, or other factors. To make future testing more efficient, it is wise to require that the testing and any remediation activities be documented.
- *Rely on Experts* – Recognize that the area of retirement plan compliance is complex and seek the advice of experts. Just as legal experts will be able to provide guidance on the rules, you should incorporate their advice with the perspective of the teams that will need to translate those rules into procedures and activities. The factual overlay and the overall environment is important.
- *Clearly Assign Compliance Responsibility* – Often during compliance reviews that I performed, I would query plan committee members as to who was responsible for compliance. They almost always indicated that their ERISA counsel owned that responsibility. When I would ask ERISA counsel the same question, they would say it was the plan committee. Don't assume you know who is responsible. It is helpful to break compliance down into components and assign responsibility for each component. For example:

  o Track legislative, regulatory, or case law that requires changes to the plan document or operations. This is a good area to assign to ERISA counsel, and their responsibility would be to notify the plan committee (or its designate) about changes and due dates.
  o Make system or operational changes required by legislative, regulatory, or case law developments. This should be owned by the process owner of the

affected area (*e.g.*, Payroll, HR, outsource vendor, and so forth). Because changes will often impact several areas that might have different process owners, the plan committee may want to assign a compliance coordinator to help manage the process among the various groups.

o   Monitoring and testing form and operational compliance. In this situation, the process owner may be the most efficient at monitoring, but they may also have a conflict in testing what they're administering. It may be possible to have the process owner responsible for some of the monitoring and testing, but periodically have a third party monitor and test independently.

o   Remediation and corrections can encompass correcting participants' accounts or benefit amounts or improving processes and controls. The individuals or entities responsible will depend on the area being remediated and will often involve a team with representatives from HR, Legal and the administrator.

Litigation Risks

Although the plan can have lawsuits with vendors, contractors, and even employees (if it has any), the largest litigation risks for retirement plans, by far, are from plan participants and the government. The plan participant litigation risk consists of three facets.

The first, which is by far the largest litigation risk, involves participant suits where they are represented by firms that bring class action lawsuits against retirement plans.[166] The bases for these suits continuously evolve and, over time, cover new legal theories and attack new types of plans and employers. The continuing evolution of this risk means the plan committee needs to periodically be updated on the litigation risks by the plan's

---

[166] Schlichter Bogard & Denton LLP is one of the best-known plaintiff law firms that bring class action lawsuits.

ERISA counsel. Knowing the newest theories will help the committee minimize the litigation risks.

For illustration, the following new legal theories, employer types, and plan types were targeted in 2016:

- Cases Questioning the *Quality* of the Fiduciary Decisions – For example, in Bell v. Anthem,[167] the fiduciaries were attacked for not negotiating harder to get an index fund charging two basis points instead of the fund they used which charged four basis points.[168]
- Church Plan Cases – These are lawsuits against large hospitals claiming that they should not be afforded the church plan exemption from ERISA. Dozens of church plan cases were brought in 2016.[169]
- Large University and 403(b) Cases – For years, 401(k) plans were attacked over excess fees and on other grounds. These attacks have now spilled over to the sibling of the 401(k): 403(b) plans for public schools and tax-exempt employers. Class actions were filed against "... Columbia, Cornell, Duke, Emory, John Hopkins, MIT, NYU, Northwestern, UPenn, USC, Vanderbilt, and Yale."[170]

The second plan participant litigation risk involves suits or claims by participants where there has been a privacy or data breach. While this hasn't been anywhere near as voluminous or expensive as the class action lawsuits brought, it is an increasing trend.

---

[167] Bell v. Anthem, filed US District Court Indianapolis Division (Dec. 29, 2015). *See also* White v. Chevron Corp., 2016 BL 281396, N.D. Cal., No. 4:16-cv-00793-PJH, 8/29/16), where the case was dismissed with the court noting that price was only one of several factors to consider.

[168] The difference in the fee charged was 0.02%.

[169] *See e.g.,* Advocate Health Care Network v. Stapleton, U.S., No. 16-74, oral argument 3/27/17; Saint Peter's Healthcare System v. Kaplan, U.S., No. 16-258, oral argument 3/27/17; Dignity Health v. Rollins, U.S., No. 16-258, oral argument 3/27/17.

[170] Clarissa A. Kang, *New Wave of Retirement Fee Litigation: The University 403(b) Lawsuits* (January 2017), available at www.tuckerhuss.com/2017/02/new-wave-of-retirement-fee-litigation-the university-403b-lawsuits/

The third plan participant litigation risk involves suits by individual participants (not class actions), based on a fiduciary breach that is specific to an individual participant. Although these actions can clearly be time-consuming and disruptive, they typically don't involve damages that rise to the amount claimed in class action suits.

Overall, participant class actions, privacy lawsuits, and suits brought by the government are the largest litigation risks. Let's take a closer look at what triggers those actions and what can be done to minimize those risks.

Class Action Lawsuits

A plaintiff's law firm can build a suit predicated on numerous potential bases. While the plaintiffs' bar has not been that creative, the majority of suits brought have been limited to the following types:

- *Stock Drop (or Reverse Stock Drop) Cases* – Stock drop and reverse stock drop cases involve plans that hold employer securities.[171] Stock drop cases typically involve situations where the employer security is publicly traded, and there was some action taken by the company or external event that caused the stock to drop significantly. The plaintiff's claim is that the plan fiduciaries should have anticipated this event and sold the employer security; their failure to take this action has harmed the participants. Reverse stock drop cases involve situations where the fiduciaries sold the employer securities before a rise in the stock price. The claim is that the fiduciaries' action caused the participants to miss this gain.
- *Employer Stock Valuation Cases* – Defined contribution retirement plans that hold stock of the employer *and* the stock is not publicly traded are at risk of being involved in an employer stock valuation case. Because the stock is not publicly traded, it must be independently valued. If the

---

[171] Over 30% of 401(k) plans with 10,000 or more participants hold employer securities. Calculated from 2011 Form 5500 data.

stock is undervalued, the participants will have a claim that the undervaluation has reduced the benefit to which they are eligible. It is possible for any defined contribution plan holding non-publicly traded employer securities to have this claim. Employee stock ownership plans, however, by definition will hold employer stock and are more likely to have this type of claim.

- *Selecting Overpriced Funds and Overpayment Cases* – The plan fiduciaries have a degree of latitude in what they pay for services. Certainly, they can pay more for better service, better options, and the like. The lawsuits typically arise where the fiduciaries select a retail, or more expensive fund or service, when cheaper options were available for the exact same fund or service. These suits are brought against defined contribution plans where the participants bear part or all of the investment or administrative costs of the plan. These suits have been fairly narrow, but due to greater disclosure of what plans are paying for various services, I would expect that the breadth of these types of suits will expand so that they don't necessarily involve only identical funds or services for different prices.

- *Defined Benefit Plan Conversions and Erroneous Benefit Calculations* – Although not as common today[172] as some of the other suits, a number of class actions have centered on claims of erroneous benefit calculations. These cases usually involve defined benefit plans, often in a situation where the benefit formula in the defined benefit plan was converted or changed. Interestingly, there are relatively few suits where the law firm has dug into the data to build a case that the benefit calculation is wrong because the wrong compensation or service is used. This type of case could be built against either a defined benefit or a defined contribution plan. As the easier to identify lawsuits are exhausted by the plaintiffs' law firms, they will begin to

---

[172] During the late 1990s and early 2000s, these suits were more common, as many companies converted their traditional defined benefit plans to cash balance or hybrid plans. That trend has subsided, and the number of suits has declined.

expend the effort to determine where these erroneous calculation cases exist.

Readily Available Data for Plaintiffs' Law firms

Services, such as Judy Diamond, compile the publicly available Form 5500 data and use it to identify areas that vendors and law firms can use. Some of the categories identified by Judy Diamond and made available are:

- Recently changed providers
- Plan recently terminated
- Reduced employer contributions
- Excessive uninvested cash
- Plan is in bottom 10% in rate of return
- Plan is in bottom 10% of plans with high administrative fees
- Plan has experienced a loss due to fraud or dishonesty
- Plan failed to provide benefits when due
- Plan's rate of return versus S&P 500

Plan committees should be proactive in seeing if their plan is identified in any of these categories and be prepared to proactively address any questions, claims, or law suits that may arise from this readily available data.

Although any law suit creates a risk, the risk of class action law suits is extraordinary because they typically involve claims for tens, even hundreds of millions of dollars and require extensive resources (in both time and money) to defend. The plan committee should consider this risk very seriously, and take action to mitigate the risk associated with these lawsuits.

The first line of defense is to remove the basis for the suit, if possible. Fund and plan expenses should be closely monitored, and where an identical or very similar service is available at a lower cost, the plan should switch or have very strong reasons for not making the switch. Additionally, they should confirm that these rationales have withstood the test of litigation.

To mitigate the risk in erroneous calculation cases, the plan committee should check there are procedures in place, with adequate controls, that are tested periodically. The goal is to avoid having a systemic error (one that impacts all calculations). There will almost always be the unique calculations with manual intervention that are prone to errors. Single errors will not trigger or support a class action. Systemic errors will.

Plans that hold employer securities pose the greatest challenge. Short of divesting the plan of all the employer securities, the plan will have the risk of stock drop suits, or valuation suits. In these situations, it is vitally important that the plan committee be able to show that it acted prudently and in the best interest of participants. Any lawsuit will look at potential conflicts of interest of the plan committee members, and how they were influenced by their "other" job with the employer and potential (stock) compensation awards. To manage these risks, I've seen employers use independent plan fiduciaries to make decisions involving employer securities.

Short of removing the basis of the suit, the second defense is to track and monitor the number, type and trends for participant complaints and aggressively address individual participant complaints. If one or more participants have complained that they think their benefit is wrong (because of a calculation, vesting, or data error), the plan committee needs to be sure that such complaints are thoroughly researched and resolved. If an error was made, own it and correct it, not only for any one participant who complained, but also for any similarly impacted participant. If an error was not made, explain the basis for the decision thoroughly and to the satisfaction of the participant. Remember, it is the plan committee that works for the participant. If there was some ambiguity in the plan communication that created the misunderstanding, correct the communication.

Good communication can help cement a favorable view of the plan committee among the participants. If participants see that the plan committee is working to protect the participants by reducing costs, managing vendors, overseeing investments, and testing controls the participants will have a more favorable perception of the plan committee. If the participants see the committee as their advocate, they'll be less likely to bring in an outsider to advocate against the plan committee.

Finally, continually improving plan governance will position the plan and the committee in the best possible position to avoid, withstand, and win against law suits.

Privacy Lawsuits

A privacy lawsuit against the plan essentially claims that the participants were injured because their personal information was obtained by a third party and can potentially be used to financially harm the participants. Some of the potential injuries range from identify theft to accessing participants' plan accounts and redirecting funds to the third party.

In addition to the direct claims made through the litigation, data breaches can bring on additional negative impacts. A major victim of any data breach will be trust. In a 2017 survey of CEOs, 55% felt that breaches in data privacy would "impact negatively on stakeholder trust levels...."[173] 53% of the CEOs felt that cyber security breaches would negatively impact trust levels.[174]

Just as the volume of data breaches is growing with companies, it is also on the rise with retirement plans. The following excerpt from a report by the Advisory Council on Employee Welfare and Pension Benefit Plans lists data breaches identified by the American Institute of Certified Public Accountants (AICPA) was provided:

- Unauthorized user hacking into the plan administrative system after gaining administrative privileges to the accounts and changing account information followed by a fraudulent distribution of funds from the participants' accounts to the unauthorized user. The

---

[173] *20 years inside the mind of the CEO... What's next?,* 20th PwC CEO Survey, 2017 at 33.
[174] Id.

hacker gained access to the system by planting a virus on the company's computer. It is believed that the virus was of a type that enabled the hacker to capture keystrokes when made by an authorized person, thereby enabling the hacker to capture login information and passwords of the plan participants;

- Unauthorized person logging into broker website, entering ID and password, and securing payment which was sent to a name different from the name on the account;
- Person hacking into database to gain access to more than 500,000 participants' PII due to failure of the plan (and administrators) to install security system updates;
- E-mail hoax (phishing attack) that directed participants to a look-alike website prompting participants to share personal data including Social Security numbers (SSNs);
- Employee downloading confidential information for more than 450,000 participants to a home computer;
- Several examples related to the ease with which PII was fraudulently obtained from laptops;
- Multiple examples involving SSNs on printed communications that were, in many cases, either mailed to wrong addresses or the information was made visible to others;
- Employee stealing electronic tapes that contained PII of plan participants and/or beneficiaries;
- Auditors who received CDs with PII of participants and beneficiaries in benefit plans they did not currently audit; and
- Payroll provider using the same password for all clients when the payroll system was established.[175]

The Advisory Council report listed the following ways to improve security for retirement plans:

---

[175] Advisory Council on Employee Welfare and Pension Benefit Plans, *Privacy and Security Issues Affecting Employee Benefit Plans* (November 2011) at 6.

- Offering participants the opportunity to lockdown their accounts so that distributions are not available until the participant unlocks the account.
- Multi-factor authentication, including:
  - Additional security questions for larger distributions and after an address change,
  - Computer software that identifies standard log-in location for the participant and imposes added security for non-standard locations,
  - Use of tokens for added security, and
  - Sending an e-mail or text message to confirm that distribution is being processed.
- Sign-offs on distributions by authorized parties.
- In defined contribution plans a spousal consent is required for a beneficiary payment to someone other than a spouse and in a pension plan the spouse must consent to an alternative form of distribution other than a joint and survivor annuity or alternative form of distribution. This spousal consent requirement does provide some additional security for such distributions because an additional signature is required.
- Mailing changes in PIN numbers and address change verifications to participants and then imposing a wait time for distributions.[176]

Individual Lawsuits

Individual plan participants can also bring suit against the plan for a fiduciary breach.[177] The basis of these suits are actions taken by the plan's fiduciaries that impair or damage an individual plan participant's account balance or benefit. The ability for individual participants to sue was validated by the US Supreme Court in the LaRue v. DeWolff. In that case, an individual participant was allowed to sue for losses because his investment transactions were not being executed timely.

---

[176] Id. at 8-9.
[177] LaRue v. DeWolff, 552 U.S. 248 (2008).

Although the threat of a suit by an individual participant is not generally as risky as a class action lawsuit, some commentators have predicted that these individual law suits could create the basis for "100 Million Potential Lawsuits."[178] The basis for a claim of such a magnitude is that participants will sue where managed funds underperform indexes, and indexes are not available investment alternatives in the plan.

> [A] case for benchmark-indexed alternatives is easy to defend as default or primary investment options, *as long as* you have a means (the option and flexibility) for participants to select from a broad array of any of the alternatives that may outperform the benchmark in the future. The risk to you as a trustee or adviser in a plan structured in this manner is very low. ERISA requires diversification and the avoidance of investment risk unless it is clearly prudent to do otherwise. The benchmark-indexed portfolio is defendable both as being diversified and as avoiding the risk of materially underperforming.[179]

The risk of individual law suits can potentially be based on claims similar to that just described, or any one of innumerable potential actions taken by the fiduciaries. Hopefully, what the plan committee and fiduciaries take away from the risk of individual lawsuits is that **they must protect participants as a class, and also individually.**

Governmental Audits and Lawsuits

If your plan is being threatened by a lawsuit by the United States government, *something has gone terribly wrong*. In most situations, the government will raise the issue and give the plan the opportunity to correct it, often making amnesty or reduced penalties available. I don't recall seeing a large employer having to litigate against the United States to defend its actions related to a retirement plan.

---

[178] The Four Pillars of Retirement Plans *supra* at 3.
[179] *Id.* at 48-49. Emphasis in original.

There are, however, many cases brought each year by the government against plans. The vast majority of these cases are against small plans and involve situations where the management of the company has been unresponsive or engaged in outright criminal behavior.[180] In these cases, once the government gets involved (because things are *that bad*), the dog has the proverbial bone and nothing will shake it lose. Expect to see management removed, businesses shuttered, and individual fiduciaries put in jail.

Who, then, are the governmental agencies involved in these investigations and audits that trigger lawsuits? How, do these audits, investigations, and lawsuits arise? What can be done to avoid or mitigate against these risks?

The main governmental agencies charged with enforcing the various provisions of ERISA, the rule governing retirement plans, are the Internal Revenue Service, the Department of Labor, and the Pension Benefit Guaranty Corporation. In general, governmental lawsuits will arise from any of these three agencies following an audit or an investigation performed by the governmental agency. Audits and investigations are usually triggered in one of three ways:

- *Government Filings* – The first and most likely trigger for a governmental audit or investigation is as a result of data reported to the government by the plan (such as on a Form 5500). Because of the risk that a governmental filing can trigger an audit, it is important that any governmental filing be reviewed by someone familiar with such filings, so the risk of an audit can be assessed.
- *Participant Complaints* – Participant complaints to their congressman or a governmental agency can also trigger an investigation or an audit. While participant complaints trigger many fewer audits or investigations than

---

[180] *See* U.S. Dep't of Labor *2014 ERISA Litigation and Significant Issues in Litigation*, available at https://www.dol.gov/sol/media/pbs/2014erisalitigation.htm. There are over 200 ERISA cases listed (not all involving retirement plans), and the abuses listed are mind boggling.

governmental filings, it does happen. In these cases, the government is obviously getting a very one-sided representation of the facts. To the extent it is possible, the goal should be to resolve participant complaints before they get escalated by the participant to the government. In FY 2016, the Department of Labor's Employee Benefits Security Administration recovered through an informal process over $394 million of benefits for participants based on calls participants made to the agency.[181]

- *Surveys and Studies* – The government will periodically conduct surveys or studies into areas that it wants to understand better. Some of the recent studies conducted have been on 401(k) plans and 403(b) plans. As a result of these studies, the government will initiate targeted audits or investigations to address problems uncovered during the survey or study.

Government Surveys and Studies Can Result in a Broad Audit Net Being Cast

During the early 1990's, the United States steel industry was suffering, plants were closing, and plans were being terminated (often with unfunded liabilities). Because of all the terminations, the government decided to conduct a study of plans in the steel industry. The government found that many of the plans were underfunded and had operational issues. As a result of the study, the government began a program of auditing plans "in the steel industry." The audit net was, however, cast much more broadly than just the steel industry, and plans that simply had "steel" in the name were captured as part of the audits.

Reputational Risks

Imagine you're an executive of a large company and serve on the retirement plan committee. Unbeknownst to you, a lower-level

---

[181] EBSA Fact Sheet, available at https://www.dol.gov/sites/default/files/ebsa/about-ebsa/our-activities/resource-center/fact-sheets/ebsa-monetary-results.pdf.

employee has embezzled plan funds through fraud. You heard about this from the staff that work on the retirement plan; they seemed to be handling it. One early morning, you're reading your industry news and there it is—an article that you've been named in a lawsuit alleging that you allowed fraud to occur. It discusses how there was a lack of oversight, a loss of funds, and to date, no action taken by the plan or the company. The article closes with quotes from investors and employees asking for your resignation. Welcome to the world of reputational risk.

Reputational risk can affect your personal brand, and also hurt the business and participants' trust in the retirement plan. Activities that can trigger reputational risk include:

- News of government audits or any law suits
- Allegations of conflicts of interest or potential self-dealing
- Reports of recurring or multiple errors, or errors being discovered and not corrected
- Claims of fiduciary misconduct or breaches

Scores of books on how to protect the reputation of a business can be extrapolated to retirement plans. The books suggest a number of possible approaches, and the right one will depend on the facts, but none of the approaches suggests doing nothing. If the plan committee meets only periodically, waiting for the next meeting can be viewed as doing nothing. Consider ways that the committee can respond to such risks without having to wait for the next meeting.

At your next risk retreat, assume you're confronted with a set of facts that will damage the plan's (and perhaps the company's) reputation. Consider how you will respond, and whether you can react quickly enough to defuse the potential risk.

In the example just discussed involving the lower-level employee who was embezzling from the plan, some of the responses might be:

- Have an emergency meeting to address the situation.

- Establish procedures in advance that will provided a measured response, such as removing the employee from any involvement on plan matters and making a demand for the restitution of the embezzled plan assets.
- The plan committee can request that the company terminate the employee.
- The plan committee can request a forensic audit of the plan to determine how the embezzlement could have occurred, so it can be prevented in the future.
- The plan committee can require tighter controls where individuals have access to plan assets.
- The options should be developed in conjunction with the company's crisis management planning experts.

Governance Risks

Hopefully, it goes without saying that inadequate governance creates risks. It is a stand-alone risk, and it also lays the foundation for every one of the risks described previously in this chapter. Governance risks will encompass a lack of oversight, poor or lacking accountability, unclear roles and responsibilities, not managing conflicts of interest, an absence of training for new plan committee members, and flawed vendor management, among others.

Administrative Risks

We began this chapter by looking at asset and investment risk, and the other bookend for this discussion is administrative risk. On the one hand, assets and investments are sexy discussions, while on the other hand the administrative risks are, well, far from sexy. Despite the mundane nature of administrative risks, they are nevertheless important.

Indeed, because administrative risks are often neglected, they can have a higher likelihood of occurring. They can also have a higher likelihood of occurring because of the volume of transactions that occur each year. For example, a 401(k) plan with 10,000 plan participants can easily have over one million transactions processed each year.

Because the potential number of administrative errors is almost countless, the following offers some approaches that can help to minimize administrative risks:

- Have processes that have controls incorporated into the process.
- Have the processes periodically reviewed and tested.
- Rely on reputable vendors that are annually audited and have comprehensive SSAE 16 reports on their plan processing.
- Avoid manual processing as much as possible, and if it is absolutely necessary, have a structured review process.
- Review and confirm that the underlying data being used is correctly mapped to the definitions in the plan (*e.g.*, the definition of plan compensation agrees with compensation pulled from payroll), and that it is tested periodically.
- Periodically review and test the processes of the vendors and those used by the company for the plan's administration.
- Review whether the terms of the plan document are followed in operation (perhaps allowing an independent third party to review the plan and check for possible "misinterpretations").

Multiple Plan Enterprise-Wide Risk

Let's step back from the individual plan for a moment, and consider the additional risks that can be created by having multiple plans. Most larger employers have multiple plans in the United States, and almost all larger global employers have multiple plans in a number of different countries. Having more than one plan creates unique additional risks that *cannot* be managed by the individual plan-level committee. These risks must be managed at the enterprise level.

The risks created by having multiple plans fall into three general categories:

- *Plans Apply Different Standards* – Imagine that your company has two similar plans for two different divisions. Each plan has its own plan committee. Now imagine that both plans are looking at their control or compliance environment, or looking at vendor costs, or assessing vendor performance, and they apply different standards. In the extreme case, one could assume that one plan applies *some* standard, while the other plan committee is passive, operating without standards and not overseeing controls, compliance, costs, or performance. In these examples, it isn't too difficult to imagine a lawsuit where the plaintiffs' counsel has plan committee members from the plan with stronger standards testify against the plan that is lacking adequate standards or has no standards at all.

  It is possible for different plans to have different standards. For example, they may have different types of participants and therefore, justify different goals. The question that management at the enterprise level must ask is whether there is justification to apply different standards among the different plans.

- *Plans with Opposing Investment Choices* – Let's assume that your company has two plans, one in the United States and one in the UK. The US plan committee decides that it should *drop* mutual fund X. At the same time, the plan committee for the UK plan decides that it should *acquire* mutual fund X. One can see that a plaintiffs' attorney will be able to argue that one of the plan committees made a bad decision. Although each plan committee can have a multitude of reasons to support its decision, if there is not clarity around the decision, or it appears they blindly followed the advisor's recommendation, or it seems they did not perform adequate due diligence, they could have a problem. It is entirely possible for different plans, with different goals, investment policies, and standards to reach opposite conclusions on the same mutual fund. The question that management at the enterprise level must ask is whether justification exists to reach opposing conclusions on the same investment.

- *Plans with Different Criteria for Selecting Committee Members or Fiduciaries, or Different Governance Structures or Standards* – Different countries have different standards for who can serve as a plan committee member.[182] Different countries can also have different governance structures (such as employee members, or independent members). These differences are potential risks. For example, if in one country there are minimum standards for knowledge and experience, or employee or independent members are required in another country, the question can be asked why the same standards were not applied to the US plan.

An approach that I have found to be helpful is to establish global governance standards, such as the 12 principles detailed in this book. This would require that all plans in all countries abide by the same governance principles. When all plans in all countries have to follow the same governance principles, then the individual country differences, such as minimum standards for the local plan committee members, do not become as much of a distinguishing factor. For example, all plans in all countries would need to meet minimum knowledge and skill standards and work to improve them. The differences would not be related to the 12 principles (which are uniform in all the countries), but related to the local application of the principles that would be attributable to local laws, customs, and practices.

How the Pragmatic Committee Approaches Risk Management

If you're feeling overwhelmed, that's understandable. There are a lot of risks, and managing those risks can be daunting. But let's pause and reflect on the plan committee's role. The committee isn't charged with having to identify all the risks or resolve all the risks. It is the oversight body and it fulfills its role by looking to the parties that it oversees and having them identify the risks and work to manage those risks.

---

[182] See discussion around footnote 185.

For example, the plan committee would ask the company staff that works on the plan and the plan vendors to assess the potential risks associated with the performance of their duties, and be sure they've addressed investment risks, economic risks, resource risks, administrative risks, reputational risks, litigation risks, compliance risks, and so on. The committee could then ask a third party (such as Internal Audit or an outside party), to provide an independent assessment. This second perspective helps ensure that the company staff and plan vendors aren't ignoring potential risks because of a conflict or possibly because of ignorance.

The key is that the plan committee needs to begin the process of having the risks identified, and have risk identification be part of the role of every party working with the plan.

Quick Hits

1. Have data related to the plan's operation compiled to compare the plan against benchmarks, such as the level of plan fees and expenses, investment return, and the like. (For example, are asset-based and other fees that are being paid competitive?) Where the plan deviates negatively from benchmarks, these areas could be identified as risks.

2. Inventory past errors that have occurred with the plan (even if they have been corrected), so they can be presented to the plan committee and the potential risks associated with those errors evaluated. This could include any recent audits by regulatory bodies such as the IRS or the Department of Labor, and any participant lawsuits.

3. Have contribution calculations (or benefit calculations) reviewed to see if these amounts are being calculated correctly. The calculation should not only consider the calculation formula, but also confirm that the inputs are correct (*e.g.*, are the correct definitions of compensation and service being used?).

4. Check that the company's systems and staff that are being relied upon for the plan's administration are both reliable and accurate.

5. Request a review of how vendors are overseen, specifically:
   a. That vendors are meeting the terms of their contract
   b. That all user controls identified in any SSAE 16's are being satisfied
   c. That there are performance measures in place, that they meet industry standards,[183] and that they are reported to the appropriate parties regularly

---

[183] Industry standard performance measures is the absolute lowest threshold. Ultimately, the plan needs to determine what performance measure it needs the vendors to have in place so the plan committee can fulfill its fiduciary obligation.

    d. The vendors have addressed potential internal risks, such as privacy, data security (redundancy), succession planning for the team, testing of their controls, and the like

    e. Review whether the vendors are capable of surviving various levels of an economic downturn

6. Ask legal counsel, HR and your administrative vendor to:
    a. Compile suggestions on how to avoid, shift, ensure against, or minimize compliance risks
    b. Identify and manage potential litigation risks (*e.g.*, related to company stock, fees, and privacy)

7. Schedule time to analyze how enterprise-wide events could create risks for the plan, such as:
    a. Acquisition of an entity and a plan that could be merged into the existing plan
    b. The influx of a large group of new individuals or the need to incorporate data from a new, unfamiliar database
    c. The conversion to a new HRIS, payroll, or another IT system that directly impacts the plan administration

8. Develop a schedule or plan to periodically have reviews performed by independent third parties of:
    a. In-house administration
    b. Outsourced operations
    c. Operation of the committee, including overall plan governance
    d. Investment portfolio risks

Knowledge and Skills

"It is possible to fly without motors, but not without knowledge and skills."
Wilbur Wright

"We are drowning in information but starved for knowledge."
John Naisbitt, author of <u>Megatrends</u>

Introduction

Serving as a plan fiduciary or a plan committee member is, in all likelihood, not the fiduciary's or committee member's primary job. In almost all instances, they have a full-time job with the plan sponsor and they are quite busy.

The plan committee members probably inherited the role as plan fiduciary either because it goes with their job title, or it was awarded to them because they have been successful in other challenges. It is, to say the least, a challenge for which they have had little prior training, and about which they are uncertain regarding their role and responsibilities. Indeed, plan committee members who have served in that capacity for years are often uncertain about the full scope of their role and have received little formal training.[184]

---

[184] Regarding the prudent expert standard, BrightScope, which ranks plans performance and provides internet-based information to plan participants, states, "[w]hether a company makes widgets, builds large and complicated machinery, sells goods or supplies a service, it's likely that 'running a retirement plan' isn't part of the mission statement. And while the company's officers are likely very good at administration, accounting, logistics and marketing, it's also likely they aren't particularly well-versed in duties such as selecting and managing investment alternatives and determining 401(k) fees are reasonable." https://www.brightscope.com/financial-planning/advice/article/5157/Erisa-Requires-That-Plan-Sponsors-Hire-Prudent-Experts-What-Does-That-Mean/

An irony in US law is that specified minimum standards that must be met for a person to serve as a plan committee member or a plan fiduciary are non-existent. The law simply requires that the fiduciary act, "solely in the interest of the participants and beneficiaries...." ERISA section 404(a). The law does *not* require that the plan committee members or fiduciaries:[185]

- Have not declared bankruptcy
- Have no inherent conflicts of interest with the plan (*e.g.,* receiving pay from a vendor, or owning a sizable interest in a vendor)
- Meet a minimum education level
- Possess or show a minimum level of knowledge or skill required to oversee a retirement plan
- Agreed to undertake certain training
- Have a minimum level of knowledge about qualified plans, plan administration, plan requirements, fiduciary duty, or plan investments

If, then, individuals who are unexperienced or untrained, or who are an outright villain[186] can become plan committee members, one might assume that the law does not set a very high standard for these positions. That is not the case. On the contrary, expectations are extremely high, as is the potential liability.

Expectation Level for Knowledge and Skills

ERISA section 404(a) establishes the basic standard for fiduciaries, and it provides that:

> ... a fiduciary shall discharge his duties with respect to a plan solely in the interest of the participants and beneficiaries and

---

[185] Other countries, such as the UK, Ireland, Australia, Germany, and the Netherlands, require certain minimum levels of knowledge and understanding, experience, or expertise. NAPF, *UK Pension Regulation Compared* (October 2008), at 6.

[186] Felons, including individuals convicted of fraud, murder, rape, kidnapping and other serious crimes, *can* serve as a fiduciary upon the later of their release from prison or 13 years after their conviction. ERISA § 411(a), 29 U.S.C. 1111(a).

... with the care, skill, prudence, and diligence under the circumstances then prevailing that a prudent man acting in a like capacity **and familiar with such matters** would use in the conduct of an enterprise of a like character and with like aims .... [Emphasis added.]

The bolded language, "and familiar with such matters," essentially raises the standard against which the plan fiduciary and committee members are held to the level of an expert. The standard is often cited as the "prudent expert" rule or standard, and the standard is described as "the highest known to the law."[187] In other words, a plan committee member will not be judged as an amateur or a novice or a part-time hobbyist, despite a lack of knowledge and experience. Instead, plan committee members are judged against this standard of behavior: that of an expert in the administration of retirement plans. In a landmark ERISA decision that developed the prudent expert rule, the Court in Donovan v. Cunningham stated, "A pure heart and an empty head are not enough."[188]

So, You Think You're an Expert?

To assess whether you are a prudent expert, or a person with the level of expertise expected by ERISA, ask yourself these questions:

---

[187] Donovan v. Bierwirth, 680 F.2d 263, 272 (2d Cir. 1982).
The standard in the US may be the highest standard in the world. A study done in the European Union on the governance of occupational pension schemes in the EU noted that,

> ... the standard of fiduciary care described in the UK is considerably weaker than the standard set in the United States. The key difference is the legal texts is that in the UK the trustee should approach the management of the scheme as '... **that of an ordinary man of business ...**' in the US the fiduciary is '...**a prudent man acting in a like capacity and familiar with such matters...**'. The US standard is more prescriptive, in that the fiduciary clearly has to have some previous experience and knowledge of the task....

Occupational Pension Stakeholder Group, *OPSG Discussion Paper on Occupational Pension Scheme Governance* (EIOPA-OPSG-13-02 July 13, 2013) at 6, emphasis in original; footnote omitted.
[188] 716 F.2d 1455, 1467 (5th Cir. 1983), *cert. denied*, 467 U.S. 1251 (1984).

- Have you ever overseen the investment of a retirement plan with the level of assets in your retirement plan?
- Have you overseen the administration of a retirement plan?
- Are you aware of the compliance requirements of a retirement plan emanating from the IRS, DOL, AICPA, SEC, and the like?
- Have you done the first three items enough to be considered an expert?

You're probably wondering, as your blood pressure rises and sweat beads on your brow, just how on earth you will ever meet this imposing standard. Fortunately, the following four-step process can help plan committee members (or other fiduciaries) meet the prudent expert standard.

Is the area subject to the prudent expert rule?
Identify the areas where the plan committee (or other fiduciary) will be held to the prudent expert standard.

Assess knowledge gaps
If the area is one where the prudent expert standard applies, determine if the plan committee has the appropriate level of expertise.

Fill knowledge gaps
If the plan committee does not have the appropriate level of expertise, fill the knowledge gap through training or using experts.

Oversee experts
If experts are used, have a process for overseeing the experts.

Is the Area Subject to the Prudent Expert Standard?

I will resist the temptation to answer this question by responding, "All areas are." While such a flippant response is neither completely accurate nor very helpful, it does reflect a visceral concern that wherever the plan committee's weakness lies, that's where you'll be sued, audited, or otherwise questioned. It is thus with some trepidation that I attempt to outline the areas where the committee should prepare to be held to the "expert standard."

Be cautious, however, that you view this list as a *starting point*, and not as a definitive list. The plan committee should look to the other experts that support them (both internal and external) to understand trends in litigation, IRS and DOL audits, and other changes that create risk. However, the experts that support the committee will likely see the plan committee's world through their lens. For example, counsel may focus on reviewing litigation updates that can show trends in where plans are sued. Counsel may not, however, focus on articles in the industry press that reflect disruption in the market (such as vendors being acquired or suffering financial difficulty, software or systems going through major updates, or the discontinuance of prior versions being supported). Getting broad-based input will benefit the committee.

Finally, before diving into the list of potential areas where the plan committee may be held to an expert standard, it is worth noting that the areas will depend on a number of factors, such as:

- Plan type (*e.g.*, defined benefit, defined contribution, cash balance, ESOP, and so on)
- Plan design (*e.g.*, investment alternatives, entry and retirement ages and requirements, distribution options, and the like)
- Systems/Administration (*e.g.*, outsourced, integrated systems, decentralized systems, and so on)
- Demographics (*e.g.*, employees/division covered and excluded, contribution/withdrawal/loan/investment/ retirement patterns, age, morbidity, and the like)
- Committee composition and experience

The following is a list of areas where the plan committee will generally be held to the prudent expert standard. For added clarification, the list is divided into three subparts: (1) Plan Committee (PC) Needs Little Expertise, (2) PC Needs Some Expertise, and (3) PC Needs Expertise.[189]

---

[189] One could debate which areas should fall into the three categories. Indeed, depending on how the plan and committee are structured, areas could shift among the three. The goal of this list and categorizing the items is to provide a

The areas that are identified under "PC (plan committee) Needs Little Expertise," are those that the plan committee can generally outsource to experts and where the committee needn't have any meaningful expertise. They do, however, have to provide vendor management and oversee the expert (*e.g.*, are they billing the right amount, following the terms of their contract, meeting performance standard, and so on). (If the area is not outsourced, the committee will clearly need to have expertise.)

The areas that are identified under "PC Needs Some Expertise" are those where the plan committee can generally rely on the services of experts, but where the committee will require more knowledge and oversight than is required for the areas that can be outsourced to experts, with the committee not needing any significant amount of expertise. For example, one of these areas involves compliance and testing. The plan committee can rely on experts, such as Legal, for assistance, but they will need to have some basic knowledge of the compliance rules, and at a minimum know when to secure the advice of counsel.

The final areas are identified under "PC Needs Expertise." These are the areas where the plan committee will generally need to be an expert. For example, the committee members will need to know what can cause a conflict of interest, since their personal behavior outside of meetings can create problems. These are also governance areas.

---

starting point for assessing where the committee will need to become an expert, and illustrate that there are a number of areas where the committee will not be able to fully escape responsibility.

Areas Committee Will Be Held to Prudent Expert Standard	PC Needs Little Expertise	PC Needs Some Expertise	PC Needs Expertise
Investing	√		
Administration (recordkeeping, valuations, etc.)	√		
Gov't reporting and participant disclosure	√		
Funding and contributions		√	
Expenses		√	
Compliance and testing		√	
Finance and audits		√	
Risk Management and Controls		√	
Knowledge, skills, and training		√	
Transparency and communication		√	
Data Analytics		√	
Vendor management			√
Performance management			√
Plan terms and rules			√
Delegation of authority; roles, responsibility, and accountability			√
Conflicts of interest; code of conduct; prohibited transactions			√
Fiduciary standards			√
Governance			√

Now that the plan committee has a list of areas to assess regarding the proper level of knowledge and skills, let's discuss how to assess the plan committee for knowledge gaps.

Assess Knowledge Gaps (Do You Have Such Expertise?)

Assessing others' knowledge and skills, and then having a dialogue about weaknesses is one of the most difficult things for plan committee members to do. The members are often all high-ranking executives and recognized experts in their field. Conversations suggesting that they have fissures in their knowledge or softness in their skills can be unexpected and even unwelcome.

Having the plan committee delegate this endeavor comes with its own set of problems. For example, let's assume you are assessing the knowledge and skills of a new committee member who happens to be the CFO. If the committee delegates the task to a staff person, who may now or potentially in the future report to the CFO, or if you hire a consultant, whose future revenue depends on being hired by the CFO for future jobs, you've created at best an awkward situation and at worst clear conflict of interest. Delegating the role may not be a good solution.

An effective way to get information about any knowledge and skills gaps is for the plan committee members to provide a self-revelation (or self-reporting) of where they have gaps (similar to the chair in the following box, "Egoless Leadership"). A successful approach is for the members to initially perform this assessment alone, and then bring their results to a gathering[190] of all the members. At this gathering, they can share results. Often the "weakness" of one member will be joined by other members, and training themes will begin to develop.

I've seen this self-revelation (or self-assessment) facilitated, or guided, with the help of a questionnaire. The questionnaire would ask about the member's training and experience in the different

---

[190] I would not have this assessment, or any training, take place at an official plan meeting. The plan committee members need to have a venue where they can ask for help in any area they deem is warranted, and "ask stupid questions" without the fear of having them in meeting minutes and later used against them. Of course, even without official recorded minutes, personal notes could be subject to discovery, and recollections of members could be queried during a cross-examination.

areas, or ask the member to provide relative ratings or scores. For example, if asking about compliance experience, the questionnaire might ask:

- How much training have you received relating to retirement plan compliance?
- How much experience do you have working with retirement plan compliance?
- On a scale of 1 to 10 (with 1 being no knowledge and 10 being total knowledge), how would you rate your retirement plan compliance knowledge?

I'm personally a little hesitant to have plan committee members document their weakness, especially if it isn't done within a clear context. I worry that this admission might later be discovered in litigation and provide the other party with an admission that some of the committee members lack the adequate level of knowledge or skill.

Instead of using a questionnaire, I've found it effective to provide the plan committee members with a menu of potential training areas so they can express interest in gaining or improving knowledge. This isn't as direct an acknowledgement that a person is "ignorant," but rather lets the member indirectly acknowledge they have gaps or are merely seeking to improve and stay current. (A list of potential training areas is outlined in the next section, "Filling the Knowledge Gaps.")

Regardless of the approach taken, the plan committee, particularly the chair, should recognize that there are inherent conflicts in having individuals assess their own knowledge and skills. This is where the chair's leadership will prove critical.

Egoless Leadership

While working with one plan committee, the issue of ego was completely neutralized, and the assessment process simplified by the chair. At the outset of the assessment process, the chair simply stated that being a plan fiduciary was not his core skill-set, and there was much that he needed to learn. He rattled off a number of areas, ranging from the terms of the plan document to investment theory and the law. Finally, he noted that as a company, they became successful by getting the best talent, and being the best they could in their industry. He felt that was a solid approach in relation to the plan, and hoped everyone would strive to be the best in every area related to the plan.

That short, heart-felt speech from an executive who truly cared about his employees engaged all the other plan committee members to be open about where they could improve and what they didn't know. It was OK to not be an expert here and to get help. On that day, that plan committee started on a journey of significant improvement.

Filling the Knowledge Gaps

Most, if not all plan committees, will have some areas where they do not have the appropriate knowledge and skills to meet the standard in ERISA section 404(a), "that a prudent man acting in a like capacity *and familiar with such matters* would use...." (Emphasis added.) Once the knowledge assessment is done and the gaps are identified, the plan committee needs to determine which of the following three possible alternatives is most appropriate to close this gap:

- *Training* – Improving the plan committee's knowledge and skill through training and study
- *Using Experts* – Relying on in-house experts or hiring external experts; this could also include outsourcing the function
- *Combination Approach* – Building on the plan committee's knowledge and skill and using experts

The plan committee will need to balance between whether it can fulfill its fiduciary duty through just training, just using experts, or if it will need to bridge the gap through a combination of the two. In almost all situations, however, supplementing the committee's training will improve the plan's performance, reduce risks, or both. One plan governance study found that committee members who "acquired knowledge and understanding about how [plans] should be run are more likely to be able to govern their [plans] well."[191]

For plans in the United States, training is often lacking. A Towers' study found that the "...lack of consistent training for internal fiduciaries presents a potential impediment to effective governance, thereby increasing liability risk." The study also found that "... a majority of respondents do not have ERISA counsel or persons with particular ERISA expertise at every committee meeting. It is therefore even more critical that internal fiduciaries receive the necessary training and keep their knowledge and skills up to date."[192]

Indeed, there is no shortage of areas in which the plan committee can receive training. The following is an illustrative list:

- Plan governance and an overview of the responsibilities of the plan committee (including fiduciary duties)
- Overseeing plan investments and investment advisors
- Primer on investment basics and theory
- Overseeing funding, contributions, and expenses
- Overseeing plan financials, plan audits, and the plan auditor
- Overseeing the plan's risk management and the control environment
- Overseeing the plan's vendors and staff (and understanding their roles, responsibilities, and accountability)
- Overseeing performance measures for vendors and others, including establishing and monitoring
- Overseeing the plan's compliance and testing
- Overseeing the knowledge and skills of the staff
- Plan communication and transparency (including government reporting and participant disclosures)
- Avoiding conflicts of interest and prohibited transactions, and complying with the code of conduct

---

[191] *Occupational pension scheme governance – A report on the 2007 scheme governance survey supra* at 14.
[192] *The New Governance Landscape supra* at 10.

- Improving familiarity with the plan document
- Improving familiarity with plan administration and operations
- Committee dynamics and traps (*e.g.,* Groupthink, avoiding hierarchical thinking, and so on)
- Uses of plan data and data analytics for the plan

For most of these areas, it would be appropriate to have introductory training in each one, and then more detailed training can be offered. For example, the last item, "uses of plan data and data analytics for the plan," could have training on the types of plan data available and the potential uses of that data, and then separate training sessions on benchmarking the plan against other plans, comparing plan expenses and costs, participant behavior (*e.g.,* loans, level of contributions, investment behavior), and so on.

There are several areas where I feel that the plan committee might benefit from a working session, rather than just a training session. These areas are:

- Identifying risks for the plan and common problem areas
- Understanding roles, responsibilities, and accountability, and the oversight and reporting framework for the plan
- Benchmarking knowledge and skills for the committee members
- Setting objectives and goals for the plan and the committee
- Performing an assessment

Training for the plan committee can be delivered economically in a variety of ways:

- **Self-taught** by reading books and articles or watching videos. The footnotes in this book provide a sampling of topics and sources.
- **Peer training**, with more experienced members training junior members. Indeed, a way to improve the knowledge of members is to have them train new members, rather

than having a staff person in HR conduct the training, which is a common approach.

- **In-house training**, where an in-house expert provides training (*e.g.*, the Internal Audit Director providing training on controls, or the Benefits Manager providing training on the plan terms). If this training is planned so that the invited expert and the plan committee both share their expertise, it has the potential to generate tremendous synergies for the plan committee and the invited expert. For example, an expert from Internal Audit can be invited to provide training on risk management and the use of controls. The plan committee can help Internal Audit understand the operation of the plan and the risks identified by the plan committee. In this way, both groups can do their jobs better.

- **Training by vendors**, such as the plan's actuary or recordkeeper, or the investment advisor. In many cases, these vendors are willing to provide training at no cost to the plan committee. Even when they've been hesitant to provide such training, they have usually been encouraged to do it for free when they learn a competitor is willing to provide free training to gain access to the committee.

- **Formal training** by a firm that specializes in training (which can be on-site at the company or at a conference with other companies' plan committee members). Although there are few plan governance training sessions, the committee can find training on retirement plan administration, current developments, and legislative and regulatory changes.

Inevitably, because of the complexity of the systems involved, the specialized skills and experience required, or the fact that training is not available or can't be completed within the time constraints, the committee will not be able to improve its knowledge and skills through training and will have to seek another option. In such a case, the solutions are to hire external experts or rely on in-house experts.

When training alone will not suffice, the plan committee will want to satisfy the prudent expert standard by using experts who will be responsible for those areas. These experts can be culled from internal or external sources.

The emphasis needs to be on finding an expert. Don't fall into the trap of using an internal resource to save on cost or to provide experience to developing staff. The standard is securing an expert that can either take the place of the plan committee or provide expert guidance to the committee, so the committee can make a decision.

Regardless of whether you're selecting an internal expert or an external expert, the plan committee should establish selection criteria for picking the expert. When establishing the selection criteria, the committee should consider:

- The role the expert is filling, or the gap the plan committee is trying to fill
- The expectations for the role and the expert's goals. For example, avoiding conflicts of interest would be one of the expectations.
- What constitutes an "expert" in the area, and whether the entity or individual meets that standard
- Whether the expert will have any fiduciary responsibilities, and whether they are accepting the risks and liability associated with the role. (Experts taking on a fiduciary role are likely to charge more for taking on this risk.)
- Performance measures or standards that will be used, and whether the expert can provide updates on performance
- What the expert will charge (and, of course, whether there are any performance guarantees, or other upward or downward adjustments that might occur)
- Whether the expert will indemnify the plan for any errors that cost the plan money

Note that for the fourth bullet, concerning whether the expert will have any fiduciary responsibilities, it may be possible in some cases for the plan committee to shift its fiduciary duty to a third party. For example, some investment advisors will act as the fiduciary and make the actual investment decisions. In these situations, they are acting as the fiduciary for such decisions. This is a good way for the plan committee to shift the fiduciary responsibility for a specific area away from the committee to the third-party expert.

Shifting the fiduciary responsibility for a specific area from the plan committee to a third party does not, however, relieve the plan committee of all of its responsibilities. The committee remains responsible for making sure that the expert remains an expert and abides by its contractual terms. The plan committee does not need to look behind any of the activity of the expert. If experts who are serving as a fiduciary make a mistake, they are liable. For this reason, an expert that is serving as a fiduciary[193] must have insurance or deep enough pockets to be able to cover what could be significant potential losses.[194]

Overseeing Experts

Once the plan fiduciaries and the plan committee tap experts in the areas where they lack expertise,[195] they no longer need to personally have expertise in those areas. Instead of being an expect in areas related to retirement plan administration, investment, and compliance, the plan fiduciary and committee members can meet these standards by being an **expert in overseeing experts.** This is where understanding plan governance and having a strong plan governance structure in place become critical.

---

[193] The non-fiduciary expert should also have insurance or sufficient assets to cover losses. When a non-fiduciary expert makes a mistake, however, the losses are not typically as great as when a fiduciary mistake is made.

[194] Governmental plans commonly require their vendors to accept unlimited liability. Because of this, the vendors that end up being hired are typically small entities that are willing to accept unlimited liability. These entities, however, have no assets and no insurance, so their acceptance of unlimited liability is a hollow promise. Don't make a mistake; be sure the vendor has quality insurance and a solid balance sheet.

[195] The Department of Labor regulation specifically states: "Unless they possess the necessary expertise to evaluate such factors, fiduciaries would need to obtain the advice of a qualified, independent expert." DOL Reg. § 2509.95-1(c)(6).

What does it mean to be an "expert in overseeing experts?" In general, this can be broken down into the following eight elements:

- ***The Expert Has the Skills*** – Assure "...that the expert actually has the skills for which he or she is being retained and, therefore, [the fiduciary] is obligated to adequately investigate the expert's qualifications."[196]
- ***The Expert is Given Knowledge of the Plan and Job*** – Ensure that the experts "...acquire sufficient familiarity with the specific nature and needs of the ... plan ... by providing them with complete, accurate and sufficient information so they can appropriately formulate requested advice or carry out delegated tasks."[197]
- ***The Expert has No Conflicts*** – Ensure that the expert does not have any conflicts of interest.[198]
- ***The Compensation Arrangement is Clear, Complete, Understandable, and Reasonable.***[199]
- ***The Expert is Monitored*** – The fiduciary monitors and reviews "...the activities delegated to assure that they have been appropriately and prudently carried out."[200]
- ***The Expert's Roles, Responsibilities, Goals, and Performance Measures are Clear*** – The plan committee or fiduciaries have been clear in detailing the expert's roles and responsibilities,[201] listing the expert's goals, and establishing performance measures.[202]

---

[196] Russell Galer, *Prudent Person Rule' Standard for the Investment of Pension Fund Assets* (OECD) available at https://www.oecd.org/finance/private-pensions/2763540.pdf.

[197] Id.

[198] The service agreement with the expert should be in writing, not "conflict with the fiduciary standard of care[,]" and represent that there are no conflicts or disclose all conflicts. The New Fiduciary Standard *supra* at 77. Conflicts, including conflicts with experts, are discussed more fully in the upcoming chapter on Ethics: Conflicts of Interest and Code of Conduct.

[199] *See Outsourcing Employee Benefit Plan Service supra* at 7.

[200] The New Fiduciary Standard at 77.

[201] Clarity of roles and responsibilities would be fundamental for the fiduciary and the expert to know what skills are required and what information would be required to do the job. *See also, Outsourcing Employee Benefit Plan Service supra* at 6: "To be an effective 'roadmap' for the relationship, a contract must

- **Is the Expert also a Fiduciary?** It should be clear whether the expert is acting in a fiduciary capacity (even if it is a limited fiduciary capacity), and for what duties and risks the expert will be responsible.
- **Expert's Organization Should Have Strong Governance –** Finally, the plan committee should check to see that the expert (and its organization) has good governance in place. This will help with all seven of the preceding elements and should include a good controls environment, meeting the compliance requirements, avoiding conflicts, driving strong transparency and reporting, having adequate knowledge and skills, and the like.

The plan committee's role as an oversight body is to be sure that the above eight areas are incorporated into the selection and monitoring of any expert. Thus, the committee would instruct the team charged with the task that, as part of its evaluation criteria, the team needs to ensure that the expert meets these eight standards. In addition, the committee could ask the team to show the committee how these criteria are satisfied.

Tailoring Your Menu of Knowledge and Skills Based on Your Plan Design and Features

The menu of knowledge and skills the members and plan committee require will differ depending on the design of the plan, its features, the demographics and make-up of the participant population, its mission, and its goals. For example, if most of the plan's administration is outsourced, you don't need to know the details related to plan administration in the same level of detail as if you had the work done in-house. However, you would need to be better at vendor management, oversight, reviews and testing.

In the United States, plans almost universally invest in mutual funds or pools of stocks or bonds. Investing in funds, stocks, or

---

lay out exactly what elements of the program are outsourced, which fiduciary functions are delegated to the provider and which are retained by the sponsor, and what other services may be provided."

[202] For the fiduciary to be able to monitor the expert, some performance standards or measures would need to be established.

bonds constitutes one class of knowledge and skills. But think about the change in the level of knowledge and skills that would be required if your plan decided to dramatically shift its investment approach. The knowledge and skill menu would need to change.

Changing Up the Menu

The Ontario Teachers' retirement plan undertook a unique investment approach (from a US perspective), according to a 2012 article in The Economist. The article stated, "the Canadians prefer to run their portfolios internally and invest directly. They put more of their money into buy-outs, infrastructure and property, believing that these produce higher returns than publicly traded stocks and bonds. They are in some ways like depoliticized sovereign-wealth funds... So far the funds' strategy has paid off. Over the past ten years Ontario Teachers' has had the highest total returns of the biggest 330 public and private pension funds in the world."[203]

Training for New Plan Committee Members

Inevitably, new committee members will join and, therefore, you should anticipate the need to train them. Ideally, this will be done proactively, with the plan committee's succession planning having identified the potential new member, and seeing to it that the individual will have had the opportunity to attend and observe meetings, review important documents, read about plan governance (and other self-study areas), and attend other training provided to the committee.

When the new member has not had a lengthy lead-up to becoming a member, the plan committee should make available the following document, training, and meetings to help the new member be effective in their role.

- Meeting with a committee member(s) to provide an introduction to the role and responsibilities

---

[203] "Maple revolutionaries," The Economist (March 3, 2012).

- Plan document and summary plan description
- Investment policy and recent investment reports
- Plan Committee Charter
- Outline of roles and responsibilities of all parties, with emphasis on the roles and responsibilities of the plan committee
- Meeting with counsel on role and risk of serving as a plan fiduciary
- Prior meeting agendas and minutes, including establishment of goals and review of goals
- Goals for the upcoming year
- Introductions and meetings with individuals in HR/Benefits, Payroll, recordkeeper/actuary, and the like who can answer questions or provide updates to current projects, issues, or risks
- Meeting with committee member(s) to identify gaps in knowledge and skills so future training can be tailored
- Other material on retirement plan governance, such as this book

That is a lot of information to cover, and for someone new to the area, it is difficult information to absorb. This is why it is very important that the new member's knowledge and skills be assessed. For any new members, the plan committee needs to ask: Do they understand the role and recognize that they are acting on behalf of the plan participants? Do they understand who is responsible for different areas, and that the committee is responsible for providing oversight? Do they understand the plan document and the investment policy? Finally, do they understand plan governance?

Unfortunately, there will be situations when a new member is not fully engaged, and has not done the requisite homework. The plan committee chair needs to step in and emphasize the importance of the role and the risk that the new member creates for the plan participants, all of the plan committee members, and the company, if the new member is not 100% committed to the role. It is best to remedy any misconceptions about the role quickly, and not have a confused, unknowledgeable, distracted committee member—who is potentially a future damaging witness in a lawsuit.

In most situations, however, the new member will only need support and guidance. The other committee members, and the committee's staff, need to provide the support needed for the new member to gain the knowledge and skills the job demands.

Knowledge and Skills Beyond the Plan Committee

The focus of this chapter has been on building and improving the level of knowledge and skills for the plan committee members. However, as one of the governance principles, the need for knowledge and skills extends to everyone who touches the plan. The plan committee will want to know that the staff and vendors have adequate knowledge to do their jobs, and that there are training programs in place or available to keep everyone current on the plan terms, systems, legal and regulatory environment, risks and controls, and goals and expectations.

Just as the plan committee members should have gaps in their knowledge and skills addressed, others involved with the plan should similarly have any gaps closed. Even in situations where more and more of the services are being outsourced, the plan committee should want to know that the vendor's team involved with the plan is as current and knowledgeable as possible.

Quick Hits

1. Ask committee members to assess their knowledge and skills and have the chair lead a discussion on possible development areas. The list on page 170 may be helpful.

2. Develop a training plan or program for members to address both the committee's gaps and individual members' gaps. The list on pages 172-173 should provide some ideas.

3. In the areas where the committee intends to use experts, it should use a selection process (similar to the one on page 175). Similarly, the committee should have a process for overseeing and monitoring the expert (like the one described on pages 176-178).

4. Finally, the committee should anticipate having to train new committee members, and develop a program that can get these members up to speed as quickly as possible. (See the list of activities and documents at pages 179-180.)

Establish and Monitor Clear Performance Measures

"The price of light is less than the cost of darkness."
Arthur C. Nielsen

"However beautiful the strategy, you should occasionally look at the results."
Sir Winston Churchill

Why Performance Measures Matter

After taking the time to establish a mission and create goals, it is essential to periodically check where you are on the journey to accomplishing your goals. Are you on track? Are you farther away? Perhaps the worst outcome is if you don't know where you are in relation to your goals. This latter situation is what happens when you don't have any performance measures in place or you are not monitoring them.

Robert S. Kaplan, renowned business author and father of the balanced scorecard used for performance measurement, has said, "If you can measure it, you can manage it."[204] It is commonplace to measure important indicators in business, such as profits, productivity, and the cost of materials so they can be managed.

Most businesses wouldn't think of operating without having a business strategy and performance measures to gauge their progress against their strategy. However, the use of performance measures tied to strategy in the retirement plan context is lax.[205]

---

[204] Robert S. Kaplan and David P. Norton, Strategy Maps (Harvard Business School Press 2004) at 6.

[205] I am not suggesting that there aren't performance measures used for retirement plans. Many plans have metrics on the percentage of time the website is up, the length of time before a call to the call center is answered, the

There are a litany of reasons for this: tying retirement plan strategy to performance measures falls outside of the primary responsibilities, experience, and skill set of most of most committee members; it is generally against the interest of third-parties involved in the plan to assist in developing good performance measures (against which they will subsequently be held accountable); and, plan committees often have not developed the objectives and strategies upon which performance measures can be built.

The lack of focus on performance measures is not unique to the retirement plans in the United States. A paper done in the UK reflects that performance measures have not been widely adopted by retirement plans in other countries:

> In the corporate world, it has long been recognized that to get to the top, and to stay at the top, an organisation needs a strong governance framework linked to a co-ordinated system of strategic performance management that together drives toward a common and clearly articulated goal. The thinking has not yet been fully embraced by the pension industry.[206]

The need to establish and monitor performance measures for retirement plan vendors is succinctly explained in a report prepared by the United States Government Accountability Office:

> [t]he hiring of any service provided is itself a fiduciary act, and under ERISA, a sponsor must act prudently when selecting one or multiple service providers and **monitor their performance.** To comply with ERISA, **the plan sponsor must have sufficient information to make informed decisions about the services, costs and**

---

number of dropped calls, etc. These metrics, however, are often not tied to or built from the plan committee's strategy related to the plan. Instead, they are simply metrics that are easy for the third party to measure.

[206] Bernard Marr, Jocelyn Blackwell and Kenneth Donaldson, *Restoring Confidence: Measuring and Managing Performance in Pensions* (December 2006, Cranfield University School of Management) at 4, http://umbraco.ap-institute.com/media/14130/pm_in_the_pensions_industry.pdf.

qualifications of the service providers, and the quality of the services being provided. The sponsor must ensure that expenses paid out of plan assets, including fees paid to service providers, are and continue to be reasonable in light of the level and quality of services provided. The sponsor must also determine whether there are conflicts of interest related to service provider compensation.[207]

How to Establish Good Performance Measures[208]

There is a classic business axiom from the legendary business author, Peter Drucker, "What gets measured gets done. Make sure you are measuring the right things!" Indeed, there is no lack of data or items that can be measured. The key is to identify those items that will tell you if you are meeting your goal: you need to establish *good* performance measures.

In theory, it shouldn't be too difficult to design good performance measures. Businesses commonly use performance measures. They are building systems and accessing data from existing systems to gain intelligence on performance areas that drive their business.

However, for retirement plans, establishing good performance measures (especially outside plan investments) is a new and novel exercise. In addition to being new, there are other hurdles. For example, much of the data exists outside of the business with third-parties and it can be difficult to get the appropriate data or have it properly aggregated with internal data. Even more

---

[207] *Private Pensions – Fulfilling Fiduciary Obligations Can Present Challenges for 401(k) Plan Sponsors supra* at 21. (Emphasis added.) A study in the UK reached a similar conclusion that the plan committee must monitor performance to achieve good governance. "In summary, we strongly believe that the protection of members' benefits ultimately depends on sound governance. This requires trustees to actively identify and manage risks and monitor performance." *Occupational pension scheme governance – A report on the 2007 scheme governance survey supra* at 6.

[208] For simplicity, I use the term "performance measure" throughout this chapter and book. It can, however, generally be thought of as synonymous with the term "key performance indicator." I refrain from using KPI to not confuse plan committee members who are not familiar with the KPI concept.

significantly, many plan committees haven't set goals or don't have a clearly articulated strategy. Good performance measures build directly off of the plan committee's strategy and goals. Thus, for many plan committees, the initial step is not to select performance measures, but rather to develop the strategy and goals upon which the performance measures can be built. Once the strategy and goals are set, it is then possible to incorporate the performance measures into the contracts.

The process for developing *good* performance measures is summarized on the following diagram, which illustrates the establishment of strategic performance measures. At the plan committee level, most performance measures for the plan committee will be strategic, as opposed to operational. However, the plan committee will want to be informed of and oversee operational performance measures, too. (More on this later.) The diagram provides a detailed example of each of the four steps.

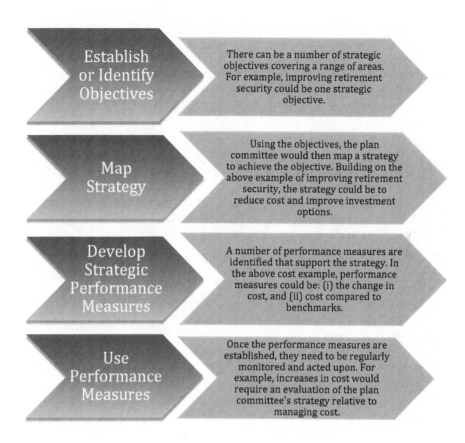

Establish or Identify Objectives — There can be a number of strategic objectives covering a range of areas. For example, improving retirement security could be one strategic objective.

Map Strategy — Using the objectives, the plan committee would then map a strategy to achieve the objective. Building on the above example of improving retirement security, the strategy could be to reduce cost and improve investment options.

Develop Strategic Performance Measures — A number of performance measures are identified that support the strategy. In the above cost example, performance measures could be: (i) the change in cost, and (ii) cost compared to benchmarks.

Use Performance Measures — Once the performance measures are established, they need to be regularly monitored and acted upon. For example, increases in cost would require an evaluation of the plan committee's strategy relative to managing cost.

If this process is applied to a plan's investments,[209] it might proceed along the following path.

---

[209] The process is simplified to illustrate the development and use of performance measures. I direct the reader interested in the development of a more robust investment management process to read <u>Prudent Investment Practices: A Handbook for Investment Fiduciaries</u> by the Fiduciary Studies Foundation, and <u>The New Fiduciary Standard</u> by Tim Hatton. These books lay out a five-step process (and 27 practices): analyze current position, diversify-allocate portfolio, formalize investment policy, implement policy, and finally, monitor and supervise. The 27 practices closely parallel the 12 governance principles detailed in this book (*e.g.*, Practice 1.1: investments are managed in accordance with applicable laws-compliance; Practice 1.2: fiduciaries are aware of their duties and responsibilities-clear roles, responsibilities and accountability; Practice 1.3: fiduciaries and parties in interest are not involved in self-dealing-avoid conflicts of interest).

Committee members who are not investment experts will appreciate these books because they demystify investing and convert it into a process which, if

Identify Objectives

To identify objectives, the plan committee (presumably with the advice and assistance of an investment advisor or consultant) should consider:

- The needs of the workforce/plan participants (age, education level, investment resources, and investment experience)
- The fiduciary duties of the committee (need to diversify, risks associated with the investments, fees and expenses associated with the investments, and liquidity)
- Limitations inherent with the plan (the value of assets available for investment, the internal resources available to oversee and manage the plan investments, and time or personnel constraints of the committee)

Establish Investment Strategy

The plan committee (with the assistance of an investment advisor) will want to incorporate the identified objectives into an investment strategy. This will allow the plan committee to identify assets or asset classes that will meet the identified objectives. For example, if the workforce is young, has little or no financial education or experience, and there are no outside investment resources available, the plan committee may decide that its strategy is to have age-based funds (or life-cycle funds) that essentially require no asset selection or balancing by participants with a limited compliment of low-cost index-based funds.

Set Performance Measures

Once the strategy is set, the plan committee (with the assistance of an investment advisor) will want to set goal and performance measures by asset class or asset category. For example, building on the above example, if the plan committee has decided to use a combination of age-based funds and index funds, representative goals could be:
- to use index funds that track the indices within certain margins,
- to have index and age-based funds that have fee or expense ratios within certain levels,
- the funds and their management teams are established, there are strong controls around both the retention of the assets and the consistency of the investment strategy (*i.e.,* loss of assets and asset strategy drift are managed),
- the fund or funds provide periodic participant communication in an easy to read and understand form, and
- the fund or funds provide periodic reports to the plan committee that address each of the committee's goals.

Monitor and React to Feedback from Performance Measures

The plan committee must periodically monitor[210] the performance measures. If possible, the information will be made available in easier to consume mediums, such as dashboards or scorecards. The committee will also want to have an established reporting frequency for each performance measure. The information on the performance measure should answer key questions for the committee:

- Is the strategy working? Is it achieving the objectives?
- Is there an issue or problem with the execution of the strategy? Does it suggest that a new vendor or system is needed?
- Is there another strategy (or way of executing the strategy) that is working more effectively (*i.e.*, the use of industry benchmarks)?
- Is the plan committee using the right performance measures? Can the performance measure be improved, or are there better data sources that will provide improved performance measures?

Continuing with the above example, the plan committee reports would provide information on:

- how close the index funds track the indices,
- the expense ratios of the index and age-based funds,
- turnover of key staff at the funds,
- level of control testing performed (areas covered, type of testing, effectiveness of the controls),
- how much the assets drifted from the underlying asset strategy (asset strategy drift), and
- participant surveys on improvement in understanding fund communications.

---

[210] This outline necessarily glosses over a number of very difficult tasks involved in actually building a good performance monitoring system: the difficult tasks of identifying *good or the best* data sources to access, aggregating and analyzing the data, and building a reporting mechanism.

Document Strategy and Goals in an Investment Policy Statement

To complete the governance process related to establishing strong performance measures for the plan's investments, it is wise to document the strategy and goals in an investment policy statement (IPS). The Foundation for Fiduciary Studies recommends that an IPS cover the following six elements:[211]

1) Purpose and background
2) Statement of objectives
3) Guidelines and investment policy
   a. Risk tolerance
   b. Time horizon
   c. Chosen asset classes
   d. Expected returns
4) Securities guidelines
5) Selection of money managers
6) Control procedures
   a. Define duties and responsibilities of all parties involved
   b. Define monitoring criteria for selected money managers
   c. Define criteria for performance reporting
   d. Define process for accounting for fees and expenses

A sample IPS for a 401(k) plan can be found in Appendix I of Tim Hatton's book, *The New Fiduciary Standard*.

Debate over IPS Detail

There exists, however, a tension between what is good governance and overall risk management for the sponsor and the fiduciaries. There is a school of thought by some ERISA counsel that the investment policy should be vague, and the plan committee should not detail the investment policy, the investment strategy, the investment selection criteria, and other details.[212] The reason given by counsel is that if the plan

---

[211] The following numbered list is quoted from The New Fiduciary Standard *supra* at 110.

committee doesn't follow the IPS and the funds underperform, the fiduciary will be held liable in a lawsuit against them (and essentially the employer).[213] The argument on the opposite side is, if you don't have any standards (or clear standards), then standards will be applied based on broad-based fiduciary standard using 20-20 hindsight.

The argument against clarity has merit if the committee does not work cohesively as a unit to achieve common goals, and if there is a chance that the members will be distracted by other responsibilities and not follow the IPS. Indeed, one can take the position that having *any* IPS may create some level of risk. This might explain why, according to the GAO Private Pension Report, only 339 of the 440 sponsors (or 77%) had an IPS.[214]

Plans with undeveloped governance may appropriately opt to have a less detailed IPS if that would reduce risk. However, the goal should be to eventually have greater detail to support strong performance measures, transparency, and the plan's strategy.

A common framework for developing performance measures rests on four fundamental components, which together compile the "balanced scorecard."[215] These components are:

---

[212] *Private Pensions – Fulfilling Fiduciary Obligations Can Present Challenges for 401(k) Plan Sponsors supra* at 18, acknowledges that this situation was raised during its survey process. I've generally seen it raised by counsel. This is a good illustration of where counsel for the employer/plan sponsor might not have the same interest as would separate counsel for the plan committee.

[213] The DOL regulations essentially provide that if you have an IPS, it needs to be followed:

> Statements of investment policy issued by a named fiduciary authorized to appoint investment managers would be part of the 'documents and instruments governing the plan' within the meaning of ERISA § 404(a)(1)(D). An investment manager to whom such investment policy applies would be required to comply with such a policy, pursuant to ERISA § 404(a)(1)(D) insofar as the policy directives or guidelines are consistent with titles I and IV of ERISA.

29 C.F.R. § 2509.94-2(2).

[214] *Private Pensions – Fulfilling Fiduciary Obligations Can Present Challenges for 401(k) Plan Sponsors supra* at 18.

[215] Robert S. Kaplan and David P. Norton, *Using the Balanced Scorecard as a Strategic Management System* (Harvard Business Review July-August 2007)

- Financial Perspective
- Customer/Plan Participant Perspective
- Internal Perspective
- Learning and Growth Perspective

Although these components are usually seen applied for businesses, they also provide a solid framework upon which to build retirement plan performance measures. The following is an example of how these four components can transition from the business environment to the retirement plan environment:[216]

- Financial Perspective
  - o Improve cost management
  - o Improve investment performance
  - o Improve plan value, or the quality in relation to cost
- Customer/Plan Participant Perspective[217]
  - o Improve knowledge about the plan benefits and investments
  - o Improve communication with participants
  - o Improve service provided to participants
  - o Improve participant perspective of value provided by plan and value it brings to being an employee
- Internal (or back-office) Perspective
  - o Improve back-office processes related to plan operation (whether they be internal or performed externally by a vendor)
  - o Improve systems to allow better measurement of investments, compliance, vendors, and the like

---

(Republication of article from 1996 HBR).

[216] The following list is illustrative since the actual strategic and operational performance measures will be based on the strategy identified by the plan committee. As Robert Kaplan, one of the creators of the balanced scorecard and KPIs said, "A good balanced scorecard should tell the story of your strategy." Robert S. Kaplan and David P. Norton, *The Balanced Scorecard – Measures that Drive Performance* (Harvard Business Review, January-February 1992).

[217] This includes having a process and a policy for managing participant complaints.

- o Improve plan governance (including overall compliance, vendor oversight, risk management, and related activities)
- Learning and Growth Perspective
    - o Improve plan committee's knowledge in areas where gaps have been identified
    - o Improve participants' awareness of retirement plan, value, investment options, and other factors
    - o Improve internal staff's knowledge in areas where gaps have been identified
    - o Identify areas where the plan's investment advisors, the plan committee, and the staff can grow and improve the benefits the plan delivers to participants

Performance Measures for the Plan Committee

Two distinct dimensions of performance measures are of interest and importance to the plan committee. The first are the performance measures related to the plan's operations and the goals outlined by the plan committee. What should the plan committee know about costs and efficiency, investment performance, vendor performance, risk management, compliance, controls, participant satisfaction, and so on? If the plan committee believes it is important, it is likely that there should be a performance measurement associated with it.

The second are the performance measures that relate to how the plan committee is performing. The plan committee's performance measures should answer questions such as:

- *What are the plan committee's goals?*
- *Is the plan committee progressing toward achieving those goals?*

The importance of the plan committee both having and actively reviewing performance measures can't be overemphasized. Very simply, this is part of the leadership role of the plan committee. If it uses performance measures, it will help drive the culture of everyone working on the plan. Vendors and staff alike will begin to think about what the drivers are for a strategy's success, and begin to *measure and focus on that area.*

Performance Measures for Vendors

Outsourcing does not remove or lessen the need to have performance measures and monitor performance. Plan committees "… should monitor performance standards regardless of whether [plan] administration is conducted in-house or outsourced."[218]

In all likelihood, your vendors will tell you that they already have performance measures in their contracts, or that they test their performance through internal testing or as part of their SSAE 16 process. They will argue that no additional performance measures are needed, or that adding additional performance measures will increase cost or detract from their performance in other areas.

Let me relay a story about a vendor that complained to me very vocally with all these arguments. They produced lists of reports on their systems that they swore should satisfy the plan committee that all cost, compliance, control, and other areas were being well addressed. Based on this information, I had to agree. Their system was well designed, well controlled, and produced stellar reports. However, neither I nor the company knew that the company's plan did not "fit" in that system and that a side system had been built solely to serve this one company. All the testing, controls, reporting, and safeguards that worked in the primary system were absent from this "shadow" system. The errors were costing the company millions of dollars and because of a lack of proper performance measurements, they were unaware of all of these problems.

There are several morals to this story. First, it is your duty to establish the performance measures that you need to test your strategies and measure your progress. This leads to the second

---

[218] *Occupational pension scheme governance – A report on the 2007 scheme governance survey supra* at 39.

moral, which is, if you're going to rely on a third party's performance measure, you should test and verify that it is measuring what you want, how you want, and when you want. Third, assume there is a correlation between how loud the vendor objects and the lack of, or ineffectiveness of, their performance measures.

Although I am advocating a strong dose of skepticism, the plan committee does need to be pragmatic. Most of the vendors have systems that are designed for many plans, and customization can be difficult, costly, and even create the risk that errors or problems will be inserted into the vendor's system. If you're not one of the vendor's largest clients, getting these changes made may take some time. Indeed, they may not make any changes until their contract is up for renewal. At a minimum, begin a dialogue with them, see what they can accomplish in the short-term, and how they might be able to assist you in other ways (such as providing you with the data needed but without the analysis).

Certain vendors also present unique challenges in establishing performance measurements. For example, what are good performance measures for the lawyer representing the plan committee, or the plan's actuary or auditor? All three are professionals who rely on their knowledge and expertise, rather than a system or a standardized process. However, these three vendors have several common responsibilities that do lend themselves to the development of performance measures. These common responsibilities are: they are typically all involved in plan compliance and filings; they have activities with deadlines; surprises from any of them are extremely frustrating; and they periodically will work on plan projects.

Building on these common themes, the performance measures for these vendors can be developed based on the following elements:

- Is the vendor's work progressing on and completed on schedule?
- Does the vendor complete the work within the prescribed budget?

- Do the deliverables meet what was described in the engagement letter, and reflect a professional level of quality?
- Were compliance, cost, risk, or other issues raised timely (shortly after the publication of the compliance requirement, the change in demographics or assumptions that affected cost, or the event that changed the risk profile)?
- Were they proactive in identifying the potential issue and quickly bringing it to the plan committee's attention?
- Did they communicate timely and clearly during the project, with explanations that allowed the committee to make decisions?

Another vendor that presents unique issues in developing performance measures are the vendors responsible for investment performance. The GAO 2008 Private Pensions Report discuss some benchmarks relative to investment performance that, while a little dated, provide good insight into measuring fund investment performance. Specifically, the Report provides that, "... monitoring funds may involve quantitative criteria that include investment returns as compared to benchmarks, risk, and fees, along with qualitative criteria such as the stability of the provider."[219] A GAO survey found that "... 362 of 448 sponsors said they benchmark the investment performance of the 401(k) plan. Of respondents who do benchmarking, 297 said they benchmark each option to the performance of a peer group as one way of monitoring performance."[220] The Report lists a number of activities included in the monitoring of funds such as, "... reviewing reports about the performance of the funds, holding meetings, placing poorly performing funds on a watch list, ultimately removing funds or replacing them with better options, and documenting their decisions."[221]

---

[219] *Private Pensions – Fulfilling Fiduciary Obligations Can Present Challenges for 401(k) Plan Sponsors supra* at 17.
[220] Id. Footnote omitted.
[221] Id.

The GAO Private Pension Report also highlighted an area that I've seen as problematic with many plans. The problem arises when the performance of the funds (or other specific investments) that are held by the plan are monitored by the entity that is sponsoring or selling the fund. Clearly, this creates a situation where there is the potential for a conflict of interest and a lack of objectivity. In my experience, the conflict and lack of objectivity have been borne out. The institution offering a fund rarely suggested that its own fund was underperforming, and rarely suggested that it should be replaced with a fund that is outside the institution's family of funds. The Report suggests that this could exist with 38% of the plans covered by the survey. [222]

Vendor Performance Measures and Contract Guarantees

Some vendors will provide contract guarantees, which essentially provide that if the vendor does not meet a certain standard in the contract, they will forego part of their fee. For example, a contract guarantee might provide: if 95% of calls to the call center aren't answered within one minute over the course of the year, the vendor will forego (or reimburse to the plan) 2%[223] of the plan fees. In theory, the vendor will provide a report to the plan showing what percentage of calls were answered within one minute. (I say, "in theory," because in my experience, after the first year or two of the contract, these reports stop being delivered, so in essence, there is no monitoring of the contract guarantee.)

As you have probably surmised, I am somewhat jaded over the "protection" provided by contract guarantees. Most are based on metrics that the vendor can easily measure and meet, and are rarely aligned with the goals and strategy of the plan committee. Indeed, I've *never* seen a vendor ask the plan committee for its goals and strategies, so it could build contract guarantees that aligned with those goals and strategies.

---

[222] Id.

[223] I've rarely seen the amount "at risk" by the vendor be anything significant that would truly be a deterrent to them.

Accordingly, don't assume that by having contract guarantees you have *good, meaningful, or useful* performance measurements in place for that vendor. Also, if you develop a set of performance measures to oversee the vendor, be sure that someone is monitoring the vendor against the terms of the contract. Even if the contract guarantee is not what the plan committee wants to monitor, it is nevertheless a performance guarantee in the contract and the plan committee (or its delegate) is responsible for overseeing that the contract terms are fulfilled.

Periodically Touching the Market to Update or Validate Performance Measures

Whether you're critically assessing the performance measures you've established for a vendor or the plan's investments, it is a good practice to periodically touch the market to see what other vendors or plans are doing. "Touching the market" might be done through a request for information, a request for proposal, benchmarking, or a commissioned study.

Reaching out and touching the market is a way to test the objective, the strategy, and the performance measurement. There might be different or better objectives, strategies, or measures that should be considered.

How Performance Monitoring Changed Strategy

On the front page of the Wall Street Journal on March 1, 2017, were two seemingly unrelated articles that lend focus to how performance monitoring has changed strategy for two entities. The first article discussed how Harvard University was changing its endowment investing strategy because its return had trailed other Ivy League institutions. [224] It was moving away from "staffers [who] specialize in specific areas, such as real estate or bonds."[225] Instead, it was moving toward "a generalist approach in which staffers look across the entire portfolio to make

---

[224] Juliet Chung and Dawn Lim, *Harvard's Endowment Chief Upends Investing Tradition* (The Wall Street Journal March 1, 2017) at A1.
[225] Id.

investment decisions."[226] About half of the staff were being laid off.

The second article, also on the front page, discussed how Fidelity Investments was looking to cut costs and increase revenue.[227] The world's largest family of mutual funds was seeing record outflows of money from its actively managed funds.[228] Its growing portfolio of index funds, however, "enjoyed a record year for new money."[229] The actively managed funds generate higher fees, but have been under pressure as retirement plans and other investors have become focused on fees. Fidelity was offering early retirement packages to about 3,000 employees.[230]

In both cases, the feedback from the performance was used to modify the strategy, arguable in very dramatic ways. If performance isn't reflecting what one would expect based on the strategy, either the execution or the strategy is flawed. If changing the execution doesn't improve the performance, the problem may be the strategy.

"However beautiful the strategy,
you should occasionally look at the results."
Sir Winston Churchill

Is an IPS Required?

The GAO Report on Private Pensions reflects the fact that not all plans have an IPS. Indeed, the Department of Labor does not require that a plan have an IPS. However, the DOL in its regulations does state, "[t]he maintenance by an employee benefit plan of a statement of investment policy designed to further the purposes of the plan and its funding policy is consistent with the fiduciary obligations set forth in ERISA...."[231] Although an IPS may

---

[226] Id.
[227] *A Painful Shift for Fidelity* (The Wall Street Journal March 1, 2017) at A1.
[228] Id.
[229] Sarah Krouse, *Fidelity Buyouts Target Older Staff* (The Wall Street Journal March 1, 2017) B1.
[230] Id.
[231] 29 C.F.R. § 2509.94-2(2) (2007).

not be *required*, at a minimum, the DOL still requires that the plan fiduciaries have a process or procedures to address the following items:

- Who is "...responsible for plan investments with guidelines or general instructions concerning various types or categories of investment management decisions...."
- Agreement by the investment manager that they accept the investment guidelines
- Policy or guidelines on voting proxies[232]

Performance Anxiety

Once the committee has established performance measures, it needs to have them *monitored*. This may seem obvious, but often the standards are established in the original contract and never visited again. Explanations range from: "the standard was in the contract and we assume they'll abide by the contract," to "we didn't have resources to monitor all the performance measures," to my favorite, "we didn't want to check, because if the standards weren't met, we'd have a ton of remedial work to perform."

It is a complete fallacy to think you have performance measures if they are not being monitored. Granted, the monitoring process can be time consuming, and hopefully the outcome of the monitoring is that there is nothing to report. Because the monitoring itself can be more of an administrative function, it is best if it is delegated, and the reporting is done on a dashboard, a heat map, or an elevator scale where only the important issues are at the top.

By periodically monitoring all of areas reported, you can ensure that they are, indeed, being monitored. By presenting them with a natural hierarchy, the plan committee can focus on the key areas. In the following example of an elevator scale, the plan committee could focus the bulk of its attention to the one area where the performance measure was not being met (the ADP test). Secondarily, it could focus on the next two areas where there is a risk that the performance measure will not be met. Having and

---

[232] Id.

monitoring performance measures gives the plan committee the opportunity to manage and take action in areas that are not performing satisfactorily, and that might jeopardize the attainment of the plan's goals.

Example of Elevator Scale

ADP Test		Failing
Financial Audit		Behind Schedule
Call Center Satisfaction		85% but Declining
Call Center Call Wait Times		Meeting
Compliance Review		On Schedule
Plan Costs		Declining on a Per Participant Basis

Key

Not Meeting PM	
At Risk of Not Meeting PM	
Meeting PM	

Quick Hits

1. Develop performance measures that will help provide insight into the attainment of the plan's and the committee's strategy and goals.
   a. Consider performance measures for the plan committee, the vendors, and staff that address the four components on pages 192-194.
   b. Schedule time to have the performance measures tested against the market (or benchmarked). Are some performance measures missing? Are the ones being used too lax or too strong?

2. Require that reports on the performance measures be delivered to the plan committee in advance of the committee meetings, and during the meetings focus only on the outliers and issues.

Compliance

"[T]his pension field is an esoteric and abstruse one, bordering on the mysterious or the occult .... And it is also truly an eye-glazing subject."
Senator John Chafee[233]

Introduction

Compliance for retirement plans is multidimensional. There are rules that relate mainly to operations, but there are also fiduciary rules that generally relate to *behavior*. The plan committee needs to address both the operational and fiduciary *behavioral* rules. However, it will need to manage them in different ways.

The operational compliance rules are complex and voluminous. They cover almost every facet of retirement plan operations, addressing areas such as participant eligibility, participation, discrimination, contributions, distributions, participant disclosure, and governmental reporting. In most respects, these rules are fairly rigid and because they are prescribed in minute detail, it is fairly easy to develop policies, procedures, and most importantly, automated systems that address these rules in a near-mechanical way.[234]

---

[233] Senate Special Committee on Aging, *A Report of Conference Proceedings, 10th Anniversary of the Employee Retirement Income Security Act of 1974*, 98th Cong., 2d Sess., 1985, p. 54 (statement of Senator John H. Chafee), cited from Karen Ferguson and Kate Blackwell, Pensions in Crisis (Arcade Publishing, 1995) at 11.

[234] The plan committee members can familiarize themselves with the operational compliance requirements for their plan by reviewing the plan document. These requirements are detailed in the plan document because IRS requires that most of these requirements be spelled-out in the document. A training session on the plan document by legal counsel (and whoever else might have been involved in its preparation), is quick way for the committee to become familiar with the operational rules for its plan.

The fiduciary behavioral compliance rules are also complex, but contrary to the operational rules, it is difficult in most cases to build the behavioral rules into automated systems. For example, these rules require that the plan committee and fiduciaries **act** in the best interest of the plan participants, or discharge their duties "with the care, skill, prudence, and diligence ... that a prudent man **acting** in a like capacity and **familiar** with such matters would use...." Although these rules generally can't be automated, it is, however, possible to have policies and procedures that assist the plan committee and other fiduciaries in staying within the behavioral bounds required by the law.

As previously noted, the goal of this book is not to provide a compliance guide for retirement plans. Rather, the goal of this chapter is to provide a strategic framework for the plan committee to oversee and achieve both operational and behavioral compliance.

The Compliance Opportunity

Compliance is always with us in the endeavors we pursue. I have often been fascinated by how some organizations struggle with compliance, and others see it as a competitive differentiator. In the forward to the book, *Essentials of Enterprise Compliance*, Mike McDuffie (VP, Public Sector at Microsoft), captured my fascination well:

"Although some organizations see compliance as a burden, others see it as an opportunity. Forward-thinking chief financial officers (CFOs) are structuring their governance policies, processes, and controls to enhance and reinforce long-term compliance. They plan not only to meet today's compliance needs but to go beyond them, and in doing so they create genuine competitive advantages for their organizations."[235]

---

[235] Susan D. Conway and Mara E. Conway, <u>Essentials of Enterprise Compliance</u> (John Wiley & Sons, Inc. 2008) at ix. (Footnote omitted.)

Operational Compliance Requirements

What are the operational compliance requirements? Simply stated, they are the rules that dictate the operation of the plan and that *can be systematized,* or built into a process. Most of the IRS rules are what one would consider operational compliance requirements because they deal with the plan's operation and the rules can be designed into a system and potentially automated.

> ### *An Example of Operational Compliance Rules*
>
> The IRS and the Department of Labor have detailed rules related to the service that must be counted for an employee to become a participant, and when an employee must be credited service for vesting. In the vast majority of cases, the definition of the service that must be counted can be extracted or tracked in the employer's HRIS or payroll system. Thus, the plan committee does not need to check how service is credited on an individual basis. Rather, it can have the programming tested to determine that it is capturing the correct service, and it can also have controls in the system to validate the service that is being captured.[236]

Having rules that can be built into a system or a process, or that can be automated (possibly through a third party's system), changes the dynamic of how the plan committee must manage operational compliance.[237] It is no longer as important for the plan committee to have the expertise related to the rules. Rather, it is more important for the plan committee to have expertise in

---

[236] Earlier, in the chapter on Risk, we discussed the idea that the plan committee can avoid risk by simplifying the plan. In this example, one can see that a single definition of service for all employees would make the programming and the testing much easier than if different groups of employees had different definitions of service that needed to be tracked and monitored. This is not to say that in some cases, such differences might not be warranted. It is, however, important to recognize that there is a cost associated with the added complexity.

[237] For a discussion on "... the role that technology should play in managing compliance..." *see* Essentials of Enterprise Compliance *supra* at 49, 51-135. Although the discussion is not specific to retirement plans, the reader will be able to extract numerous adaptable insights.

overseeing plan systems, controls, processes and testing. I would argue that most executives serving on a plan committee already have these skills and can translate them from their "regular" job to their role as a plan committee member.

Using this approach, even a novice plan committee member can open the plan document or summary plan description, identify an operational compliance area, and ask:

- Is there a process to ensure the operational compliance of an area?
- How is the process controlled?
- Have the controls been tested (and how recently)?
- Are the controls working effectively?
- Have we seen any issues or problems that would suggest that the process or the control isn't working properly?
- Are the process, the control, and the testing of the control documented?

Another advantage of this approach is that, because it focuses on the oversight of systems, processes and controls, the plan committee can leverage the systems, controls, validations, testing, and experts used by the employer. For example, determining whether employees can enter the plan or participants can earn vesting is probably tracked and calculated in the employer's HRIS or payroll system. For many employers, these systems already have processes and controls built into them that the plan committee can use, or leverage, to ensure the plan's compliance.

When the Employer's Systems, Processes, and Controls are Weak or Lacking

The operation of the plan is often tied to many of the employer's systems, processes, and controls. For example, the plan will rely on the employer for pay, employment service, breaks in service, leaves, and demographic data. If the employer's systems, processes and controls are weak or lacking, then the data being used by the plan can be inaccurate. This could result in employees being wrongly denied participation in the plan, incorrect payments being made, compliance deficiencies, and fiduciary breaches.

The plan committee needs to understand if the employer's systems, processes, and controls are strong or weak. If they are determined to be lacking (and the employer will not improve its systems, processes, or controls), the plan committee needs to evaluate possible corrective approaches and take remedial actions. This might include the addition of controls, supplementing the data, or other actions.

Fiduciary Behavioral Compliance Requirements

The fiduciary compliance requirements are, perhaps, the most difficult of all the compliance requirements to understand. They are not easily navigated or mastered, and they can't be systematized, automated, or managed by adding a control. They depend on the behavior of the plan committee or the fiduciary.

How can these rules be so difficult to understand when the Department of Labor has so succinctly defined them? The DOL has described these rules as follows:

> The primary responsibility of fiduciaries is to run the plan solely in the interest of participants and beneficiaries and for the exclusive purpose of providing benefits and paying plan expenses. Fiduciaries must act prudently and must diversify the plan's investments in order to minimize the risk of large losses. In addition, they must follow the terms of plan documents to the extent that the plan terms are consistent with ERISA. They also must avoid conflicts of interest. In other words, they may not engage in transactions on behalf of the plan that benefit parties related to the plan, such as other fiduciaries, services providers or the plan sponsor.[238]

---

[238] Department of Labor website on Fiduciary Responsibility, https://www.dol.gov/general/topic/retirement/fiduciaryresp

But what does this mean? When selecting a vendor, for example, what does the plan committee need to do to meet the requirement that it is running the plan solely in the interest of the participants or for the exclusive purpose of providing benefits?

I've seen and heard numerous presentations by consultants and attorneys describing the "exclusive benefit rule" and "prudence expert rule," but they never explained how to apply these rules to real situations. Granted, they would often say the plan committee needs to evaluate all the facts and circumstances, but generally without much more guidance. The plan committee and the fiduciaries are often left with abstractions and ambiguity.

Struggling with Abstractions and Ambiguity

What do the exclusive benefit and prudent expert rules *mean?* For example, when picking a vendor to perform the daily recordkeeping for the plan, what should the plan committee do and consider in order to act "solely in the interest of the plan participants?" What does the committee need to do to be sure that the exclusive purpose is the providing of benefits and paying expenses? Does that inherently mean paying benefits accurately? Does it imply that expenses will be managed and paid only when appropriate? And what does it mean when one overlays the concept of acting prudently on these activities?

Unfortunately, there isn't a simple answer, but these questions are explored in this chapter and the chapter on fiduciary duty.

It is for these reasons that the fiduciary behavioral compliance requirements are more difficult for plan committee members and fiduciaries to master. Unlike the operational compliance requirements, they cannot easily be built into a system or automated. Also, since the rules can't be systematized or automated, the plan committee members and fiduciaries can't rely on areas where they already have expertise, such as overseeing and testing controls, processes, systems, and outsourced vendors. The following are, however, several approaches and tools that will help the plan committee and the plan fiduciaries navigate through these dangerous waters.

Study and Receive Training on Fiduciary Duty

Fiduciary behavioral compliance is a complex area and clearly outside the experience and expertise of most plan committee members. The first step is to recognize this and then have the individual committee members and the plan committee collectively get training and become more knowledgeable about fiduciary principles and practices.

Assessing the Knowledge and Skills Gap

If the plan committee has been working through the 12 principles detailed in this book, it will have assessed the members' *knowledge and skills*, including the committee members' knowledge and skills related to compliance. A program of training and the use of experts would then be applied to address the committee's knowledge and skill gaps in this area.

The challenge is to structure and deliver training that goes beyond simply repeating the fiduciary principles and discussing abstractions. The fiduciary principles should provide a basis for the training. However, the abstract fiduciary concepts, which are difficult to understand for most committee members who are not steeped in trust law, need to be translated into practical concepts that can be applied in practice.

As a starting point, less experienced plan committee members should review the following Department of Labor, Employee Benefits Security Administration (EBSA) publications:[239]

- Meeting Your Fiduciary Responsibilities
- Understanding Retirement Plan Fees And Expenses
- Selecting An Auditor for Your Employee Benefit Plan
- Selecting And Monitoring Pension Consultants – Tips for Plan Fiduciaries

---

[239] EBSA publications can be found at
https://www.dol.gov/agencies/ebsa/employers-and-advisers/plan-administration-and-compliance/retirement

- Tips for Selecting And Monitoring Service Providers For Your Employee Benefit Plan

More experienced and ambitious committee members and plan fiduciaries can tap into a number of books on compliance that are available on ERISA.[240] Most vendors, particularly ERISA counsel, provide training on fiduciary duty upon request, usually for a fee. The training ranges from covering the basics (or an introduction to fiduciary duty) to updates on recent cases and developments, to more consultative discussions that are focused on the plan committee's performance.

A number of companies provide external training, and the number is growing. A good starting point for external training, however, is to go to the source: The Department of Labor, Employee Benefit Security Administration (EBSA). The EBSA sponsors seminars to help plan sponsors and fiduciaries, and the sessions are held in a variety of cities free of charge.[241] A good source for video training is the Plan Sponsor Council of America.

The key is to know that there is always more to know, and build learning about fiduciary compliance into the plan committee's schedule. There are a multitude of ways to get this information, and many are free or low-cost.

Build Fiduciary Behavioral Requirements into the Decision-Making Process

Although one cannot automate the fiduciary behavioral requirements, it is possible to follow a process that helps meet these requirements. By following a process, it is possible to take fiduciary behavioral requirements from an abstraction to something practical. It is, in general, simply a matter of converting the governance principles into a process. The more robust the process, and the more they reflect and incorporate the

---

[240] *See e.g.,* Marcia S. Wagner, Stephen J. Migausky, and Daniel L. Blynn, The ERISA Fiduciary Compliance Guide (The National Underwriter Company 2012), and Tess J. Ferrara, ERISA Fiduciary Answer Book (7th ed. 2015).
[241] Seminars and webcasts can be found at the EBSA's website: https://www.dol.gov/agencies/ebsa

governance principles, the more they will help the plan committee meet its fiduciary behavioral requirements.

In its most abbreviated form, the process is based on the following activities:

1. *Identify the goal for the activity* – What is it that the plan committee wants to accomplish? It could be reviewing or replacing a vendor, or having the plan's controls tested.

2. *Identify the decision-making criteria, or the standard that will be applied* – What will drive the committee's decision from one option to another? What are the most important factors to consider in making the decision? If the plan committee is looking to review or replace a vendor, it should identify the criteria that it will use in making its decision. For example, how important is price, the range of functions in the systems, the availability of live support, the availability of on-site advisors, built-in controls, reporting features, and the like? If the plan committee is testing the plan's controls, what standard should be used? Is evaluating the description of the controls adequate, or does the committee expect that the controls will be tested? Is it important to test all the controls, or just certain key controls that have a more profound impact?

Using Agreed-Upon Criteria to Get the Committee on the Same Page

Another benefit of establishing criteria for the plan committee to use in the decision-making process is that it aligns all the members of the plan committee with the same set of criteria. If, for example, the plan committee is later sued for the decision it made, having the committee members able to look at the clearly identified criteria to explain their decision is very important. Imagine if there were no criteria, and each committee member felt that different criteria were the most important. This lack of harmony could make the plaintiff's case for them.

3. *Obtain the Necessary, Objective (Expert) Support* – Determine if the plan committee lacks the expertise or knowledge in the area, and supplement the committee's expertise or knowledge. For example, if the committee is having difficulty in determining the key criteria to use to select a vendor, then its expertise and knowledge could be supplemented by studies, benchmarks, or the use of experts. However, even when relying on supplemental information or experts, the plan committee should still approach the information critically. The goal here isn't only to get support, but that the support should be *objective.* If relying on an expert to help with the selection of a vendor, the committee should question whether the expert receives any benefit, financial or otherwise, if they are selected. Similarly, the committee should see if the expert has any bias or preferences: do they always select the same vendor or the same type of vendor? Finally, it is important to get feedback from their prior clients about their process and whether they incorporated the specific needs and goals of the client's plan into the selection process.

4. *Strive to have, and work from, quality data and information* – Compliance decisions will often turn on data or information. One of the most frustrating positions for a plan committee is to be asked to make a decision, but not be provided with complete, accurate, or relevant data and information. "[D]ata quality ... [is] at the core of any reliable compliance program...."[242]

5. *Establish Performance Criteria* – When the plan committee makes a decision, whether it is the selection of a vendor or to achieve some other goal, at the time of making the decision it should establish the performance measurement or criteria. How will the new vendor be measured? What are the key elements that the plan committee will want to be apprised of periodically? For example, if price was a key component of the decision, the plan committee may want to know if the fees for the vendor deviate in any material way from what the vendor proposed.

---

[242] Essentials of Enterprise Compliance *supra* at 3.

6. *Verify There are No Conflicts of Interest* – The plan committee should be able to look at the decision and feel comfortable that it was made in the best interest of the plan participants. The committee should be able to see that conflicts didn't exist for any committee members, staff, or vendors. The steps related to establishing objectives, selection criteria, and performance criteria will help to make decisions and show that those decisions were objective and not influenced by self-interest.

Seek the Counsel of Experts

On numerous occasions in this book, it has been suggested that the plan committee rely on experts where it lacks the knowledge, experience, or expertise in an area. In this situation, however, the reliance is broader. In this context, the plan committee should consider using the expertise of someone who can help it make a *fiduciary* decision.

Typically, whether or not an activity is meeting the fiduciary standards under ERISA is a legal determination. Accordingly, the plan committee should consider using an attorney with experience in *fiduciary* decision-making.

The plan committee needs to be cautious that it isn't getting its fiduciary advice from an individual who has a legal background but who is not acting as an attorney. Numerous attorneys are working as consultants but not as attorneys. Giving fiduciary advice would be outside the area that they could advise on. Indeed, many of the consultants who have a legal background will have a disclaimer in their engagement letter or deliverables stating that any legal advice should either be ignored or given to another attorney for their legal opinion. In other words, they may give legal advice, but they will deny that they could serve in such an expert capacity—leaving the plan committee completely exposed.

The second area of caution for the plan committee is in the selection of an attorney. The committee will clearly want an attorney who has expertise relative to fiduciary decision-making.

There are, however, many ERISA counsel who are experts on the IRS rules but not on the fiduciary rules. The goal is to engage an attorney with experience working with plan committees making fiduciary decisions.

Understanding Historical Trends and Staying Abreast of Current Retirement Plan Developments

The decisions that the plan committee and fiduciaries make exist within the environment of the time when they are made. They have as a backdrop the history of the plan, the law, and the industry. Therefore, the plan committee and the fiduciaries should understand and look to the history of the plan, the law, and the industry for guidance on current decisions. In addition, having an appreciation for trends and developments will help the committee in making a decision.

Example of History and Trends

During the 1980s and into the 1990s, there were not many class action lawsuits against 401(k) plans. Starting in the 1990s, the number of class action lawsuits began to grow. Initially, most of the lawsuits involved cases where the plan committee selected more expensive "retail" funds when identical and cheaper "institutional" funds were available. At that time, this was a trend, but now it is part of the history. The plan committee members began to look with skepticism at which funds were being used and their pricing.

More recently, however, a trend in class action lawsuits has involved situations where the plan committee has not negotiated to have revenue-sharing dollars reduced, and therefore, the investment cost to the plan and its participants reduced.

In both situations, the class actions have involved fiduciaries' decisions about the cost the plan is paying for a service or a fund. Plan committee members should not only take into account the past results of class actions, but also the broader trend that focuses on the plan cost for funds and services.

The three best approaches for staying abreast of historical trends and current developments are:

- Provide training to the committee members.
- Use experts who provide both historical context (*e.g.,* lessons learned from history) and who can provide updates on current trends.
- Provide tools to the plan committee members where they can keep current on developments.

To develop effective training, it helps to understand what the plan committee members know and where there are gaps in their knowledge. To assess the members' knowledge and understand the gaps, one could ask if the plan committee members know:

- The basis for historical or recent class-action lawsuits
- The current enforcement efforts of the Department of Labor
- Actions that trigger DOL investigations or inquiries
- Actions that have caused fiduciaries to be removed by the DOL or imprisoned
- Actions that have caused prohibited transactions

From there, well-tailored training can close any knowledge gaps that are identified.

Using experts can be a way to both accelerate the training and improve the knowledge of the plan committee members, and also provide insight from individuals with deep knowledge and broad experience in specific areas. A good expert will not only instruct the plan committee on the historical trends and current developments, but they will also make both the trends and developments relevant to the plan's specific situation. Their discussion will answer the inherent question of why the trend or development matters to *your* plan.

When seeking out the advice and counsel of experts, the plan committee should view "experts" broadly. Experts are not limited to attorneys who are experts in fiduciary law. Rather, it also includes experts who have knowledge, experience, and perspective in other areas, such as investing, administration, vendor management, and the like. While plan committee attorneys may be expert in ERISA and fiduciary law, they may not know the nuances or best practices in the practical areas where fiduciary decision-making is often embedded.

Using Experts: An Example

What must be done to prudently select a vendor? In practice, this means going beyond the obvious superficial criteria of looking at price, quality, and experience. While these are valid measures, this approach ignores the practical steps of identifying the universe of potentially qualified candidates, then applying a process of narrowing the population of potential candidates to a reasonable pool of possible options. Legal counsel may not know the universe of candidates, or tools and processes that can be used to reduce the selection pool using reasoned selection criteria. This is where experts who have experience in vendor searches are immensely helpful.

Shift Fiduciary Responsibility Where "Prudent"

In the chapter on managing risk, we discussed the advantages of using vendors or outsourcing providers, and how the committee can shift some of the risk to them. Shifting risk might seem somewhat absurd, however, when discussing compliance. After all, legal counsel will not typically take ownership of decisions made based on legal advice (they'll just own the responsibility for the accuracy of the legal advice). But what if the plan committee could shift the decision to a third party? What if it was the third party's responsibility to get the appropriate legal advice upon which to make the decision?

Let's take the example of a plan committee that makes the final selection (or approval) of the funds held in the plan. They develop a process to review funds and managers. They have ERISA counsel review the process. The plan committee then develops an investment policy statement, oversight structure, and a regimen for overseeing the managers. Again, they have ERISA legal counsel draft or review the documents. Even though ERISA counsel is drafting, reviewing, or advising on each facet of the investment selections, the *decision* is owned by the plan committee. ERISA counsel has merely provided the legal context.

The plan committee can shift the compliance burden away from itself if it shifts the underlying responsibility for making the investment decisions (and the associated fiduciary duty) to a third party. Although there is a trend toward third-parties being willing to accept more of the fiduciary duty, this is an area where the plan committee should proceed with caution. Some third-parties that say they are accepting the fiduciary responsibility are actually only accepting some responsibility or they are otherwise limiting their liability. Any carve-outs that are not accepted by the third party will undoubtedly fall back on the plan committee.

Insuring Against Fiduciary Breaches Where Possible

Unfortunately, even well-run plans and well-governed plan committees can make mistakes. This is why it is important to acquire fiduciary insurance to help protect the plan and the committee when mistakes do happen. The protection provided by fiduciary insurance isn't absolute, but it is clearly better than nothing. For a more detailed discussion on the topic, please refer to the text at and following footnote 136.

Periodically Have the Plan Committee's Structure and Operations Critically Reviewed

It is possible that the plan committee structure or the member composition of the plan committee may hinder compliance. Stated another way, it is possible that fiduciary compliance might be improved by structural, composition, or operational changes. Does the committee have the right structure to facilitate fiduciary compliance? The right people? Does the committee's approach or operation hinder the committee in meeting its fiduciary responsibilities?

Answering these questions may be difficult for the plan committee. This is why it is sometimes helpful to get outside assistance to see if fiduciary compliance can be improved by structural, personnel, or operational changes.

Here are examples where the committee's structure hindered compliance:

- The plan had two committees: one for investments and one for administration. There were no overlapping members, and the two committees didn't meet together. Because their activities weren't coordinated, compliance activities that weren't clearly the responsibility of either committee were overlooked.
- The retirement plan and the health plan committees were the same. When the committee met, almost all the time was spent discussing medical claims and appeals. Very little attention was spent on retirement plan matters.

Looking at the committee's operation from the outside, it was clear to see how the committee's operation could be improved. However, because the members were not familiar with any other structure, they were oblivious to any improvement opportunities.

Rely on and Apply the Governance Principles

It may seem self-serving in a book on governance to suggest that the plan committee should rely on and apply the governance principles outlined here. There is, however, a shift in focus from compliance to governance that recognizes that compliance doesn't exist alone, and needs to be addressed with risk management, establishing controls, clear definition of roles and responsibility, effective oversight and accountability, the avoidance of conflicts, and so on.

An article published by the International Organization of Pension Supervisors (IOPS) reflects this trend. It states that the IOPS "recognizes that financial services supervision has been moving rapidly from a world where the supervisor was a compliance officer to becoming a 'governance supervisor,' i.e. a supervisor who ensures, in forward looking manner, that sound governance practices are applied in supervised entities."[243]

---

[243] John Ashcroft, Nina Paklina and Fiona Steward, *Governance and Performance Measurement of Pension Supervisory Authorities* (International

This trend is also happening in corporate America, where companies are changing the role of the chief compliance officer to one that is more broadly focused on governance and overall risk. Indeed, even the stalwart of compliance, the IRS, has begun to shift its focus from strictly compliance to one incorporating risk management and governance. The movement to governance is not, however, abandoning the importance of compliance. Compliance is a part of governance, and remains important. By embracing governance, however, each of the governance elements are also given import within a structure that can be consistently applied.

Organization of Pension Supervisors, Working Paper No. 10, Nov. 2009) at 5.

Quick Hits

1. Verify that the parties who are responsible for the various components of compliance are identified. Who is responsible for identifying new developments, and to whom is this information communicated? Who is responsible for day-to-day operational compliance? Who is responsible for fiduciary or behavioral compliance of the committee? (In this latter area, if it is the committee, training may be required to assist the committee with this compliance responsibility, or they may need to access experts/legal counsel.)

2. Operational Compliance
   a. Have the operational compliance requirements tested to ascertain:
      i. If they are built into the processes and systems that administer the plan
      ii. If the controls associated with the processes and systems are sound
      iii. If the controls are working effectively
      Require that a plan be developed to address any gaps in any of these areas. Also, confirm that areas that are processed (in whole or in part) manually or have weaker controls are identified and monitored and tested more frequently.
   b. Confirm that compliance failures or issues are escalated, and that there is a mechanism for tracking the frequency and type of problems, so the proper corrections can be implemented.
   c. Confirm that there is communication and coordination between Legal and others with responsibility related to compliance (*e.g.,* the recordkeeper or actuary), concerning new compliance requirements so changes can be made to existing processes, controls, and systems.

3. Fiduciary/Behavioral Compliance Requirements
   a. Assess the knowledge and skills of the plan committee members and other fiduciaries regarding the fiduciary/behavioral compliance requirements.
      i. Provide training to address any gaps (such as those described on pages 211-212).
   b. Develop processes for good fiduciary decision making:
      i. Using the 12 governance principles
      ii. Building decisions from established goals
      iii. Using agreed-upon standards and criteria for making decisions
      iv. Soliciting and using objective and expert-based information
      v. Requiring that performance criteria be included as part of the monitoring and accountability for all decisions

Ethics: Conflicts of Interest and Code of Conduct[244]

"Relativity applies to physics, not ethics."
Albert Einstein

"Ethics is knowing the difference between what you have a right to do and what is right to do."
Supreme Court Associate Justice Potter Steward

"There no such thing as business ethics – there's only ethics."
John C. Maxwell[245]

Introduction

In any governance scenario, there are certain minimum ethical requirements that would be expected of the overseeing body. For example, the overseeing body of a for-profit business or a not-for-profit enterprise is expected to avoid conflicts of interest. Most plan committee members approach their role on the committee with the same general ethical framework applicable to for-profits and not-for-profits. The ethics standards for retirement plans that is imposed by ERISA, however, raises the ethical standards for plan committee members and other fiduciaries above what would be expected in a typical governance situation.

Because ERISA has an elevated and different standard for fiduciaries in a number of areas, ethical concepts span across two of the governance principles and two chapters. This first chapter

---

[244] Ethics involves more than just conflicts of interest and codes of conduct, but those are the two areas of focus for this chapter. To avoid repetition, other areas of ethics such as ERISA's duty of loyalty, duty of prudence, and exclusive purpose duty, are discussed in the chapter on Fiduciary Responsibilities at page 254.

[245] There's No Such Things as "Business Ethics", *supra* at xi. This book was later published under the title, Ethics 101 – What Every Leader Needs to Know.

deals primarily with conflicts of interest. As will be seen, the duty to avoid conflicts extends far beyond the plan committee to include most individuals and entities that deal with or work on the plan.

The second (and next) chapter deals primarily with fiduciary responsibilities that apply *exclusively* to the plan committee and other plan fiduciaries. These rules are specific to individuals who are fiduciaries and involve unique duties. They do not apply to most vendors and individuals working on or for the plan who are not fiduciaries.

Ethics and Integrity

Integrity is sometimes used in this book and by others (*e.g.*, the OECD), to describe ethics. Integrity has been defined as "the quality or state of being of sound moral principle; uprightness, honesty, and sincerity."[246] In *Integrity Works*, integrity was described as having 10 characteristics:

"1. You Know That Little Things Count
2. You Find the White When Others See Gray
3. You Mess Up, You Fess Up
4. You Create a Culture of Trust
5. You Keep Your Word
6. You Care about the Greater Good
7. You're Honest But Modest
8. You Act Like You're Being Watched
9. You Hire Integrity
10. You Stay the Course"[247]

Because it may be impossible to memorize all the fiduciary and ethical rules that spring out of ERISA, it may be easier to approach your plan committee and fiduciary rules with *integrity*. You may find the moral standard an easier one to navigate (and a higher standard) than the legislated and litigated standard applied under ERISA.[248]

---

[246] <u>Webster's New World Dictionary</u> (The World Publishing Co. 1968).
[247] Dana Telfor, <u>Integrity Works</u> (Gibbs Smith 2005) at 15.

The Cost of Conflicts to the Plan

The existence of conflicts of interest create ethical dilemmas and the risk of inappropriate behavior; it "can inhibit open discussions or result in decisions, actions or inactions that are not in the best interests of beneficiaries[;]"[249] it diminishes the trust that plan participants have for the plan, and potentially reduces the rate of return for the plan. It is for these reasons that the *duty* to avoid conflicts is imbedded in ERISA and the law of trusts that underpins it. Thus, to meet the legal requirements of ERISA, one must avoid certain activities that are deemed to create conflicts.

The very real negative impact that conflicts can have on the performance of plan investments has been investigated. A study done by the U.S. Government Accountability Office "revealed a statistical association between inadequate disclosure [of conflicts of interest] and lower investment returns for ongoing plans, suggesting the possible adverse financial effect of undisclosed conflicts."[250] The GAO study was extensive, looking at 1,111 plans with total assets of $183.5 billion.[251]

---

[248] Dana Telford, the author of Integrity Works, said, "In today's world, few things seem to shock people anymore – except integrity." When serving as a plan fiduciary and a plan committee member, every decision, every day needs to be approached with the utmost integrity. Integrity Works at page 34.

[249] The Pensions Regulator, *Conflicts of Interest Consultation Document* (February 2008) at 3. Footnote omitted.

The document has a nice definition of what constitutes a conflict of interest:

> A conflict of interest may arise when a fiduciary is required to take a decision where (1) the fiduciary is obliged to act in the best interests of his beneficiary or principal and (2) at the same time he has or may have either (a) a separate personal interest or (b) another fiduciary duty owed to a different beneficiary or principal in relation to that decision, so that there is a conflict with his first fiduciary duty.

Id.

[250] U.S. Gov't Accountability Office, GAO-09-503T) at 5. Testimony Before the Subcommittee on Health, Employment, Labor and Pensions, Education and Labor Committee, House of Representatives, Statement of Charles A. Jeszeck, Acting Director, Education, Workforce, and Income Security. (March 24, 2009). *Private Pensions: Conflicts of Interest Can Affect Defined Benefit and Defined Contribution Plans.*

[251] *Id.* at 5-6.

How much of an impact did the study find? The difference in the rate of return was "a statistically significant 1.2 to 1.3 percentage points...."[252] A loss of 1.2% on $183.5 billion represents a *$2.2 billion loss* experienced by the participants in these plans—or an average of nearly *$2 million per plan.*

Are conflicts with fiduciaries for retirement plans really that prevalent? Although there isn't a comprehensive study of the area, one study done by the SEC found that, out of 24 registered investment advisors reviewed, **over 50% had significant ongoing conflicts of interest.**[253] Of the 13 investment advisors that had conflicts, nine of them were among the top 25 (ranked by assets managed) in the country.[254] If you're a plan committee member for a larger retirement plan, the chances are good that you use one of these investment advisors.

The underlying point is that the existence of conflicts is probably greater than you think. Simply asking about conflicts during meetings in a general, non-specific way, will probably not uncover the conflicts. The plan committee needs to collect the appropriate data and conduct ongoing rigorous due diligence into all relationships with the plan.

Have You Established 100% Trust with Your Participants?

As you being to think about ethics, conflicts, and having a code of conduct, step back and put yourself into the participants' shoes. In many cases, they are handing over all the investment assets they have (other than their home). If you were in their shoes, *what would you require before handing over all of your assets?*

---

[252] *Id.* at 5.

[253] *See* U.S. Securities and Exchange Commission, Office of Compliance Inspections and Examinations, *Staff Report Concerning Examination of Select Pension Consultants* (Washington, D.C.: May 16, 2005.) Thirteen of 24 consultants had significant unreported conflicts. See http://www.sec.gov/news/speech/spch120505lr.htm.

[254] *Private Pensions: Conflicts of Interest Can Affect Defined Benefit and Defined Contribution Plans supra* at page 5.

Bob Bingham, CEO of The Little Gym (a company that "offers curriculum-based, physical skill-building programs for children"), summed this up in an analogous situation: "When you drop off your child with someone, you can't *almost* trust them, you have to have 100 percent trust in them."[255]

How do you establish 100 percent trust when taking almost all of a person's liquid assets? Perhaps you can establish 100 percent trust by showing the participant that you will avoid conflicts, that you have embraced ethics, that you train to promote ethics, and that you have a strong code of conduct.

The ERISA Framework for Conflicts (Prohibited Transactions)

Because ERISA is built upon trust law, it incorporates rules that prohibit certain transactions that inherently have conflicts. These activities are called "prohibited transactions" under ERISA (both the IRS and DOL provisions). ERISA considers the enumerated activities as so bad that they are simply prohibited (with several exceptions that will be discussed shortly). Engaging in a prohibited transaction can result in an excise tax by the IRS, a penalty the DOL, or a civil suit by the DOL to remove the party that engaged in the transaction. In cases where the activity is severe or egregious, the DOL has brought criminal charges and put the party in jail.

To have a prohibited transaction under ERISA, a fiduciary must cause the plan to engage in certain prohibited activities with a party, called a "party in interest."[256] Thus, to have a prohibited transaction, you must have (i) a party in interest, (ii) who has

---

[255] John Marchia, The Accountable Organization: Reclaiming Integrity, Restoring Trust (Davies-Black Pub. 2004) at 7.

[256] "Party in interest" is the term used by the Department of Labor. ERISA § 3(14), 29 U.S.C. § 1002(14). The IRS uses the term "disqualified person." IRC § 4975(e)(2). The parties or persons covered by these terms are essentially identical. For simplicity, "party in interest" is used throughout this book. Labor and the IRS can impose separate and different sanctions for prohibited transactions.

engaged in a prohibited transaction with the plan, and (iii) a fiduciary who caused the plan to engage in the transaction.

Parties in interest "include the employer, the union, plan fiduciaries, service providers, and statutorily defined owners, officers, and relatives of parties in interest."[257] In practice, this definition encompasses almost everyone dealing with the plan: the plan committee and other fiduciaries, the recordkeeper, the actuary, the auditor, and individuals acting on behalf of the employer. For good measure, the definition reaches out even further and covers family members and related companies.

Absent a statutory or DOL granted exemption,[258] the following activities between the plan and a party in interest are **prohibited** under ERISA:[259]

- A direct or indirect sale, exchange, or lease
- Direct or indirect lending of money or other extension of credit

---

[257] U.S. Dep't of Labor, Employee Benefits Security Administration, *Meeting Your Fiduciary Responsibilities*, (February 2012) at 7.

[258] DOL Class Exemptions can be found at https://www.dol.gov/agencies/ebsa/employers-and-advisers/guidance/exemptions/class#2002-13.

[259] Morton (Mort) Klevan, one of my professors at Georgetown, authored an excellent article on the development of the prohibited transaction rules from common law. As someone who was involved in both the drafting of ERISA and the regulations, Professor Klevan's article provides unparalleled insight into the law. In a key passage, he states:

> ... the drafter of ERISA consciously intended section 406 to prohibit 'structural conflicts' that were not always addressed by the common law. Structural conflicts occur if a fiduciary acts on behalf of a plan in a situation in which the fiduciary ... may benefit from the transaction to the potential detriment of the plan. The conflict may be characterized as structural because the law is more concerned with the structure or form of fiduciary behavior than with the substantive result. The theory behind the prohibition is that it is easier to simply prohibit a fiduciary from acting in any situation in which it has an interest that may adversely affect its ability to exercise disinterested judgment on behalf of the plan than it is to determine whether a result adverse to the plan actually occurred....

Morton Klevan, *The Fiduciary's Duty of Loyalty Under ERISA Section 406(b)(1)*, 23 Probate and Trust Journal 561, 561-2 (Winter 1988).

- Direct or indirect furnishing of goods, services, or facilities[260]

Once again, the scope of the definition of prohibited transaction is so broad that it covers almost every activity in which the plan might engage. Activities that are swept up in its scope include purchases of stocks, bonds, or mutual funds, and purchasing goods or services from vendors. In other words, most (indeed, almost all) of the plan's activities are potentially prohibited transactions. The sole remaining question is whether any exemption applies.

There are a number of statutory exemptions (and one can apply to DOL to have a transaction exempted), but the primary ones[261] that cover most of the situations that arise are for:

- Service providers where the service is necessary to operate the plan, and the compensation paid and the contract are reasonable[262]
- Loans to participants that are secured and charge a reasonable rate of interest
- Buying or selling employer securities from the employer, an employee, or another party in interest if the price is the security's fair market value and no commission is charged

Don't Let the Employer Make These PT Mistakes

- Buy stock for the plan outside of an established exchange (such as from an officer)
- Borrow money from the plan, even if the loan is secured and the interest rate is better than what the plan would otherwise earn
- Loan money to the plan, even if the interest rate is lower than

---

[260] ERISA § 406(b), 29 U.S.C. § 1106(b).
[261] ERISA § 408(b), 29 U.S.C. § 1108(b). ERISA section 408(b) lists 20 statutory exemptions. Only the most common three are mentioned above. The Department of Labor also has the authority to grant an exemption in certain circumstances if certain conditions are met. ERISA § 408(a), 29 U.S.C. § 1108(a).
[262] The reasonableness of the contract is discussed in further detail at footnote 268.

> market and it results in the plan earning a large profit
> - Fail to deposit employee 401(k) deferrals (elective deferrals) timely;[263] this is considered a loan between the plan and the employer and is a prohibited transaction
> - Use plan assets for business purposes, including using money from the plan, or not deposited into the plan, to pay business expenses
>   - Have the plan invest in business assets (*e.g.*, real estate, inventory, equipment)
> - Buy artwork with plan assets, and use the artwork to decorate the company offices
>   - Make in-kind (non-cash) contributions to satisfy a required contribution[264]
>   - Transferring real or personal property to the plan by a party in interest if the property has a mortgage or similar lien that the plan assumes[265]
>   - Contribute a promissory note to cover a contribution to the plan

Managing Vendor Conflicts and Prohibited Transactions

The challenge for the plan committee is how to manage conflicts and prohibited transactions if almost everyone dealing with the plan is a party in interest, and almost all transactions are prohibited (unless there is an exemption). This challenge is exacerbated because the plan committee has two roles. First, it needs to ensure that the committee members and the employer have no conflicts and don't engage in any prohibited transactions.

---

[263] The rule for timely depositing employee elective deferrals is often misstated as the 15th day of the month following the deferral. 29 C.F.R. § 2510.3-102(b). Except for plans with less than 100 participants, that is the *latest* day on which the deposit can be made. The rule actually requires that the deposit be made "as soon as administratively feasible." In most cases, this will correspond with how quickly the employer makes payroll tax deposits (usually 1-3 days after payroll is run). If you're not making your deposits as quickly as you make your payroll tax deposits, you may have a prohibited transaction. Late contributions are required to be disclosed on Form 5500, and reporting late contributions can trigger an IRS or DOL audit.

[264] DOL Interpretive Bulletin 94-3.

[265] ERISA § 406(c), 29 U.S.C. § 1106(c).

Second, it needs to ensure that its vendors, service providers, and agents[266] have no conflicts.

To understand the complexities involved with managing conflicts for vendors, service providers, and agents, it helps to consider the challenges. Typically, the first step in trying to manage conflicts and prohibited transactions is to identify the parties in interest. Although the earlier description of parties in interest[267] is relatively simple, it becomes quite complex when trying to apply the definition in practice to an array of service providers, vendors, and others on an ongoing basis.

Plan Service Provider's Extended Party in Interest Family

To illustrate the complexity of identifying the parties in interest for a service provider, one must look at *every* service provider and identify the following additional individuals and entities because they are *also parties in interest:*

- Relatives of the service provider,
- Employees, officers, directors and 10% or more shareholders of the service provider,
- 10% or more partners or joint ventures in the service provider,
- 50% or more owned subsidiaries (either corporations, partnerships, trusts or estates),
- Employees, officers, directors and 10% or more shareholders of a 50% or more owned subsidiary, and
- 10% or more partnership or joint venture interest in the 50% or more owned subsidiary.

This is obviously a daunting challenge for the plan since it lacks most of the necessary data. This is one of the primary reasons why it is suggested that this burden be shifted to the service provider.

---

[266] This would include employees of the company that are acting at the direction of the plan committee or on behalf of the plan.
[267] *See* description at footnote 257.

As the plan changes its vendors and service providers, and as the vendors and service providers undergo organizational changes (*e.g*, mergers), it can be difficult to keep up with even their most basic data. Furthermore, keeping that data regularly updated often becomes overwhelming. Because of these struggles, I've often seen plans begin the process of identifying their parties in interest, only to become bogged down and never complete it. When this first step is incomplete, the committee ends up with no processes through which to identify parties in interest or to identify and avoid conflicts.

There is an alternate approach that is simple and builds on the governance framework (leveraging the fact that the plan committee is, of course, an oversight body). Under this approach, the plan committee *directs* its service providers, vendors, and agents to establish policies and procedures (and controls) that will identify and prevent the occurrence of potential conflicts.

This direction is built into the roles and responsibilities of the service providers, vendors, and agents. It requires them to have a process for identifying their parties in interest and potential prohibited transactions, updating this information regularly, and reviewing it for completeness and accuracy. It also means that they understand and acknowledge that any activity that would constitute a prohibited transaction and that doesn't fall within an exception is avoided. Finally, the service providers, vendors, and agents need to be accountable to the plan committee for accomplishing these processes, and report on them as the plan committee deems appropriate.

Their Facts, Their Exemption, Their Responsibility

One of the primary reasons for shifting the responsibility for identifying and managing potential prohibited transactions to the service provider or vendor is that they know their industry, their facts, and presumably the exemptions under which they can operate. For example, there are numerous prohibited transaction class exemptions dealing with banks, brokerage firms, and insurance companies. The exemptions involve complex transactions that are familiar to that industry. The party that should be best positioned to analyze the facts and the class exemption will be the service provider or vendor in that industry.

Unfortunately, the service providers and vendors typically do not want to take responsibility for their actions and may attempt to limit their liability for prohibited transactions they cause. This is an area where the plan committee will want to consider having additional terms negotiated into the contract or shift to another vendor that would be more amenable.

Examples of some of the requirements that the plan committee may want its service providers and vendors to accept are:

- Acknowledge that the plan is an ERISA plan and that different conflict standards apply, that they are aware of the standards and have processes and control in place that will ensure that they will avoid violations of the prohibited transaction rules. Unfortunately, many advisors apply the conflict standard that applies to their industry, rather than the higher standard that ERISA demands.
- Recognize the areas where it may be acting as a fiduciary and agree to apply the appropriate fiduciary standard of care in those areas. Again, it should acknowledge that if it is acting as a fiduciary, it has processes and control in place to avoid violations of the prohibited transaction rules or the fiduciary responsibilities discussed in the next chapter. (It may state that it is not serving in a fiduciary capacity, which is why the following requirement is important.)
- Realize that if it exercises discretion, the exercise of such discretion can cause it to be a fiduciary in such area, and that it will apply the appropriate fiduciary standard of care in those areas and have processes and controls in place.
- Agree that it is a party in interest based on its role, and that it cannot engage in certain transactions without qualifying for an exemption. It should have in place a process and controls whereby the applicable exemptions that allow it to take such actions (which could constitute a prohibited transactions) are identified and documented.

- Understand that its status as a party in interest will cause certain relatives of employees and related businesses also to be a party in interest, and that the plan committee (or the sponsoring employer of the plan) cannot know the identity of these individuals or entities. Accordingly, it needs to accept the responsibility of either tracking the activities of these individuals and entities to prevent prohibited transactions, or informing the plan committee of these individuals and entities so it can track activities of the plan with them.
- Appreciate that it has an ongoing duty to disclose all of its fees or compensation paid for providing services to the plan, including fees or compensation paid indirectly (by soft-dollars or through third parties). It would be nice if they would also agree to represent that the fees are reasonable (which would help exempt the activity), but it is probably unlikely they would make such a representation.
- Realize that if they engage in a prohibited transaction as a party in interest, or if they are serving as a fiduciary and breach their duty, then they are responsible for the error and will take such action as is necessary to keep the plan and the participants whole.

The statutory exemption that allows vendors to provide services to the plan also has a number of conditions. The primary condition is that the contract be reasonable.[268] There are also a number of provisions that the service provider must disclose (either in the contract or another document), and that the plan committee should require that its staff verify:

- The contract allows for termination without penalty[269]
- The service provider will provide (either through the contract or another document) a description of any direct or indirect compensation that they reasonably expect to receive,[270] including shared compensation based on soft-

---

[268] ERISA § 408(b), 29 U.S.C. § 1108(b).
[269] 29 C.F.R. § 2550.408b-2(c)(3).
[270] 29 C.F.R. § 2550.408b-2(c)(1)(iv)(C)(1)-(2).

dollars, commissions, or "...similar incentive compensation based on business placed or retained...[,]" or charged against the plan's investments[271]

- The services to be provided[272]
- If any services will be provided by the vendor as a fiduciary[273]

Although not directly required by ERISA or the regulations, the plan committee, under the rubric of good governance, should also ask that its staff seek to include in the contract the following:[274]

- That all individuals serving the plan are licensed or have the proper designations, and have cleared background checks to ensure that the plan's assets and information are secure. In addition, that all individuals or entities are not prohibited from serving as an ERISA service provider.
- There are performance measures and guarantees that indicate the level of performance expected (regarding items such as quality and accuracy, timeliness, risk management, and the like).
- The vendor will provide reports to the plan committee or the committee's staff that the committee expects.
- The vendor agrees to monitor for prohibited transactions and fiduciary breaches, and to report the same promptly upon discovery to the plan committee.
- The vendor accepts liability for engaging in prohibited transaction or any fiduciary breach.

Managing Plan Committee and Employer Conflicts and Prohibited Transactions

If the plan committee is successful in shifting the conflict management for vendors and service providers to those groups, the plan committee is left to manage its own conflicts and those of

---

[271] 29 C.F.R. § 2550.408b-2(c)(1)(iv)(C)(3).

[272] 29 C.F.R. § 2550.408b-2(c)(1)(iv)(A).

[273] 29 C.F.R. § 2550.408b-2(c)(1)(iv)(B).

[274] Some of these provisions might be reasonably required by a prudent fiduciary depending on the facts and circumstances.

the employer. Avoiding these conflicts consists of more than plan committee members simply declaring they will avoid conflicts or having good intentions. To truly avoid conflicts, the committee needs to implement a two-part process:

- Developing a process to *identify* potential conflicts
- *Monitoring and managing* potential conflicts

Identifying Potential Conflicts

Identifying potential conflicts requires that one know *who* can have a conflict and *what* activities can potentially trigger conflicts. Identifying "who" may have a conflict is not as pedestrian an exercise as one may think. Each one of the groups that can qualify as a party in interest has its own complexities. Because identifying the "who" is neither clear-cut nor easy, many plans don't put forth the effort to identify all the parties that are parties in interest. Omitting this vital step means they can't, and don't, catch potential conflicts of interest.

The first step in identifying who can have a conflict is to inventory your parties in interest. Parties in interest are:

- The **employer**[275] (and members of its controlled group),[276] whose employees are covered by the plan
- The **union** whose members are covered by the plan[277]
- Plan **fiduciaries**[278] (discussed in more detail shortly)
- **Service providers**[279]
- Statutorily defined **owners,**[280] **officers, directors,**[281] **and relatives of parties in interest**[282]

---

[275] ERISA § 3(14)(C), 29 U.S.C. § 1002(14)(C).
[276] ERISA 3(14)(G), 29 U.S.C. § 1002(14)(G). The controlled group rules extend the definition of party in interest to parents and subsidiaries with 50% or more interest. The ownership can be in a corporation, partnership, trust, or estate.
[277] ERISA § 3(14)(D), 29 U.S.C. § 1002(14)(D).
[278] ERISA § 3(14)(A), 29 U.S.C. § 1002(14)(A).
[279] ERISA § 3(14)(B), 29 U.S.C. § 1002(14)(B).
[280] ERISA § 3(14)(E), 29 U.S.C. § 1002(14)(E).
[281] ERISA § 3(14)(H), 29 U.S.C. § 1002(14)(H).
[282] ERISA § 3(14)(F), 29 U.S.C. § 1002(14)(F). Relative "means a spouse,

When trying to identify the parties in interest, the inclusion of relatives and various owners and subsidiaries greatly complicates the analysis. The complex and lengthy rules associated with these areas create conceptual speed bumps that often slow down or stop the identification process of the parties in interest.[283]

The table below[284] simplifies this complex analysis, but even the simplified version is complex. The first step is to identify the "primary" party in interest, which are individuals and entities in the left hand column. The top row lists the "secondary" parties in interest, who attain their party in interest status from the primary party in interest. For example, an employer or service provider can trigger all four types of secondary parties in interest. A plan fiduciary or plan counsel can only trigger two types of secondary parties in interest. It is a rigorous exercise.

	Relatives	10% Shareholders	10% partner, joint ventures, and employees, officers and directors	50% or more owned subsidiaries, and 10% shareholders, 10% JV's, and employees, officers and directors
Employers	√	√	√	√
50% Owners of the Employer	√	√	√	√
Service Providers	√	√	√	√
Fiduciaries (including trustees/custodian and named plan administrators)	√			√
Plan Counsel	√			√
Plan Employees	√			√
Unions	√		√	√

ancestor, lineal descendant, or spouse of a lineal descendant." ERISA § 3(15), 29 U.S.C. § 1002(15). It does not include siblings.

[283] ERISA counsel can be helpful with both the technical analysis, and also keeping the identification process moving forward.

[284] The table is built off the rules in ERISA § 3(14), 29 U.S.C. § 1002(14). The IRS rules differ slightly.

Even the "simple" task of identifying the "primary" party in interest can be deceptively difficult. For example, if we examine who are the plan fiduciaries for a plan, the process appears to be easy. After all, it is often the company's board or executives that name or create the fiduciaries. Accordingly, identifying who the fiduciaries are seems like it should be a simple process. Yet, as we look at who is defined as a fiduciary, we see that it isn't all that simple.

ERISA states, as a given, that the following individuals or parties are fiduciaries:

- *Named fiduciaries*[285] – ERISA requires that every plan have a "named fiduciary."[286] These individuals are identified in the plan document (or elsewhere) as the "named fiduciaries" and are, by definition, plan fiduciaries. To determine who the named fiduciaries are, check the plan document and summary plan descriptions, which routinely have a definition of "named fiduciaries." Once you've identified the named fiduciaries, be sure they are aware they are fiduciaries and are willing to serve as a fiduciary. If it is not intended for the individual or entity identified as the "named fiduciary" to be a fiduciary, or they are unwilling to serve, that will need to be changed. For example, it is common for the plan document or the summary plan description (SPD) to name the company, the employer, or the board as the "named fiduciary." This can shift fiduciary duties to an unaware board.
- *Trustees* – A plan trustee typically holds the assets of the plan and exercises some discretionary control over the assets (such as directing investments). Because the nature of a trustee involves holding the plan assets and exercising discretion, the Department of Labor views trustees as being fiduciaries.[287] Custodians, who also hold the plan

---

[285] The Department of Labor regulations state that certain titles, by their very nature, carry fiduciary status. The titles that carry such fiduciary status are named fiduciary, trustee, and plan administrator. 29 C.F.R. § 2509.75-8, FR-3.
[286] ERISA 402, 29 U.S.C. 1102.
[287] *See* footnote 285.

assets but typically do not exercise discretionary authority over the assets, are usually not fiduciaries. (Directed trustees are more complex, and whether they are a plan fiduciary should be discussed with legal counsel.) To identify the trustee (if the plan has one), look at the plan document or a separate trust document covering the plan.

- *Person or Entity with Control Over Plan Assets* – Similar to the trustee, individuals who exercise control over plan assets are fiduciaries.

- *Plan Administrator* – Because the Department of Labor views the plan administrator as having discretionary authority related to the plan, they are by definition a fiduciary. There is, however, a lot of confusion in the use of the term "plan administrator." For most plans, an external company (such as Fidelity, Aon-Hewitt, or Prudential) administers the plans. Because these external companies do not want to potentially be liable as a fiduciary, the contracts for these external companies almost universally state that they are *not* serving as the plan administer as that term is used by ERISA, and they are not serving as a fiduciary. What does this mean? The bottom line is that the company sponsoring the plan or some group within the company is acting as the plan administrator (knowingly or not). If no one is named in the plan document, it is the plan sponsor (or employer).[288] If the company, employer, or plan sponsor is not named as the plan administrator, the retirement plan committee is often named as the plan administrator. This would make the plan committee a fiduciary.

- *Any Person or Entity Rendering Investment Advice for a Fee.[289]*

- *Investment Managers that Acknowledge that they are a Fiduciary* – and are typically registered by the State or under the Investment Advisers Act.[290]

- *Any Person or Entity with Discretionary Authority* – Identifying any person or entity with discretionary authority or control over the management of the plan, the

---

[288] ERISA § 3(16)(A), 29 U.S.C. § 1002(16)(A).
[289] ERISA § 3(21)(A), 29 U.S.C. § 1002(21)(A).
[290] ERISA § 3(38), 29 U.S.C. § 1002(38).

administration of the plan, or disposition of plan assets[291] is a facts and circumstances test. Because of the need to apply the facts and circumstances to a complex legal standard, this is an area where the plan's ERISA counsel should be deployed. In general, however, individuals performing ministerial tasks or following the direction of a fiduciary do not have discretionary authority and, therefore, are not a fiduciary.[292] Functions that are typically considered ministerial include:

- Applying eligibility rules
- Calculating service or compensation
- Preparing communication material
- Maintaining plan records
- Preparing reports required by the government
- Calculating benefits
- Conducting new participant orientations
- Processing claims
- Making recommendations upon which others will make a decision[293]

The committee needs to have these areas analyzed critically, however, because an individual or entity that is supposed to be performing ministerial functions and is not supposed to have any discretion can, without the knowledge of the committee, be exercising discretion.[294] Indeed, often times the individual or entity is not aware that they have encroached on the fiduciaries' domain and become a fiduciary. I call these "poltergeist" fiduciaries because they are often invisible and cause havoc behind the scenes. For example, in an effort to save the plan committee time and trouble, the company's retirement plan manager may routinely make decisions related to the plan (interpreting the plan language, resolving ambiguous questions related to eligibility to participate, creating new

---

[291] ERISA § 3(21)(A), 29 U.S.C. § 1002(21)(A).
[292] 29 C.F.R. § 2509.75-8, D-2.
[293] *Id.*
[294] Yeseta v. Baima, 837 F.2d 380 (9th Cir. 1989).

rules on calculating benefits, or other areas). While these well-intended activities may save the committee time, they are usurping the discretionary fiduciary function of the plan committee and creating a fiduciary that is not known, and may unwittingly have conflicts that cause prohibited transactions.

Activities that often involve discretionary authority and trigger fiduciary status include:

- Appointing or removing plan fiduciaries
- Interpreting plan provisions
- Approving or denying claims for benefits
- Establishing criteria for the selection, monitoring, management, or removal of vendors[295]

There are, however, a number of areas where the company or its management can exercise discretion without becoming a fiduciary. These include adopting the plan, modifying the plan, or terminating the plan.[296]

As one can see from this summary definition of who is a fiduciary, it can be a challenging endeavor to identify even the simplest groups that are parties in interest.

You May Rely on Experts, But You May Still Be the Fiduciary for the Decisions They Recommend

Typically, the following individuals are not fiduciaries unless they have either accepted fiduciary responsibility in their contract or are acting with discretion:

---

[295] "Note that ... [ERISA] imposes fiduciary duties only if one exercises *discretionary* authority or control over plan *management,* but imposes those duties *whenever* one deals with plan *assets.* This distinction is not accidental--it reflects the high standard of care trust law imposes upon those who handle money or other assets on behalf of another." (Emphasis in original.) FirsTier Bank, N.A. v. Zeller, 16 F.3d 907, 911 (8th Cir.), *cert. denied sub nom.* Vercoe v. Firstier Bank, N.A., 513 U.S. 871 (1994).

[296] *See* Lockheed Corp. v. Spink, 517 U.S. 882, 889-891 (1996). See the text around footnote 102 for a discussion of settlor functions.

- Accountants/Auditor
- Actuaries
- Attorneys
- Consultants
- Recordkeepers
- Third-party administrators

Relying on the advice of these groups or individuals does not shift fiduciary responsibility to them (unless they accept it in their contract or are exercising discretion). This is why it is so important to provide these individuals or groups with the criteria they should be using to structure their advice and to understand how they should operate.

Although these parties are typically not fiduciaries, they are service providers and therefore they are parties in interest and must avoid prohibited transactions.

Identifying *what* activities can create a potential conflict is the second step in the identification process. As noted previously, the following activities between the plan and a party in interest are **prohibited** under ERISA:

- A direct or indirect sale, exchange, or lease of property
- Direct or indirect lending of money or other extension of credit
- Direct or indirect furnishing of goods, services, or facilities[297]

Since most activities of the plan constitute a prohibited transaction, it is paramount to have the vendor, service provider, or agent identify and track the exemptions that apply to their activities. (See prior discussion at pages 231-236.)

---

[297] ERISA § 406(b), 29 U.S.C. § 1106(b).

Monitoring and Managing Potential Conflicts

For many plan committees, if a member doesn't self-identify and raise a potential conflict, then the potential conflict is essentially ignored. If there isn't a process in place to identify potential conflicts, it will probably be rare for the committee to pauses its deliberations to discuss and explore the potential for conflicts.[298]

Let me present a different perspective. If every sale, exchange, lease, loan, and contract with a service or goods provider is potentially a prohibited transaction, then practically *every transaction entered into by the plan is a potential prohibited transaction.* There needs to be a process adhered to by the committee whereby potential conflicts are sought out.

Clearly, if the plan committee had to get involved in reviewing every potential transaction or stock trade, the operation of the plan would come to a grinding halt. Instead, the plan committee needs to have a process for monitoring and managing conflicts. Once facet of the process, as discuss earlier, is to shift the burden to the vendors and service providers to identify potential prohibited transactions and structure the transaction or stock trade so that it meets an exemption.

Although the plan committee can shift much of the work on avoiding prohibited transactions to its vendors and service providers, it can't shift the identifying, monitoring, and managing of prohibited transactions from the plan committee and its members. The committee needs to take the time to identify where potential conflicts might exist.

As in the evaluation of any other action or decision, having quality information and data is essential. One approach to help the committee have access to quality information and data is to annually solicit and collect information from the plan committee

---

[298] In the GAO Report on Fulfilling Fiduciary Obligations, 60% of the respondents monitor investment decisions for potential conflicts of interest. 38% have committees monitor for conflicts, and 22% have external advisors monitor for conflicts. *Private Pensions – Fulfilling Fiduciary Obligations Can Present Challenges for 401(k) Plan Sponsors supra* at 19.

members on potential points of conflict. Depending on the plan type and design, the information and data gathered might include items such as:

- Employment relationships of family members
- Investments held by the committee members and family members
- Board memberships or ownership interests in businesses
- Sources of gifts, awards, trips, seminars, or other items of value

Although these four items can make the process seem relatively simple, in practice it can be complicated and require detailed investigation. For example, when identifying the employment relationships of family members, committee members will probably be able to easily identify the company for which their spouses work. But what if that company is a subsidiary of a larger organization? And what if that company also owns other companies or has large ownership interests in other companies? Identifying these parent and subsidiary relationships (sometimes called the controlled group) and other interests *may* be important to avoiding potential conflicts, but they can also be time-consuming.

One solution is to have the plan committee members identify the specific relationships of which they are aware, and have a staff person research and identify other companies that are in the entity's controlled group. The mirror image of this process would take place when evaluating vendors for conflicts. A staff person will research the vendor and identify other companies that are in the vendor's controlled group.

Conflicts from Non-Ownership Interests

Ownership, or being part of the same controlled group, is not the only potential source of conflicts. It is possible that a potential conflict can exist in other situations. For example, a board member's spouse worked for Company X, and Company X's largest customer was Company Y. There was no ownership interest between the two, but Company X received a significant portion of its revenue from Company Y. Indeed, Company Y's interests could sway decisions at Company X.

In this situation, the plan committee decided that the member with a spouse at Company X also had a potential conflict at Company Y.

A difficult area for identifying conflicts relates to gifts, trips, seminars, and awards. Vendors often send calendars, books, and guides to committee members and these have value. There are also the occasional lunches or dinners, or free training sessions. In some situations, members might be offered free trips to attend conferences or seminars. Does accepting them create a conflict?

Most businesses have rules for addressing these types of potential conflicts. If they are fairly rigorous, I've found that applying the same or similar rules can be a good approach (following a review by ERISA counsel). This way, the members of the management team who serve on the plan committee don't need to learn a second set of conflict rules.

It is worth exercising some "prudence" and caution. The conflict rules established by the business are for business ethics. The conflict rules that the plan committee members need to apply are derived from the fiduciary standards, which may very well be a higher standard than that which is used for mere business ethics.

Conflicts Rules Related to Gifts and Entertainment

The Form 5500, Schedule C requires that gifts and entertainment be reported unless they are of "insubstantial value." Determining if the aggregate of gifts received from a vendor is insubstantial is, of course, a complex endeavor.

In general, gifts from a single source that are valued at less than $10 can be ignored.[299] (A single source would be considered

---

[299] Promotional items such as coffee mugs with the company logo are generally deemed by the Department of Labor as having a value of less than $10. U.S. Dep't of Labor, *Supplemental Frequently Asked Questions about the 2009 Schedule C,* (Updated October 2010) Question 2, available at

multiple gifts from different individuals at the same vendor.) Also, gifts between $10 and $50 don't have to be reported if the aggregate of such gifts from a single source don't exceeds $100. Thus, gifts over $100 will always have to be reported, and gifts over $10 will have to be reported if the aggregate value of all gifts from a single source reaches $100.

But be warned. The above reporting requirements for the Form 5500, Schedule C are not a safe-harbor for whether one has a conflict. The Schedule goes on to say, "*[t]hese thresholds are for purposes of Schedule C reporting only. Filers are strongly cautioned that gifts and gratuities of any amount paid to or received by plan fiduciaries may violate ERISA and give rise to civil liabilities and criminal penalties.*"[300]

After identifying the potential conflict, the next step is to monitor and manage the potential or actual conflict. The approach will likely vary depending on whether the conflict is an actual conflict or a potential conflict. In the case of an actual conflict, plan members or fiduciaries may need to remove themselves from the matter (by resigning or recusing themselves from the decision-making process).

In the case of potential conflict, there are additional, less dramatic ways to manage the potential conflict. These can include:

- Engaging an independent plan committee member or fiduciary that is devoid of any potential conflicts
- Having the plan committee member or fiduciary withdraw from both the decision and the deliberations related to the matter
- Securing legal advice from the plan's counsel on the existence of the conflict, appropriate action for the committee member to take to manage the conflict, and potentially to assist in the decision-making process related

---

www.dol.gov/sites/default/files/ebsa/about-ebsa/our-activities/resource-center/faqs/faq-sch-C-supplement.pdf.
[300] 2016 Instructions for Schedule C (Form 5500), *Service Provider Information*, at 25. (Emphasis in original.)

to the matter to which the conflict related
- Establish "an executive subcommittee"[301] that can take responsibility for the decision or action
- Having the plan committee member resign where the conflicts are "acute or pervasive"[302]

Prohibited transactions will occur on occasion. In such cases, they need to be reported to the government; they will typically require that a penalty be paid; and they will need to be corrected or undone. In addition, however, the process that allowed the prohibited transaction to occur needs to be reviewed and modified to prevent the occurrence of the prohibited transaction in the future. Were controls missing? Was there manual intervention that created the issue? Was the process incomplete or not followed (*e.g.*, parties in interest not identified)? Did system changes create a flaw? Is there a need for increased training?

Potential Conflicts of Executives Serving on the Committee

The plan committee has one set of objectives and is accountable to the plan participants and beneficiaries. The company's executives will have a different set of objectives and are accountable to the owners or shareholders. For most companies, there will be individuals who are in both roles: a plan committee member and an executive with the sponsoring company. Because the same person can be wearing "two hats," it is likely that at some point, these individuals will have conflicts between their role as a company executive and their role on the plan committee or as a plan fiduciary. [303]

---

[301] *Conflicts of Interest Consultation Document supra* at 3.
[302] Id.
[303] For any executive, plan committee member, or fiduciary that doubts this probability, let me direct you to the book, *Retirement Heist,* by Ellen Schultz, a well-known Wall Street Journal reporter. It is the equivalent of a Stephen King novel set in the retirement world, with the difference being that it's nonfiction. The transactions described in *Retirement Heist* highlight the inherent conflicts that often exist between the company's goals and those of a plan fiduciary.

Companies have tremendous discretion when managing *certain* aspects of their pension plan, unrestrained by any of the fiduciary constraints. These are the previously discussed "settlor functions," [304] which are areas that are owned by the employer or company, and are not governed by ERISA and its fiduciary standards. The list of such areas includes:

- Designing, creating, or establishing the plan
- Designing activities in advance of the adoption of a plan amendment, such as plan design studies or cost projections. (Studies and design activity could be for early retirement windows, participant loan programs, or plan spin-offs.)
- Making the decision to terminate the plan (but "...activities undertaken to implement the plan termination decision are generally fiduciary in nature...."[305])
- Making the decision to merge the plan
- Increasing or decreasing future benefits under the plan
- Increasing employer contributions under the plan
- Changing eligibility criteria for participation in the plan

The importance of avoiding conflicts that might arise because of confusion about one's role is discussed in detail in the chapter on roles, responsibility, and accountability. To recap, a few of the suggestions are:

- Keep fiduciary and settlor decisions separate.
- Have settlor decisions made outside of plan committee meetings. This way, it is clear that they are not made by a plan fiduciary or part of the committee's deliberation process.
- Manage conflicts for committee members by removing the source of potential conflicts, such as decisions related to benefit levels, plan design, and the like. Keep these decisions with management, which doesn't have a duty to

---

[304] *See* footnote 102 and surrounding discussion.
[305] Department of Labor Advisory Opinion 97-03A at 3.

act in the best interest of the plan participants or avoid conflicts.

There will still be situations where conflicts will arise, such as when selecting a vendor. For example, some vendors will charge less in direct fees, but will have greater charges against investments. If the company pays the direct fees but the plan participants bear charges against their investments, the plan committee may be tempted to select the vendor that will cost the employer less, especially if higher profits by the employer could result in incentives for members of the plan committee who are on the management team.

This dilemma is not unique to the United States. In the UK, the Pension Regulator, in its consultation document on conflicts, noted the inherent nature of conflicts between members of management and the plan:

> The regulator recognises that in certain circumstances, there may be some benefits from appointing senior members of staff of the employer as trustees or to the trustee board.[306] However, *if representatives of an employer are trustees of a scheme (or directors of a trustee) conflicts are inherently likely to arise.* It is therefore vital that those conflicts are appropriately identified, monitored and managed, if they cannot be avoided completely.[307]

Despite the dire warning that conflicts are "inherently likely" to occur when "senior members of staff of the employer" are on the plan committee, the Pension Regulator also notes that there are advantages to having such senior members involved. "Having senior staff of the employer on the trustee board may also bring some benefit to the effectiveness of the trustee board, particularly in terms of their knowledge and expertise."[308]

---

[306] The trustee board would be comparable to the plan committee in the U.S.
[307] *Conflicts of Interest Consultation Document supra* at 3. Footnote and emphasis added.
[308] Id. at 6.

The Ethical Path Forward

As an executive in your company who is serving on the plan committee, you probably believe that you behave ethically. Indeed, in your role as a plan committee member, you likely see yourself as bending over backward to act in the most ethical manner possible. That, however, is *your perspective of your behavior.* What do your plan participants believe? What is their perspective? How might their view color their opinion of decisions made by you and the rest of the plan committee? How might their view impact their decisions, such as whether to contribution to the plan or how to invest?

Consider for a moment that the level of trust given to executives by their employees is at an all-time historic low.[309] The financial crisis that started in 2007, and the movements it spawned, such as Occupy Wall Street, reflect some of the concern and distrust held by employees. The question is, as a plan fiduciary, what can you do to avoid conflicts, act ethically, and improve the trust of the participants?

The plan committee can begin on the path to building the trust of participants by:

- Making the right decision, not the easy one.
- Not placing business goals ahead of plan goals when acting as a plan fiduciary.
- Being clear and open with participants. Transparency helps to promote and drive ethics.
- Setting an example and provide an ethical "compass"[310] that will help guide everyone working on the plan.

Ethics involves treating everyone fairly. The plan committee should ensure that the participant with the smallest plan benefit is treated no differently than participants with large benefits;

---

[309] 2017 Edelman Trust Barometer, available at http://www.edelman.com/news/2017-edelman-trust-barometer-reveals-global-implosion/.
[310] There's No Such Things as "Business Ethics" *supra* at 29.

executives should not be treated better than rank-and-file employees.[311] A plan committee member or an officer of the company should not be given preferential treatment, such as being allowed more time to make deferral or investment elections, or having one-on-one investment consultations with the plan's investment advisor.

Being on the plan committee should not bestow any special benefits on you. As one plan committee member told me, "I should be the humblest participant, and the last one in line for anything coming from the plan."

---

[311] These basic principles are reflected in the IRS nondiscrimination requirements, which *generally* prohibit discrimination in favor of highly compensated employees. Although any good consultant will be able to identify numerous exceptions for executives to get around the IRS nondiscrimination rules, this does not mean that the plan committee should treat certain participants differently.

Quick Hits

1. Confirm that the vendors and service providers have established procedures and controls for avoiding prohibited transactions. (If they don't, require that they establish such procedures and controls.) This includes having them identify parties in interest within their organization.

2. Begin the dialogue with the vendors and service providers about the requirements on pages 234-236, and work to have these requirements included in their contracts to the extent feasible.

3. Assign Legal and HR the task of identifying parties in interest for the plan committee and others within the company.
   a. Establish an annual process for updating this list and obtain verifications from parties in interest that they are aware of their status and the prohibition on prohibited transactions. See the list on pages 237-243.

4. Have ERISA counsel evaluate the rules related to conflicts of interest and gifts (travel, seminars, other items received from actual and prospective vendors and service providers), so ERISA counsel can report on whether additional guidance or rules are needed for the plan committee (and other parties in interest).

Meeting Fiduciary Responsibilities

"Any person who is a fiduciary with respect to a plan who breaches any of the responsibilities, obligations, or duties imposed upon fiduciaries by this subchapter shall be <u>personally liable</u> to make good to such plan any losses to the plan resulting from each such breach...."
ERISA section 409(a)[312]

"In FY 2016, EBSA closed 333 criminal investigations. EBSA's criminal investigations ... led to the <u>indictment of 96 individuals</u> – including plan officials, corporate officers, and service providers – for offenses related to employee benefit plans."
Employee Benefits Security Administration, Fact Sheet[313]

Introduction

In addition to the conflicts of interest and prohibited transactions discussed in the preceding chapter, plan committee members and other plan fiduciaries have additional ethical requirements they must meet. These additional fiduciary requirements trigger potential personal liability and criminal exposure for plan committee members and plan fiduciaries who don't meet these responsibilities.

Unfortunately, the fiduciary responsibilities can be somewhat ambiguous and confusing, especially for a lay person. This is where the governance principles come into play. They help to clarify these standards and provide principles that the plan

---

[312] 29 U.S.C. § 1109(a), underlining and italics added.
[313] Available at https://www.dol.gov/sites/default/files/ebsa/about-ebsa/our-activities/resource-center/fact-sheets/ebsa-monetary-results.pdf. Underlining and italics added.

committee and its members can follow to meet their fiduciary responsibilities.

This chapter discusses what is meant by fiduciary responsibility, explores each of those responsibilities, and looks at which fiduciaries for the plan are held to the fiduciary standard.

What are Your Fiduciary Responsibilities?[314]

The fiduciary responsibilities are described in ERISA very simply, even eloquently:

> (1)... a fiduciary shall discharge his duties with respect to a plan **solely in the interest of the participants and beneficiaries** and—
>> (A) **for the exclusive purpose of**:
>>> (i) **providing benefits** to participants and their beneficiaries; and
>>> (ii) **defraying reasonable expenses** of administering the plan;
>> (B) **with the care, skill, prudence, and diligence under the circumstances then prevailing that a prudent man acting in a like capacity** and familiar with such matters would use in the conduct of an enterprise of a like character and with like aims;
>> (C) **by diversifying the investments** of the plan so as to minimize the risk of large losses, unless under the circumstances it is clearly prudent not to do so; and
>> (D) **in accordance with the documents** and instruments governing the plan insofar as such documents and instruments are consistent with the provisions of [ERISA].[315]

---

[314] We've already discussed in some detail two of the fiduciary responsibilities required by ERISA: the avoidance of conflicts of interest and certain prohibited transactions. ERISA §§ 406(a) and (b); 29 U.S.C. §§ 1104(a) and (b). Because they've been covered in detail, we won't be revisiting them here, but they nevertheless remain core fiduciary responsibilities. *See* the chapter on Ethics: Conflicts of Interest and Code of Conduct at page 224.

This language describes four duties, which are often summarized as:

- **The duty of loyalty:** to act solely in the interest of the plan participants and beneficiaries, and for the exclusive purpose of providing benefits and defraying reasonable expenses under the plan[316]
- **The duty of prudence:** to act as a prudent person familiar with such matters[317]
- **The duty to diversify investments:** unless it is prudent not to do so
- **The duty of obedience:** requiring that the plan documents be followed, provided the documents are consistent with ERISA

Volumes have been written on each of these duties, and they are subject to change and evolve based on new regulations and guidance, and new case law. Our goal, however, is not as ambitious as trying to make you an expert on these duties. Instead, it is to provide a primer on these duties, and also fit them into the overall governance framework. Once it is clear how they are naturally integrated into the governance framework, the complex and shifting nature of the duties will be less intimidating.

Fiduciary Responsibilities Amplify the Governance Principles

Most enterprises and endeavors that are seeking to accomplish a mission or have goals will have some form of governance in place. In many situations, the "governing body" will not have any fiduciary duties or responsibilities.

In other situations, however, the governing bodies will have fiduciary duties to those they serve. The corporate and non-profit

---

[315] ERISA § 404(a); 29 U.S.C. § 1104(a).

[316] Sometimes this is described as three separate duties: duty of loyalty, exclusive purpose duty, and duty to defray reasonable plan expenses.

[317] The duty of prudence is also discussed in the chapter on Knowledge and Skill starting at page 166. The duty of prudence is sometimes referred to as the duty of care.

boards are governing bodies, and they are also fiduciaries. Trustees and guardians similarly are governing bodies and fiduciaries.[318] In all of these cases, the governing body is responsible for the oversight of the endeavor and for making sure the endeavor is properly governed (roles and responsibilities are clear, risks managed, all have adequate knowledge and skills, and so forth).

When the governing body also has fiduciary responsibilities, however, it is in a trusted position to the group it is benefiting. The law has historically held the governing body for these trusted relationships to a higher standard than that which would be required of one who is just an overseer. One court succinctly summarized it by saying, "... [t]he distinguishing or overriding duty of a fiduciary is the obligation of undivided loyalty."[319]

Although the fiduciary responsibilities add several new dimensions to the governance principles, they generally serve to amplify the already existing governance elements. The four fiduciary duties can be mapped to the 12 governance principles as follows:

Fiduciary Duty	Corresponding Governance Principles
Loyalty	Ethics and conflicts of interest Transparency Periodic assessments Oversight
Prudence	Mission and goals Roles, responsibilities, accountability Risk management Knowledge and skills Performance measurement Compliance

---

[318] Fiduciary relationships also exist for the personal representative of an estate, partners, and agents. It often involves a party holding or managing the property of another. Restatement (Second) of Trusts § 2.

[319] Australian Securities and Investments Commission v. Citigroup Global Markets Australia Pty Limited (No. 4) (2007) FCA 963, paragraph 289 (2007) 62 ACSR 427, Federal Court (Australia). Cites omitted.

	Meeting fiduciary duties
	Succession
Diversification	Risk management
	Performance measurement
	Periodic assessments
Obedience	Roles, responsibilities, accountability
	Compliance
	Transparency

The fiduciary responsibilities are, however, more than a reiteration of the governance principles. By adding the fiduciary dimension to the governance principles, the standards are strengthened and elevated. For example, the duty of loyalty raises the requirement of avoiding conflicts to an absolute, undivided loyalty. And as discussed, the duty of prudence promotes the knowledge and skills standard to "the highest known to the law."[320]

Duty of Loyalty

The duty of loyalty has been called "[t]he most fundamental duty of ERISA plan fiduciaries…" and "… a duty of *complete* loyalty…."[321] It requires that the plan fiduciary act *solely* in the interest of the participants, *and* for the exclusive purpose of providing benefits and defraying reasonable expenses of administering the plan.

This means that plan fiduciaries, including plan committee members, must hold the interest of plan participants above their own interest or the interest of the company. It also requires them to "exclude all selfish interest and all consideration of the interests of third persons."[322] Inherently, this requires the avoidance of conflicts of interest.[323]

---

[320] Donovan v. Bierwirth, 680 F.2d 263, 272 (2d Cir. 1982). *See* discussion following footnote 186.
[321] In Re Enron Corp. Securities, Derivative & ERISA, 284 F. Supp. 2d 511, 546 (S.D. Tex. 2003).
[322] Pegram v. Herdirich, 530 U.S. 211, 235 (2000).
[323] Mertens v. Hewitt Assoc., 508 U.S. 248, 251-52 (1993).

> ### *You Shouldn't Do That!*
>
> 1. Loan yourself, your business, or family members money from the plan, even if it is at the market rate of interest (or better), unless you get permission from the DOL.
> 2. Select a plan vendor because they provide you with some personal benefits (like trips, holidays, access to clubs, or memberships).
> 3. Have the employer provide services for a fee to the plan (unless you get permission from the DOL).
> 4. Select a service or a vendor because a committee member's family member is an employee or owner of the business.

Duty of Prudence[324]

The duty of prudence, or the prudent man rule, requires the plan committee and the fiduciary to act "with the care, skill, prudence and diligence under the circumstances then prevailing that a prudent man acting in like capacity and familiar with such matters would use in the conduct of an enterprise of a like character and with like aims...."[325] From a governance perspective, there are two major lessons the plan committee and other plan fiduciaries need to take from the duty of prudence standard.

First, when reading articles or cases about the duty of prudence, one will see that most of them focus on plan investments. This is, quite simply, because investments are important to the plan, tremendous fees are generated from investments, and poor or costly investments generate much of the litigation involving retirement plans. The duty of prudence is not, however, limited to plan investments. It applies to all decisions made by the plan committee and other fiduciaries. Thus, it encompasses vendor

---

[324] The "prudent expert" standard is discussed in detail in the chapter on Knowledge and Skills at page 166. The high, expert-like standard to which fiduciaries are held, and the need to utilize and oversee experts is not repeated here. Instead, the focus here is on the broader ERISA prudence standard.
[325] ERISA § 404(a)(1)(B), 29 U.S.C. § 1104(a)(1)(B).

selection and oversight, monitoring plan costs, and of course, selecting investments. This begs the question: what is prudence?

Second, prudence, which depends on all the facts and circumstances, looks at the *process* used by the plan committee to reach its decision.[326] Indeed, it is often said that *"prudence is process."*[327]

When focusing on prudence, courts look at "whether the fiduciary, at the time of the transaction, utilized proper methods to investigate, evaluate and structure the [transaction] ...."[328] In discussing prudence in the context of an investment, one court summarized the duty of prudence as follows:

> "[ERISA's] test of prudence ... is one of *conduct*, and not a test of the result of performance of the investment. The focus of the inquiry is how the fiduciary acted in his selection of the investment, and not whether his investment succeeded or failed." Thus, the appropriate inquiry is "whether the individual trustees, at the time they engaged in the challenged transactions, *employed the appropriate methods* to investigate

---

[326] "[F]iduciaries are judged not by a retrospective assessment of whether their investment decisions were successful, but by whether they followed a reasonable process in reaching their decision. As one U.S. court succinctly stated, "The focus of the inquiry is how the fiduciary acted in his selection of the investment, and not whether his investments succeeded or failed." Galer, Russell, *"Prudent Person Rule" Standard for the Investment of Pension Fund Assets* (OECD) at 5, available at https://www.oecd.org/finance/private-pensions/2763540.pdf, quoting Donovan v. Cunningham, 716 F.2d 1455 (5th Cir. 1983).

[327] "Since the future is unpredictable, a decision made today, even with the best of advice and soundest of judgment, may turn out poorly. This does not negate the prudence of the decision. Thus subsequent returns are not the basis by which prudence is judged. Instead, it is judged by the degree of care with which the decision was made. So fiduciaries have a duty to themselves to document with care the consideration that guided any decision of theirs. Essentially, this means that the relevant facts and opinions must be considered as part of a process that is relevant to reaching the decision, and they must keep an adequate record of all this. Hence the snappy summing up of the standard: 'Prudence is process.'" Keith P. Ambachtsheer and Don D. Ezra, Pension Fund Excellence (John Wiley & Sons, Inc. 1998) at 35.

[328] Laborers National Pension Fund v. Northern Trust Quantitative Advisors, Inc., 173 F.3d 313, 317 (5th Cir.), *cert. denied* 528 U.S. 967 (1999).

the merits of the investment... (citations omitted)." (Emphasis added.)[329]

The courts continually emphasize that when judging prudence, the focus is on the process, and not on the ultimate success of the decision. While individual cases may focus on singular elements, such as not using an expert or not adequately assessing risk, there is **an overarching process that is inherently prudent**. That process, of course, **is embodied in the 12 governance principles.**[330]

Prudence is Process
Governance Creates the Ideal Process

By following the 12 governance principles, the plan committee can work to develop an ideal process and act prudently. Granted, not every principle will be relevant in every decision. But by considering whether each principle is potentially relevant, and having a process that continually invokes all the principles, the plan committee will be as prudently positioned as possible. Here is a brief recap of the principles and how they support prudence:

1. *Mission statement and goals* - Does the decision or transaction support the plan's mission and goals? Often, individual decisions can be attacked when viewed in a vacuum. One can always find a vendor that is cheaper, or an investment that is better. If, however, the plan committee can elevate the discussion to one related to achieving the broader mission (and the criteria used to make the selection supported the mission), then narrow considerations will have less weight. Striving to achieve the plan's mission can explain why individual decisions are made. If, for example, the plan committee has decided that low investment cost is not the most important factor in selecting investments because the

---

[329] Laborers National Pension Fund v. Northern Trust Quantitative Advisors, Inc., 173 F.3d 313, 317 (5th Cir.), *cert. denied* 528 U.S. 967 (1999).

[330] On occasion, I have been asked if all 12 of the governance principles are needed to be prudent. I would usually respond rhetorically by asking, if you were a participant, which of the 12 governance principles would you want your fiduciary to ignore and still feel that they were acting prudently?

participants need help with investment education, better advice on planning for retirement, and easy access,[331] then the decision of selecting higher-cost funds with greater services can be supported.

2. *Clarity about roles, responsibilities, and accountability* – Is each parties' role and responsibility and how they will be held accountable clear in the decision? Certainly, engaging a vendor where there is ambiguity related to who will be making particular decisions, or possibly having discretion and fiduciary responsibilities, is not prudent on many levels. Tasks could go unfulfilled, and the services provided may not be commensurate with the amount charged when there is a lack of clarity related to roles, responsibilities, and accountability.

3. *Risk management* – Is the plan committee aware of the risks related to the decision or transaction, and taking appropriate steps to mitigate the risks? For investments, this typically involves diversifying, liquidity needs, projected return and the risk of loss, using experts, and aggressive monitoring against standards imbedded in an investment policy statement (to name the major risks).[332] Failing to investigate, ignorance, or turning a blind-eye to risks will not absolve a fiduciary from its duty.[333]

4. *Knowledge and skills* – Are there any knowledge or skill gaps that should be closed, and is it necessary to use experts?[334] Also, the plan committee should be using the best information available when making decisions or engaging in a transaction.

5. *Clear performance measures* – Are the expectations, goals, and roles clear and able to be measured and monitored? It is expected that there will be standards when making decisions, and those standards will be continually monitored against the expected outcome of the decision, transaction, or vendors performance.

---

[331] It would be helpful if the mission was supported by surveys or feedback from the participants.

[332] 29 C.F.R. § 2550.404a-1(b)(2).

[333] Katsaros v. Cody, 744 F.2d 270, 279 (2d Cir.), *cert. denied*, 469 U.S. 1072 (1984), and Donovan v. Cunningham, 716 F.2d 1455, 1467 (5th Cir. 1983).

[334] Bussian v. R.J.R. Nabisco, Inc., 223 F.3d 286, 300-301 (5th Cir. 2000) (fiduciaries who lack expertise should seek the assistance of experts, but should not blindly rely on their advice).

6. *Compliance* – Are the decisions expected to be, and actually carried out, in compliance with all applicable laws and the plan document?
7. *Ethics: Conflicts of interest and code of conduct* – Are the decisions conflict-free, and is anyone who is carrying out the mission for the plan also conflict-free?
8. *Transparency and disclosure* – Is it required that, as decisions and transactions are carried out, there is transparency and disclosure on the progress and any issues or problems that are encountered?
9. *Meeting fiduciary duties* – Is it clear that fulfilling any decision or accomplishing any transaction should not violate any of the four fiduciary duties?
10. *Succession planning* – Will the plan be able to carry out its mission if a plan committee member or other key player leaves unexpectedly?
11. *Periodic assessments* – Are critical areas periodically assessed to ensure that they are functioning properly and to identify areas for possible improvement?
12. *Oversight* – Does the plan committee hold all the players accountable while motivating them and driving the mission of the plan?

Finally, having proper documentation related to the process is the bow that ties these process neatly together. It is always best to have a record of the decision-making process that is contemporaneous with the decisions.

Well governed plans inherently have a prudent process, and a prudent process is by definition good governance.

Executive Life Insurance GICs: A Prudent Choice

In *In re Unisys Savings Plan Litigation*, the court considered whether the plan fiduciaries breached their duty by investing in guaranteed insurance contracts issued by Executive Life, which later went bankrupt. The court found that the fiduciaries fulfilled

---

[335] 173 F.3d 145 (3d Cir. 1999).

their duty by conducting a reasonable investigation and hiring an expert.[335]

Another plan that made a similar investment but didn't hire an expert and didn't conduct any due diligence would likely be found to have breached its fiduciary duty.

Duty to Diversify

To understand diversification under ERISA, one must first distinguish diversification for participant-directed defined contribution plans and all other plans (such as defined benefit plans).[336] In a defined benefit plan (and other non-participant directed plans), the plan committee and its investment advisors work at achieving diversification by taking an investment theory or strategy, selecting the individual investments that support that strategy, and deciding on an asset allocation[337] between the various investments. There is a single plan, executed by a single group that controls all the elements of the process.[338]

What are Acceptable Investment Theories or Strategies?

The Department of Labor and most of the case law view the use of Modern Portfolio Theory (MPT) as an acceptable approach for investing the plan assets.[339] Indeed, MPT might be the only

---

[336] It also includes any non-participant directed defined contribution plans.

[337] Asset allocation is the way that one divides their portfolio between different asset classes.

[338] The Department of Labor has not provided a safe-harbor type of diversification for defined benefit plans, like it has for participant investment directed defined contribution plans. Accordingly, it is left to the plan's investment committee and investment advisor to craft an appropriate investment strategy. Failing to diversify in defined benefit plans generally does not trigger any participant lawsuits. This is largely due to the fact that poor investment results in a defined benefit plan will be borne by the company, not the participants. Despite the lack of risks from litigation related to failing to diversity, the plan committee will want to meet its duty to diversify and the company will want to maximize investment results and minimize risk.

[339] DOL Advisory Opinion 2001-09A (December 2001) (modern portfolio theory is generally accepted); Laborers National Pension Fund v. Northern Trust Quantitative Advisors Inc., 173 F.3d 313 (5th Cir. 1999); Franklin v. First Union Corp., 84 F. Supp. 2d 720 (E.D. Va. 2000); Crowhurst v. California

acceptable approach, as reflected by the Department of Labor's statement in the preamble to the regulations on investment advice:

"While several commenters described theories and practices they believe to be generally accepted, there did not appear to be any consensus among them, with the exception of modern portfolio theory, which the Department believes is already reflected in the rule's reference to investment theories that take into account the historic returns of different asset classes over defined periods of time."[340] (Footnote omitted.)

Labor's bias toward MPT is understandable. "The central plank of MPT is the concept of diversification – the fact that a well chosen group of assets can achieve a higher rate of return with a lower level of risk than any asset taken in isolation."[341] Since diversification is required by ERISA "unless under the circumstances it is clearly prudent not to do so," MPT and its emphasis on diversification sync well with ERISA.

There are, however, many other investment theories, variations to MPT, and critics of MPT. The plan committee should continually look for better investment theories or refinements to MPT.[342] Similarly, if the plan's investment advisor suggests an alternate approach, the plan committee should evaluate it critically:

Institute of Technology, 1999 WL 1027033 (C.D. Cal. 1999).

[340] Investment Advice –Participants and Beneficiaries, 76 Fed. Reg. 66,135, 66,140 (Oct. 25, 2011), quoting the preamble to the regulations later codified at 29 C.F.R. § 2550.408g-1.

[341] Morningstar Glossary, Modern Portfolio Theory (MPT), available at www.morningstar.co.uk/uk/glossary/98207/modern-portfolio-theory-(mpt).aspx.

[342] Modern investment theory does not require that one invest solely in passive or indexed investments. "One of the primary reasons for drafting the Restatement [3rd of Trusts] was to incorporate the concepts of the Modern Portfolio Theory. ...[T]he Restatement is clear that passive as well as active investment strategies are prudent. However, there is a greater burden of proof for those utilizing active strategies to show that their efforts are in fact adding value." The New Fiduciary Standard supra at 13-14.

- Is the alternate strategy achieving greater reward with less risk?
- If it isn't as diversified as an approach under MPT, then is it "clearly prudent not to [be as diversified]"? If the plan committee deviates from a diversified strategy to another strategy, it needs to recognize that the burden of proof will shift to the committee to show that the strategy was "clearly prudent."[343]
- Is the investment advisor willing to indemnify the plan for any loss caused by a lawsuit by participants or Labor if it is found that the alternate strategy was not clearly prudent?

The process is dramatically different for participant directed defined contribution plans. In a participant directed defined contribution plan, the plan committee has to provide a selection of investment options without knowing how they will be assembled by any of the plan participants. The allocation by each participant of their assets among the options provided by the committee is entirely up to them. They may choose not to diversify, they may not follow any investment theory, indeed, they may not follow any sound investment approach.

This presents two significant challenges for the plan committee. First, how can the plan committee limit its exposure if the assets are not being diversified? Second, how can the plan committee provide a menu of investment options that can make it easier for the participants to maximize return while minimizing risk (or, diversify), if they don't know how the participants will allocate their assets?

---

[343] "The language in ERISA regarding diversification does not require prudent fiduciaries to make bets against being fully diversified in an attempt to produce higher returns, or less risk, than the fully diversified benchmark. It requires trustees to be able to prove that if they make bets against diversification, they need to meet the criteria of an expert making a clearly prudent decision. Thus, the standard isn't that a bet against diversification is OK because it has a *chance* of being beneficial. Instead, the standard is that if you are making a bet against diversification, you need to have exceptionally compelling evidence that it is more prudent than diversifying (i.e., clearly prudent.)" The Four Pillars of Retirement Plans *supra* at 69.

As discussed earlier,[344] the plan committee can shift the risk of participant investment decisions to the participants if the investment portfolio is designed to meet the requirements of ERISA section 404(c). (The plan committee or fiduciaries selecting the investment options that are made available to the participants remain responsible for the selection and monitoring of the chosen options.) If the requirements of section 404(c) are not met, the risk of the poor investment decisions made by the plan participants will fall back onto the plan committee. This is why it is so important for the committee to be sure that a plan that permits participant directed investments is compliant with section 404(c).

Summary of Requirements for Section 404(c) Compliance[345]

1. The participant is given the opportunity to direct the investment of the assets in their account.
2. The participant can make investment decisions and receive written confirmation of their investment directions.
3. The person receiving the investment direction is identified as a plan fiduciary and is required to comply with the participant's direction.
4. The participant is provided by the identified plan fiduciary with the following:
a. An explanation that the plan is intended to be an ERISA section 404(c) plan
b. An explanation that the fiduciaries may be relieved of liability for losses caused by the participant's ability to direct investments
c. A description of the investment options that are available under the plan
d. A general description of the plan's investment objectives and the risks and return characteristics of each of the designated investment alternatives
e. An identification of any designated investment managers

---

[344] *See* discussion following footnote 76.
[345] 29 C.F.R. § 2550.404c-1.

f. An explanation about how to give investment instructions
g. A description of any transaction fees and expenses that will affect the participant's account balance (such as trading fees, 12b-1 fees, and the like)
h. The name, address, and phone number of the plan fiduciary responsible for providing the information
i. Information regarding investing in employer securities
j. Copies of the most recent prospectuses for the investments that are subject to the Securities Act of 1933
k. Any material provided to the plan relating to the exercise of voting, tender or similar rights
5. The participant is able to obtain upon request:
a. A description of annual operating expenses of each designated investment alternative
b. Copies of any prospectuses, financial statements, and reports provided to the plan
c. A list of the assets comprising the portfolio of each designated investment alternative
d. Information concerning the value of shares or units in designated investment alternatives
e. Information concerning the value of shares or units in designated investment alternatives held in the account of the participant
6. The plan must permit participants to give investment instructions with a frequency that is appropriate in light of market volatility (but at least once per quarter)
7. The core investment alternatives consist of a broad range of options (at least three of which are diversified and have materially different risk and return characteristics)

The second challenge is how to select the best investment options from which participants can build their portfolio. ERISA section 404(c) provides the minimum threshold requirements: at least three options, direction at least once every three months, and an array of disclosures. However, from a governance perspective, the plan committee can do more.

For example, the plan committee can take into consideration the information it gathered as part of developing the plan's mission and goals. This could include participant data such as:

- Age
- Education
- Financial investment experience and sophistication
- Language skills (will material need to be translated, and, if so, into how many languages?)
- Actual participant investment selections and performance[346]
- Access to a computer and the internet

Depending on the answers to these items, the investments selected by the plan committee could be a complex array of varied and sophisticated funds that require regular review by the participant, or lifecycle funds that can be selected by the participants and thereafter essentially be ignored by the participants. From a governance perspective, the funds must meet the needs of the participants and the plan mission—not just the bare bones of ERISA section 404(c).

The duty to diversify is critically important because poor investment results (or excessive investment costs) can be huge liabilities for the plan fiduciaries and the company. This is an area where the committee will want to emphasize its governance by:

- Improving the investing knowledge and skills of the members – do they all understand modern portfolio theory and any other investment strategy being used by the plan?
- Having clear performance measures—for both the investments and the advisors.
- Avoiding conflicts for both the committee members, the investment advisors, and the investment managers. This goes beyond having everyone confirm annually in writing that they have no conflicts, but also extends to conducting reviews to identify potential conflicts.

---

[346] It can help the plan committee and its advisors build a pool of investment options if they know, for example, that historically some of the participants have not diversified (they only select one fund or put the bulk of their assets in one fund), have not changed funds or rebalanced, or have not downloaded any research on the funds (such as historical performance, prospectuses, etc.).

- Insuring compliance with section 404(c) and the diversification requirement by having counsel periodically opine on the plan's compliance.
- Having identified investment roles so it is clear which advisors are serving as a fiduciary and where their liability ends, and the plan committee's exposure begins.

Duty of Obedience

The duty of obedience requires that the plan committee follows ERISA, the plan document and other instruments governing the plan, and valid directions they receive, in that order. If the plan document or a direction is inconsistent with the law, the plan committee or other fiduciaries must comply with ERISA.[347]

The duty of obedience requires that the plan committee:

- Understands the ERISA rules and framework (discussed extensively in this and the prior chapter), and that training is conducted to close any knowledge gaps
- Understands the plan document and the other governing instruments (again, with training as necessary)
- Ensures that the plan document and the other governing instruments are kept current, both with the law and with actual practice
- Confirms that roles and responsibilities are clearly defined and followed, so that directions (or orders) come from the proper source and can be fulfilled

Unfortunately, the profound complexity that surrounds both ERISA and the plan documents are the reason why the plan committee members need to embrace them, and the reason why the plan committee keeps them at a distance. But despite the complexity, as a plan committee member, you need to be familiar with both to fulfill your duty of obedience.

---

[347] ERISA § 404(a)(1)(D), 29 U.S.C. § 1104(a)(1)(D). *See also,* <u>Kuper v. Lovenko</u>, 66 F.3d 1447 (6th Cir. 1995).

Recognizing neither ERISA nor the plan documents will be a fun read, an interesting read, or a quick read, here are several suggestions to help the plan committee begin to eat this elephant:

- Start by reading the summary plan description (SPD), but don't stop there. The SPD omits everything related to your duties and powers, the committee structure, and any reporting relationships. For that, you'll need to read the plan document.
- The plan document[348] is the controlling instrument on the plan design and structure.[349] Don't be intimidated by its length; it will only take a few hours to read and there are a few helpful hints:

  o A lot of the most significant items are hidden in the plan definitions (usually at the beginning of the plan document). For example, "employee" might be defined to exclude union employees or temporary employees. "Compensation" may also be defined to exclude bonuses, overtime, or stock options. The "company" may also be defined to exclude or include related companies, such as parents or subsidiaries.

  o There are typically only three-to-five articles or chapters that deal with participation, contributions, or benefits, and payouts. These can be a quick read, especially after reading the SPD.

  o There are also usually one or two articles or chapters on the plan committee, its powers, and duties. As a committee member, you can approach this with a critical eye and as a governance expert. Is the delegation of powers to the committee clear? What does the plan document contemplate should be addressed outside the document, perhaps items such as a plan committee charter or detail on avoiding conflicts?

---

[348] Often, the "plan document" will consist of multiple documents, such as the original document and a variety of amendments.
[349] CIGNA Corp. v. Amara, 131 S. Ct. 1866 (2011).

- o Much of what is left relates to the hoops that Congress requires businesses to jump through in order to get a tax deduction. These articles or chapters address areas such as contribution limits and discrimination rules. If you're up for a challenge, give them a read. Whether you read them or not, you may want to flag these areas as topics that are outside of the committee's expertise, and recognize that experts will be required to help with compliance in those areas. (Also, note that you'd like to see recent test results for these areas, and an explanation of any exceptions.)
- o Finally, toward the end of the document, there is a discussion on how the plan can be amended and terminated. It is possible that the plan committee will have limits to its power to amend or terminate the plan.

- Learning about ERISA can be a challenge. Not many books have been written to explain it to non-lawyers, and the statute and regulations can be a brutal read, even for the most devoted attorney. I have four recommendations that will help plan committee members gain a foothold in ERISA:

  - o Look at the Department of Labor, Employee Benefits Security Administration website, specifically www.dol.gov/agencies/ebsa. Also, check out the IRS Employee Plans website: www.irs.gov/retirement-plans/about-employee-plans. At a minimum, this will inform you of the government's thinking on what you should know. Labor also gives information to your participants, and it can be helpful to see the perspective your participants might be receiving from the government.
  - o Read books on ERISA. Unfortunately, there aren't too many options. As of my last check, there were under 200 hits on Amazon for ERISA, and only a handful were overview books. I've found an

excellent introductory read by the U.S. Congressional Research Service, which is available for free online.[350]

- o Subscribe to periodicals that provide updates on rules, regulations, and cases involving ERISA. Most of the larger employee benefits and HR consulting firms will provide periodic newsletters and updates electronically for free.
- o Secure experienced ERISA counsel.

Duty to Monitor - Co-Fiduciary Liability

In addition to the above four duties, there is a fifth that relates to participating in, concealing, or having knowledge of a breach by another fiduciary.[351] It may seem obvious that as a fiduciary, one should not conceal or participate in breaches by other fiduciaries. The harder standard is the one related to knowledge. Under this standard, if a fiduciary has knowledge of a co-fiduciary's breach, and the fiduciary does not take any action to remedy the breach, then the fiduciary is also in breach. This raises difficult questions about when a fiduciary has knowledge of a co-fiduciary's actions that might constitute a breach, and what actions a fiduciary should take to obtain such knowledge.

The standard of having knowledge also extends to situations where the fiduciary's failure to monitor or oversee another fiduciary (particularly one that he or she appointed), allowed the other fiduciary to commit a breach.[352] The Department of Labor has specifically stated that, "At reasonable intervals the performance of ... fiduciaries should be reviewed by the appointing fiduciary in such manner as may be reasonably expected to ensure that their performance has been in compliance with the terms of the plan and statutory standards, and satisfies the needs of the plan."[353] The regulations don't provide any

---

[350] Patrick Purcell and Jennifer Staman, *Summary of the Employee Retirement Income Security Act (ERISA)* (Washington, DC 2008), *available at* http://digitalcommons.ilr.cornell.edu/key_workplace/505/.

[351] ERISA § 405(a), 26 U.S.C. § 1105(a).

[352] *Id. See also,* Leigh v. Eagle, 727 F.2d 113 (7th Cir. 1984).

[353] 29 C.F.R. § 2509.75-8.

guidance on what would be a reasonable interval, or exactly what should be reviewed.

For the duty to monitor, as well as the other fiduciary duties, adhering to the 12 governance principles can provide a solid framework toward meeting one's fiduciary responsibilities. The governance framework will help insure that delegations are clear, accountability and reporting exists, performance measurements and standards are created, there are periodic assessments, there is a process to promote compliance, and there is on-going oversight. Finally, recognize that this is a complex area and there will probably be a need to seek the assistance of legal advice and other expertise.

Quick Hits

1. Approach fiduciary decisions with a *process* that is built around:
    a. The plan's mission and the specific goals[354] that are being accomplished
    b. Clear evaluation criteria
    c. Supported by each of the governance principles as illustrated on pages 261-263.
   Decisions should be reflected in contemporaneous documentation.

2. Verify (using experts) that the plan's investments are *diversified.*
    a. If the plan has participant directed investments, have ERISA counsel review the plan and opine on whether the plan meets ERISA section 404(c). (See the requirements at pages 267-268.)
    b. Investment diversification should be supported by:
        i. Training for committee members related to plan investments
        ii. Establishing clear performance measures for the investments and advisors
        iii. The avoidance of conflicts
        iv. Maintaining compliance (*e.g.,* with section 404(c))
        v. Having clearly identified investment roles (*e.g.,* whether advisors are serving as fiduciaries, and where their liability ends)

3. Assess the plan committee's knowledge of ERISA and the plan.
    a. Develop a plan to close any gaps.
    b. Check that the document and supporting procedures are accurate.

---

[354] Considering the current litigation environment, reasonable plan cost and fees should be one of the goals considered.

Transparency and Disclosure

"Honesty and transparency make you vulnerable. Be honest and transparent anyway."
Mother Teresa

"Speak the truth. Transparency breeds legitimacy."
John C. Maxwell

Introduction

Transparency is critical to governance because it causes the plan committee actions and decisions to be visible, and thereby helps to hold the committee accountable to the plan participants. Transparency is the disinfectant of ill-advised fiduciary behavior.

In general, transparency requires that the plan committee creates an environment in which its "objectives, frameworks, decisions and their rational, data and other information are provided to stakeholders in a comprehensive, accessible and timely manner."[355] In many ways, transparency strengthens all the other governance principles. Objectives are articulated more clearly, committees strive more vigorously to achieve their goals, vendor accountability is intently monitored, and potential risks are attacked with unparalleled intensity.

Because transparency shines such a revealing light on both the accomplishments and failures of the plan committee, committees that are not yet well-governed can be hesitant to be fully transparent. They often embrace transparency later than the other governance principles. Transparency can be a harsh light, and the plan committee may want to have its house in order before shinning this harsh light in. But just because the committee

---

[355] John Ashcroft, Nina Paklina and Fiona Steward, *Governance and Performance Measurement of Pension Supervisory Authorities* (International Organization of Pension Supervisors, Working Paper No. 10, Nov. 2009) at 7.

might not be ready for all of its actions to be fully exposed, doesn't mean that it can't begin to shine the light of transparency on some of the plan's activities and on those that report to the committee.

Obfuscation Objective

Retirement plans are costly to fund, can represent significant liabilities on corporate balance sheets, constitute tremendous pools of assets, and generate significant fees for vendors. By making certain changes to retirement plans, companies can improve their income statement and balance sheet, and thereby improve profits and incentives for executives. The ability to impact profits and incentives can create significant pressure, and serve as strong drivers for companies, executives, and their business advisors to make changes to the plan (such as reduce benefits or plan services) that aren't necessarily beneficial to the plan participants.

In *Retirement Heist,* Wall Street Journal reporter Ellen Schultz described a litany of transactions where financial pressures caused management to make retirement plan changes. One transaction she described had the objective of obfuscating the plan change.

> In 1997, Cigna executives held a number of meetings to discuss their pension problem. At the time, the plan was overfunded, but the executives ... suggested cutting the pensions of 27,000 employees in an effort to boost the earnings they could report on their bottom line. The only hitch? How to cut people's pension ... by 30 percent or more, without anyone noticing?
>
> ... The challenge was how to cut pensions without provoking an employee uprising.
>
> ... Cigna's solution to this communications challenge? ... [P]repare the written communication to Cigna employees describing the changes without disclosing the negative effects.[356]

---

[356] Schultz at 29-31.
The CIGNA case has been litigated and appealed for over 15 years.

There have been, and surely will be in the future, situations where members of management will make decisions that are permissible under ERISA, but negatively affect participants. It will then be left to the plan committee members (who may be the same individuals as the members of management or their peers) to execute or implement the decision of management, including communicating management's decision to plan participants.

Good governance dictates that decisions be clearly communicated to plan participants. The fact that the decision may be received negatively or with resistance, or create employee or HR headaches for management, does not justify obfuscating the message so it cannot be understood. In egregious cases, courts may find that the company's "successful efforts to conceal [the truth] ..." damaged the participant.[357] Indeed, in 1996, the Supreme Court found that misinformation provided to participants amounted to deceit and a breach of fiduciary duty.[358]

The Tension Created by Wearing "Two Hats"

As discuss earlier,[359] companies can make changes to retirement plans in a variety of ways that are legal and don't violate any fiduciary duties to the plan participants. Some of the situations described by Schultz, and the hundreds of other situations where companies have taken legally permitted actions that are not necessarily beneficial to plan participants, reflect the ongoing tension within US retirement plan administration. The companies and members of management can make certain decisions related to the retirement plan, regardless of how they impact participants. It's permissible for management to reduce benefits, delay vesting, limit participation, or even terminate the plan. These actions are not fiduciary decisions and management does not need to act in the best interest of plan participants. In a vast majority of cases, however, the same members of the management team making decisions that are contrary to the

---

[357] Amara v. CIGNA Corp., 534 F. Supp. 2d 288, 354 (Conn. 2008).
[358] Varity Corp. v. Howe, 516 U.S. 489 (1996).
[359] See discussion surrounding footnote 102.

participants' interest are the plan committee members who must make decisions that are in the "best interest of plan participants."

The conflict arises when the same individual wears two different hats: a management non-fiduciary hat, and a plan committee member fiduciary hat. The tension that can exist between the two hats, or roles, can be significant in certain situations.[360]

The "two-hat" doctrine is made more difficult because it is unique to ERISA.[361] A trustee or fiduciary in a non-ERISA context can wear only "his fiduciary hat when he acts in a manner to affect the beneficiary of the trust...."[362] However, in ERISA, it is possible that a fiduciary "may wear many hats, although only one at a time, and [the fiduciary] may have financial interests that are adverse to the interest of the beneficiaries but in the best interest of the company."[363]

Because inherent conflicts are permitted by ERISA (embedded in the "two-hat" doctrine), it is even more important that the plan committee strives to be as transparent as possible to keep the two hats separate and easily identifiable.

Moving Toward Transparency

Transparency can expose the plan committee's warts and flaws. It isn't something that most committees working toward improving their governance will initially embrace. But it is something that committees can strive for, even if it is gradual. As the committee's overall governance improves, its transparency can become broader and brighter.

So, how does the committee begin to improve its transparency? A way to begin is to increase the level of transparency of all the

---

[360] *See* discussion around footnote 101 for suggestions on how to minimize the risks associated with individuals wearing two-hats.

[361] The two-hat doctrine was first espoused in Curtiss-Wright Corp. v. Schoonejongen, 514 U.S. 73, 78 (1995).

[362] In Re Enron Corp. Securities, Derivative & ERISA, 284 F. Supp. 2d 511, 550 (S.D. Tex. 2003).

[363] *Id.*

staff, vendors, and others that the committee oversees. This is a relatively easy initial step since transparency below the committee level is essentially just heightened accountability and oversight. The committee can, however, build on the heightened accountability and oversight of those it oversees by getting the information the committee will need to be more transparent.

What is a good way to launch a program to increase transparency with those that report to the plan committee? A very simple start is to ask each party to suggest what they see as the most important areas across the following three dimensions:

1. Key **Oversight Areas,** which can include:
   a. Systems (websites, information systems, calculation systems)
   b. Personnel (staff working on the plan for the company, staff in call centers, and the like), including items such as succession planning and training
   c. Performance management and contract-term management
   d. Compliance, including legal compliance, conflicts, and fiduciary responsibilities
   e. Other Risks
2. **Evaluation Criteria** Used to Assess these Oversight Areas, including:
   a. Quality – including accuracy of processing, certifications, review results (*e.g.,* SSAE 16s)
   b. Pricing/Cost – such as unexpected costs, contract overages, cost of corrections and adjustments
   c. Participant and Customer Satisfaction
3. Strive to Evaluate these Areas and Criteria along the Following Four **Indicators**:
   a. Monitoring (such as tracking numbers, completion)
   b. Efficiency Indicators – not only whether it is done, but ensuring that it is done efficiently (timely, quickly)

c. Leading Indicators – to show progress toward various goals and determine whether the current path is the best

d. Predictive Indicators – can it predict trends, problems or issues, resource needs?

Improving Vendor Transparency: An Example

Your plan committee has decided to embark on the path of improving transparency, and they want to begin by improving the transparency of the plan's 401(k) recordkeeper. The recordkeeper is a reputable company that has been in the recordkeeping business for decades. Indeed, the plan has used the company for over 20 years. The longevity of the relationship is more a testament to the strength of its account manager and the difficulties involved in changing recordkeepers than a reflection of the lack of problems over the years.

Since this is a new undertaking, the plan committee reaches out to the recordkeeper, the HR and IT staff who work on the plan, ERISA counsel, and others[364] to get their input into the areas in which the committee should build greater transparency. The committee reminds all the parties about the plan's mission and the identified roles and responsibilities of the recordkeeper, so the recommendations can be kept focused and relevant.

These groups identify the following areas (among others):

- The plan committee specifically charges the HR staff and the company's in-house contract attorney to review the contract for areas that should be *monitored* to ensure compliance with the contract and performance measures in the contract, plan manuals or SSAE 16 reports (which relate to quality, pricing,[365] and participant satisfaction).

---

[364] Others could include procurement, other vendors that interact with the recordkeeper, Internal Audit, or other parties that might have reviewed the performance of the recordkeeper and, of course, plan participants.
[365] Each of these areas can be explored in much greater detail than this example provides. To show how one might drill down more into pricing, an illustration is provided at the end of this chapter titled, "Pricing Transparency

- The HR staff and ERISA counsel identify issues related to errors that have been occurring at the call center. The cause of the errors is not known, but the call center has high turnover, and some of the calls are handled offshore. The focus is on *personnel* (training, experience, supervision). These errors affect quality, costs, and participant satisfaction. The recordkeeper is charged with (i) surveying participants one week after a call on whether the advice they received was accurate, (ii) having a sample of all calls reviewed by supervisors, and (iii) developing a *predictive model* from the data (*e.g.,* are the errors related to new representatives, offshore workers, workers under a specific manager, workers trained by a certain individual, certain types of calls or questions, and the like).

- The plan committee has also asked the recordkeeper to provide a quarterly report that addresses: the recordkeeper's timeliness (on reports, allocations, transfers, distributions, and the like), projected discrimination test results, variances in contribution amounts (including annual changes), warnings from edit checks, major data discrepancies, data security verifications, staffing changes, staff losing certifications, missed goals or deadlines, and other areas.

Transparency Lite for the Committee

Unfortunately, in today's litigious world, the plan committee will need to expand its level of transparency carefully so as not to promote an unwarranted law suits. Therefore, it is important to develop and begin with a transparency plan. The plan should explore what can be communicated now without undue risk, and what will need further refinement before being communicated. It should also address the best ways to communicate with the plan participants (the manner of communicating, such as a website, emails, payroll stuffers, and so on), the frequency of the communication, who will be responsible for the communication, and who will be involved in its development.

Illustration."

Two other important considerations are what do the participants want to know about, and what are the areas that will hold the committee accountable. Ultimately, it is the information that will most benefit the participants, and the information that will most improve the plan's governance that are important. Work toward these last two items. These can be giant steps, which may need to be preceded by baby steps as the committee is improving its transparency.

One way to achieve transparency is by having clarity related to the roles and responsibilities of the plan committee, the vendors, management, and staff supporting the plan. If the board or management created the plan and the plan committee, what powers and authority did the board or management retain, and what was delegated to the plan committee, members of the management team, or others? What types of reporting are expected by the board or management?

For example, it should be easy and low risk to provide a listing of committee members, make available the plan documents, provide access to commonly used forms, identify contacts (website, emails, or phone numbers) for questions or certain actions, and list frequently asked questions.[366]

As the plan committee begins upon the path of greater transparency, it needs to be transparent about this change. All members of the committee, vendors, service providers, and also members of the company's management team that interact with the plan need to know that there will be greater transparency, and that interactions with the plan may be publicized. In many

---

[366] Other areas the plan committee can consider, which are a little more complex and have somewhat greater risk, are: publicizing goals, the committee structure, committee meetings agenda and minutes, detail on roles and responsibilities, and accountability, plan financials, investment performance, plan costs and expenses (including investment costs), participant communications, and the conflict of interest policy and code of conduct. In general, any action that impacts participants is worth considering, such as changes in investment funds, how to make investment elections, funding levels, and plan design changes.

cases, just the threat of greater disclosure will help to sanitize many actions.

The Gold Standard in Transparency

Often, governmental plans are subject to the government's freedom of information rules.[367] Because what they do is publically available, they naturally do a good job being transparent. Perhaps it is because transparency is imbedded in how they operate that one finds the gold standard for transparency is owned by two governmental plans.

The first plan is CalPERS. If one scans through the CalPERS website,[368] you will see that *anyone* can see and read about:

- The Board of Administration (which is the oversight body), including the board members and their biography, the Board Committees,[369] and which members serve on which committee
- Board Meetings and Committee Meetings, including notices of meetings, agendas (going back to 2014), handouts from the meetings
- Governance and Policies, including an education policy, governance policy, delegations, gift policy, travel policy, and various policies relating to ethics and conflicts. There are also separate actuarial, financial, investment, and ethics policies
- Benefits Overview, which describes the various benefits available under the program[370]

---

[367] In general, freedom of information laws exists at the Federal level and in most states. The freedom of information laws allow individuals to request information from the government (with certain exceptions). For governmental retirement plans in a state with a freedom of information law, this means that the plan committee agenda, meeting minutes, reports, documents, financial reports, expense reports, and other information can be requested.

[368] https://www.calpers.ca.gov/page/about.

[369] The website gives information on each of the plan's seven committees: Board Governance, Finance & Administration, Global Governance Policy Ad Hoc (subcommittee), Investment, Pension & Health Benefits, Risk & Audit, and Performance, Compensation & Talent Management.

[370] In addition to retirement benefits, CalPERS provides for death, disability,

- Education Center, which covers education events that occur throughout California and online courses
- Forms and Publications, ranging from election forms to historical reports
- Frequently Asked Questions on 61 topics
- Resources for asking questions and contact information
- Information Request (Public Information Request), which allows participants to request information that may not be available through the website

If your committee wants to become fully transparent, then what CalPERS does is an excellent example. If, however, you want to take a small step initially, as you peruse CalPERS' website you will probably find a number of areas that will expand your transparency and be relatively simple to accomplish with lower risk.

The second plan that I see as having a gold standard for transparency is the Ontario Teachers' Pension Plan. The Ontario Teachers' website[371] is about as complete as CalPERS', but it has a more accessible feel. It doesn't feel like a government website, but a website designed by a private company seeking to pull one in and sell one business. Indeed, it has a heading titled, "Our Product," which it goes on to describe as, "[w]e administer a defined benefit pension plan. It pays lifetime pensions to eligible members and their survivors."[372] When introducing their "brand," they have an entertaining one-minute video,[373] which describes their history and their mission, going from a single county focus, to being involved in 50 countries. Like other great slogans, they've captured their mission in a short phrase: *"Pensions mean the world to us."*

Both the CalPERS and Ontario Teachers' websites will be educational and informative. The Ontario Teachers' may also be

---

health, long-term care, and other benefits.

[371] https://www.otpp.com.

[372] https://www.otpp.com/corporate/about-teachers.

[373] Other videos include their annual meeting webcast. *See* https://www.otpp.com/corporate/ontario-teachers-reporting/annual-meeting-webcast.

entertaining, and even inspiring for plan committee members seeking to differentiate themselves, their plans, and their companies from the pack.

Final Thoughts on Transparency with Plan Participants

Like many other areas, communicating with plan participants has been outsourced to third parties. Communications now are often generic discussions watered down from layers of legal review. Reading them, one senses that the writers hope they won't be read or retained.

Granted, the plan committee probably doesn't have its own communications department, or writers that are versed in retirement plan intricacies. This makes it difficult for the plan committee to draft its own communications that are clear, unambiguous, and relevant to the plan participants. But the fact that it is difficult shouldn't mean that the lower standard currently being delivered should be accepted.

I would propose that the plan committee ask itself the following questions regarding participant communications:

- *From whom should the communication come?* For most companies, they are generic mailings or postings on a website, and not from the plan committee or its chair. Instead of coming from a nameless source, you may want to consider having the communication come from or have a letter or preface from an individual (such as the committee chair or a member, or even the CEO). These have been among the more effective communications I've seen.
- *What should be covered in the communication?* Rather than generic information, address items and areas specific to the company and the plan. What's changed (like investment lineups), and *why.* I've found that participants are typically impressed to understand that there is a process for overseeing investments and selecting new alternatives. Plan design changes, vendor changes, website changes, or service changes are specific topics that are

often of interest to participants (beyond the routinely communicated investment performance). The names and background of who is overseeing the plan can be comforting when there is a skilled, credentialed, and experienced team on the plan committee.

- *What questions are coming from participants?* Tracking and then responding to common or recurring questions from participants can be helpful. A question asked by several participants is probably on the minds of many more.

- *Related to what questions are coming from participants is where does the participant stand in relation to its retirement accumulation?* Interactive modeling is ideal if available, but at a minimum, the plan committee can provide guidance on how to calculate what would be an adequate savings target or caution participants who are clearly not saving enough (*e.g.,* nothing or a low percentage).[374] I'm not suggesting the plan committee give investment advice, but it can work to educate the plan participants.

- *Do participants have misperceptions that can be cleared up?* There are numerous misperceptions about retirement plans, from participants who have been misinformed by a relative or friend to a plain lack of understanding or having never received information. I've seen participants think their money wasn't in a trust; their 401(k) assets would be lost in the case of bankruptcy; their contributions ultimately decreased their Social Security benefits; they couldn't borrow their money; and they couldn't direct their own investments (thinking that it was managed by "Wall Street").

- *How can communication alleviate concerns that might exist about conflicts?* For many participants, the scandals of the early 2000s are still fresh, and the market drop caused by Wall Street in 2008 creates pause if not outright distrust.

---

[374] I've seen scenarios where a very low-paid individual would receive a relatively high level of replacement income just from Social Security. Just because one is saving zero percent for retirement does not mean they will have inadequate retirement income.

The plan committee should address the process it follows and the actions it takes to avoid conflicts at the committee level, and also what it requires of vendors and advisors to attempt to avoid conflicts.

A Radical Idea: Meet with the Participants!

It is uncommon, indeed it is unheard of, for plan committee members to meet with plan participants. This just seems so bizarre to me.

If someone was holding your largest assets (other than your house), wouldn't you want to meet with them? It is like a lawyer, an architect, an engineer, a painter, or a builder not meeting with their client. Where else does one see a relationship like this where the person charged with doing the work doesn't meet with the people for whom the work is getting done?

If you're in the participant's shoes, wouldn't you want to be able to provide feedback on whether the web-portal was easy to use or hindered your participation, whether the plan communication and education were clear and encouraged participation, and whether the investments were appropriate for individuals with your background and education level? Wouldn't you think that the plan committee might want to understand the participants' perspectives before establishing a mission or goals?

These are clearly potential benefits for meeting with participants (or getting more direct feedback). Indeed, imagine the plan committee meeting with participants and getting glowing feedback about the plan's administration, communication, education, portal, cost-management, and investments. It seems that might make it harder for a class-action lawsuit to gain a foothold. The opposite point is also true; it would help if the plan committee gets feedback that the participants don't understand the communications or the investments. Then the committee understands that it might need to work on those areas and address the participants' concerns before they fester into a lawsuit.

Of course, a reason why you don't see many plan committees meeting with participants is that having those meetings can raise their own set of risks. If the committee members become aware of problems, they may feel that they have the burden of having to confront the problems. Also, the participants might have conflicting views, which can be unhelpful or even distracting. Finally, the plan committee members might make inappropriate comments or make promises that are hard or impossible to keep.

This is another area where it might be possible to move forward gradually. For example, surveying a sample of participants to get feedback can provide some data, as can having small focus group sessions that delve into participants' thinking. The results can be published in a summary or a newsletter that solicits feedback.

Granted, your recordkeeper or actuary may have experience with similar plans, which can provide some insight. Insight from other plans, however, is not a substitute for what *your* participants think about *your* plan. At the end of the day, you're a fiduciary for *your* plan, and what matters most is what *your* participants think.

Pricing Transparency Illustration

How might greater transparency in plan pricing work in practice? Let's assume that the plan committee would like to be more transparent about the fees and costs the plan pays, and how these fees and costs benchmark against similar plans with similar missions.[375] To begin getting the necessary information, the committee can start requiring that vendors and service providers provide more detail related to their fees. The following are several data points that the committee might request:

- How the fee is charged or calculated, such as whether it is charged by the time incurred (and what is the hourly rate), by the number of transactions, based on the amount of assets in the plan, or in another manner. Some examples of these types of charges include:

    o Plan design changes or mergers of plans are often charged based on the hours the changes will take (or a flat fee based on an estimate of how long the changes will take).
    o Qualified domestic relations orders[376] (QDROs) are often charged a flat fee for each order processed.
    o Investment advisory fees are often based on the amount of assets in the plan.
    o The recordkeeping fee (which usually covers accounting for contributions, distributions, and earnings), is often based on a blend of the amount of assets in the plan and the number of participants.

---

[375] Greater transparency is definitely needed in the area of plan costs. A GAO report found that 80% of plan participants do not know what they pay for their retirement account. U.S. Gov't Accountability Office, *Private Pensions: Changes Needed to Provide 401(k) Plan Participants and the Department of Labor Better Information of Fees*, GAO-07-2 (November 2006), www.gao.gov/new.items/d0721.pdf.

[376] QDROs are court orders pursuant to a divorce that split plan assets. These orders need to meet certain requirements under ERISA and there is often a fee charged by the recordkeeper or counsel it uses to review the QDRO.

- A listing of activities that are bundled and not charged separately. For example, recordkeepers will often perform plan contribution limit testing, discrimination testing, and prepare a Form 5500 for the plan "for free" or as part of the total cost of the plan's administration.
- How the fees have changed over time. For example, if a fee is based on the level of plan assets, and assets are rising, are fees rising without any additional work being performed by the vendor?
- Benchmark information to compare what the plan is paying compared to like plans. This is usually not secured from the vendor or service provider that the committee is analyzing. They naturally have conflicts in comparing their fees and costs, so it is best to get independent advice. It is important to compare like plans (similar number of participants, similar level of assets, and similar complexity) that have a similar mission.

Quick Hits

1. Ask vendors and service providers to increase their transparency by providing greater information about key oversight areas, using the evaluation criteria and applying one of the indicators outlined on pages 280-281.

2. Develop a transparency plan for the plan committee that:
   a. Provides participants with the information they desire
   b. Progresses gradually in a way that promotes transparency and manages risk

Succession Planning

"I try to buy stock in businesses that are so wonderful that an idiot can run them. Because sooner or later, one will."
Warren Buffett

"One of the things we often miss in succession planning is that it should be gradual and thoughtful, with lots of sharing of information and knowledge and perspective, so that it's almost a non-event when it happens."
Anne M. Mulcahy, Prior CEO of Xerox

Introduction

Succession planning has nothing to do with the attainment of current goals and immediate success. It is all about the future, and a change that will occur at some indeterminate, potentially distant time. For these reasons, succession planning can seem to be a low priority, unimportant, and even mundane because it lacks any immediate impact. That perspective would be misplaced.

This is because succession planning isn't about planning for an isolated event, such as the replacement of one plan committee member. It is about developing a process for having the entire next generation of leaders and key players for the plan identified, trained, and prepared to drive the plan's future success.

Succession for plan committees can be complicated and confused by the company's succession planning. For example, plan committee member status is often dictated by one's company title, such as CFO or VP-HR. At first blush, having this pre-defined structure appears to make succession planning easier. However, if the company isn't proactive in planning for succession for these positions, then there is a succession gap for the committee. No company successor can mean no plan committee member successor.

Similarly, a company with a culture that is weak in planning for succession will have to overcome inherent inertia related to the plan's succession. If the successors for executive roles are not identified, it may be difficult or impossible to identify plan committee member successors for those same executives. The failure of the company to identify successors for its executive positions will not, however, excuse the plan fiduciaries from their obligations.

Resolving weaknesses in a company's culture for succession planning is beyond the scope of this book, but there are pragmatic ways to help the plan committee drive success, regardless of the environment in which it finds itself.

Corporate Succession Planning

Succession planning is clearly recognized as an important principle for corporate, private business, and not-for-profit entities.[377] It's been called "... perhaps the most important job of corporate boards."[378] Preparing the next generation of plan committee members for the challenges they'll have to address makes succession planning one of the most important jobs of the plan committee.

In a study on CEO succession, PwC's group, *Strategy&,* found, "[f]ailed CEO successions are usually a result of boards having allowed succession planning to fall off their regular agenda. This happens a lot, because many boards treat succession as a discrete

---

[377] *See e.g.,* OECD, *G20/OECD Principles of Corporate Governance* (OECD Publishing, Paris 2015) *at 48, available at* www.oecd-library.org/docserver/download/2615021e.pdf?expires=1504749225&d=id&accname=guest&checksum=7826fd4e6f7d248C25464ae511207acd, and Business Roundtable, *Principles of Corporate Governance – 2016* at 3, *available at* https://businessroundtable.org/sites/default/files/Principles-of-Corporate-Governance-2016.pdf.

[378] Donald Delves, *The Critical Task of Succession Planning*, Forbes (March 31, 2011).

event, not as a process...."[379] Ignoring succession planning means that you are temporarily enjoying success now, but securing failure at some point in the future. Keep it on your agenda.

Planning for Whose Succession?

Succession planning is a clear need for a corporate Board or the company's executive officers. Because the plan committee is essentially the Board for the retirement plan, succession planning is equally important for it. The plan committee should, however, extend its interest in succession planning beyond the committee to cover key staff, vendors, and advisors.

The questions asked by the plan committee need to go beyond who will replace each of our members and how can we ensure they are well prepared? The committee also needs to ask who will replace the key people working on the plan should they leave, and what entity could replace a vendor that suddenly goes out of business or loses its focus? From this perspective, succession planning is risk management for turnover.

When planning for succession, the committee should include in its review any entity or individual whose loss would impact the accomplishment of the plan's goals and mission. For most committees, this would generally encompass:

- The plan committee members
- The investment advisor
- Other individuals who are plan fiduciaries
- Investment funds (with an eye toward any key investment managers at those funds)
- The vendor handling the plan's recordkeeping and administrative functions and key individuals at the vendor handling the plan
- Plan actuarial firm and the key individual actuary

---

[379] Ken Favaro, Per-Ola Karlsson and Gary L. Neilson, *The $112 Billion CEO Succession Problem*, Strategy + Business (May 4, 2015, Issue 79) *available at* https://www.strategy-business.com/article/00327?gko=8dfe1.

- External plan advisors and consultants, especially those with intimate knowledge of the plan's operation and history
- ERISA counsel for the plan
- Internal staff who are intimately familiar with the plan administration and history, such as manager of benefits and potentially individuals in Finance, IT, or Payroll who support plan functions

This list may not be appropriate for your plan. It might not be comprehensive enough, or it might be too long. It can, however, serve as a starting point or a straw model to build upon or deconstruct as the plan committee considers succession.

It is noteworthy, however, that the plan committee is just one of the nine areas on this list for succession planning consideration. Even if the company has done a poor job in identifying the successor for an executive and thereby created a gap in the succession for the plan committee, the committee can nevertheless close the succession gap in the other eight areas.

Ways to Prepare for and Simplify Succession

If your company has succession planning as part of its culture, then you're ahead of the game. There's an existing process for developing executives, and staff and individuals are ready to step up and assume more responsible roles.

If, however, you don't have a succession planning culture, here are some actions the committee can take to prepare for and simplify succession planning, and reduce the risk of unexpected turnover.

- *Identify the roles that are critical* – Some of the roles that potentially are critical are discussed in the bullets above. Don't just rely on that straw model. Have the staff that reports to the plan committee look at the various roles, individuals, and vendors, and determine if they vanished, how difficult it would be to replace them. If the void caused by their disappearance can be cured by better documentation of their roles, processes, and tools, then the challenge is defined and can be overcome relatively easily with some solid discipline. If, however, better documentation won't help and it is necessary to find and prepare a potential replacement, the challenge is different and will require a different approach.[380]

- *Clearly document the roles, responsibilities, and accountability of key players* – Having clarity about roles, responsibilities, and accountability is essential to have successful succession. Such clarity makes transition easier by providing a clear path for development, specificity about the duties, and clarity related to the expectations.

- *Outsource succession planning where possible* – There may be roles that are being done by staff within the company that can be outsourced. If these roles are outsourced, the committee can require the vendor to develop and provide a succession plan for that role. Examples of roles that could be, and often are, outsourced are the investment advisor and ERISA counsel.

- *Develop a plan to accelerate the transfer of knowledge and skills* – Plan, prepare, and execute the best knowledge and skills transfer you can muster. Be prepared to quickly assess the new individual's knowledge and skills and be prepared to supplement those areas where there are gaps. This can include having the assessment tools completed; training material established; key documents related to the plan (or the areas where they are responsible) well documented and organized;[381] allowing sufficient time for reading the material; and access to advisors, consultants, and ERISA counsel to bring the material to life. If there is

---

[380] Compare the loss of a person in payroll who processes the employee payroll deductions to the loss of legal counsel who has advised the committee on fiduciary issues. One succession might require only better documentation, but the other might require that a second attorney be introduced and made familiar with the committee and its deliberative process.

Another approach to consider is rotating positions on the committee, so new members shadow for a year and then serve for a prescribed time.

[381] Having *complete* documentation *easily accessible* is very important when trying to acclimate a new member or other individual assuming a new role. The last chapter in this book touches on documentation that will help with these transitions.

some period of overlap between the old and new individuals, provide opportunities to attend meetings or participate in the work done by the outgoing individual. Let the training to transfer the knowledge and skills be multidimensional: reading, meetings, hands-on, and formal.

- *Plan for succession where you can* – Even if you can't identify the successor for plan committee members, you can plan for succession for individuals at vendors and in internal roles. Although this sounds simple, this too can be difficult. It is not always easy to have succession in place for key plan roles where that individual reports to someone who isn't on the plan committee. For example, there may be some individuals in IT or Payroll that have critical roles, but the department heads have other priorities. To achieve good governance (and potentially fulfill your fiduciary duties), committee members need to try to improve succession planning and avoid the potential risk of unexpected turnover. They may run into obstacles or they may not be able to achieve their goal in certain situations. The plan committee can only work toward achieving its goals; there are things it won't be able to control, and the committee shouldn't (in theory) be judged based on things outside of its control.

- *Manage the risk associated with transition and personnel or vendor disruptions* – Even with the best planned successions, there can be risks and problems. Mike Tyson once said, "Everyone has a plan, until they get punched in the mouth." So, you have a succession plan? Assume your plan just got punched in the mouth and is on the canvas out cold. What's your plan now? Before this happens, take the time to identify ways to manage the risk when there is a void during a transition. For example, should other members take on more responsibility, more meetings, or temporary outsourcing of select functions? Plan B shouldn't be hoping someone has smelling salts handy.

- *Keep succession on the agenda* – At least annually, have time dedicated to reviewing succession (at all levels) for the plan. This can include reviewing the succession plan, the succession process, revisiting documentation, and determining whether succession planning was successful when it's happened.

Succession Planning Beyond the Committee

Running a retirement plan is a team sport. It takes strength in all the positions to be successful, and it takes bench strength to have long-term success. A weakness in one position can seriously handicap the team, and losing a key player without backup can be catastrophic.

All too often, however, plan committees focus on their individual superstars. Perhaps you feel like your investment advisor or ERISA counsel is a superstar in their area. They seem to always know the way to reach the goal and never fumble or commit an error. Maybe they are superstars, but if anything happens to them, how deep is your bench? Even if they stay on the team and remain healthy, do they have quality players supporting them in the other positions to help them achieve the plan's goals?

The plan committee is like the general manager, picking the coaches, scouts, and trainer to execute the day-to-day. The GM holds the coaches, scouts, and trainers responsible for fielding a strong team for every game and with enough depth to do so for a long season. The difference between most sports teams and a retirement plan, however, is that the retirement plan's season never ends. Are you prepared to go the distance?

The plan committee should have as one of the responsibilities of the key vendors and internal company staff that they will have clear documentation about their roles and responsibilities, that someone is trained to take over those roles and responsibilities during temporary absences or disruptions, and they have a process for training a permanent successor. Periodically, the vendor or staff members should report to the committee on their preparation for these initiatives. In addition, periodically the vendor or staff member should have their successor or temporary replacement assume their role so they can experience fulfilling the actual roles and responsibilities. The successors or replacements should get their hands on the ball in controlled situations so their first live interaction isn't during a crisis.

Quick Hits

1. Identify the individuals, entities, and roles where a succession plan is needed. See the list on pages 295-296 for guidance.

2. Have the roles and responsibilities for key players documented to make succession easier.

3. Have a plan developed to accelerate the transfer of knowledge and skills following a succession.

4. Keep succession on the agenda!

Periodic Assessments

"There is surely nothing quite so useless as doing with great efficiently what should not be done at all."[382]
Peter Drucker

"[T]he entrepreneur always searches for change, responds to it, and exploits it as an opportunity."[383]
Peter Drucker

Introduction

We've come to the next to last of the 12 governance principles. The principle of periodic assessments has been saved for near the end because it is literally the opportunity to look back and critically reflect on all that the plan committee has done. It ranges from the simple and obvious assessments of the goals and objectives the committee has set, to the broadest assessments of the committee's governance of the plan. Indeed, the Department of Labor regulations provide:

> At reasonable intervals the performance of trustees and other fiduciaries should be reviewed by the appointing fiduciary in such manner as may be reasonably expected to ensure that their performance has been in compliance with the terms of the plan and statutory standards, and satisfies the needs of the plan.[384]

The assessment process is the way in which the committee paves the path for future improvements in all areas, even in areas where it believes it is performing well.

---

[382] Peter Drucker, "Peter Drucker on Managerial Courage." Harvard Business School, Working Knowledge (June 12, 2006), available at https://hbswk.hbs.edu/archive/peter-drucker-on-managerial-courage.
[383] Peter Drucker, Innovation and Entrepreneurship (Routledge Classics 2015) at 33.
[384] 29 C.F.R. § 2509.75-8 FR-17.

Types of Periodic Assessments

Retirement plan assessments can take a number of forms and involve many facets of plan governance. I've spend a good part of my career conducting or assisting plan committees with assessments spanning a variety of areas. Areas the plan committee can assess include:

- Governance[385]
- Objectives and strategy
- Risk management and controls
- Compliance and fiduciary responsibility
- Vendor management (including performance and billing)
- Investments (assets and liabilities) and investment advisors
- Technology and systems
- Costs, fees, and billing
- Conflict management
- Process reviews[386]
- Participant complaints
- Efficiency and quality

Periodic assessments should not, however, stop at the plan committee level, but should be incorporated by every group or individual with responsibility for the plan. Most plans have annual assessments done for the plan's investments, but it is also important to have this done in areas involving plan administration. Just as it is important to assess how the plan's investments are performing against benchmarks, it's also important to consider:

- How many errors or mistakes have occurred (in enrollments, elections, distributions, call center advice, amendments, compliance, data transfers, and the like)?

---

[385] Governance can include committee structure, delegations, committee operations, and effectiveness of the plan committee charter.
[386] Process reviews can compare actual operations to existing processes and procedures, and also existing processes and procedures to best practices.

- Have benchmarks or goals been met in areas such as transmitting participant contributions, making distributions, up-time for participant-facing systems, reconciliations of data, and the like?
- Have vendors met contracted minimum standards?
- Is there training designed to improve quality, understanding, responsiveness, timing, cost and risk management, and rates of return? Is it effective and actually driving improvements in those areas?

Who Performs the Assessments, and How Frequently Should They Be Done?

A periodic assessment can be an internal review, a review done by an independent internal group (such as internal audit), or by an outside third party. Indeed, it is helpful to use all three to gain the advantage of different perspectives, the experience of specialized expertise, and share the load of doing the reviews among different groups.

Except in rare situations, the plan committee does not have dedicated staff that can oversee or perform these audits or reviews. Accordingly, a solution is to leverage existing audits or reviews whenever possible. For example, the annual ERISA audit (performed for the Form 5500 filing) can be expanded so there is additional testing performed related to risk management, data transfers, data integrity, enrollments, or other areas. Similarly, an internal audit being performed on HR can include a review of some of the areas related to the plan.

Although it is enticing to attempt to try to expand an existing review to include every possible area, that approach isn't practical from a timing, budget, or expertise perspective. An approach that works well when the plan committee is unaware of the relative risks or priorities is to perform a high-level risk assessment. This high-level risk assessment will help the plan committee understand the larger risks and allow it to prioritize future reviews. In situations where the plan committee has questions or concerns, or is already aware of risks, it can undertake a detailed review of those areas.

Other ways to add efficiency to the reviews is to try to address similar areas simultaneously, and try to have a cycle for the reviews. For example, assume the plan committee has determined that the compensation data being used by payroll to calculate participant deferrals in a 401(k) plan might be inaccurate.[387] When reviewing this compensation data, it might be efficient to also examine other payroll data that is being used for plan purposes, such as compensation data used to determine who is highly compensated or for testing purposes.

Once a review area is identified, it can help to build that review into a cycle or long-term schedule. In the prior example, the review of compensation being used by payroll might be something that is reviewed once every five years (or sooner if issues are identified or there are payroll system changes). This avoids subjecting the same groups or vendors to constant reviews, allows them time to improve their processes and controls, and allows for other areas to be assessed.

The frequency of the reviews depends on the environment. For example, higher risk areas (such as areas where the plan has had compliance problems), will need to be reviewed more frequently. The following is a list of environmental factors and higher risk areas that may increase the frequency of when an area is reviewed:[388]

- New laws or regulations
- Changes in the plan design or terms
- Change in vendors, the type of vendors, their service, or contracts
- Change in the company or plan personnel responsible for the plan operations, controls, or compliance
- Changes (including degradation, outsourcing, or automation) to processes or controls

---

[387] This can easily occur when payroll codes are added, changed, or removed and are not properly mapped to the plan definition of compensation.
[388] The first six of these environmental factors are the same "risk events" that are discussed starting on page 18.

- Changes to the company's or vendor's systems or technology involved in plan operations (calculations, data storage or management, and the like)
- Plan merger or split off
- Areas with higher degree of manual intervention
- Change from insourced to outsourced, or vice versa
- Areas identified as higher risk or that have had problems or issues
- Areas that are higher cost, higher volume, or higher frequency

I've found that if the plan committee is reviewing the plan environment carefully and critically, in most years it will identify that a number of these risk or environmental factors have occurred or are occurring. The illustration in the following box shows how the plan committee would identify and address these areas.

Identifying and Addressing "Environmental Factors"

Sue, the plan committee chair, calls the first plan committee meeting of the year to order. The agenda, as always, is quite aggressive, but the committee has scheduled more than enough time to address all the items.

Sue is pleased at how well the committee is working together and proceeding proactively. At the last meeting of the prior year, the committee asked representatives from the vendors, HR, Internal Audit, Finance, and Legal to prepare summaries of areas where there were changes in systems, personnel, vendors, rules, control, procedures, and the like (*i.e.,* environmental factors). The committee also asked for a report on areas where problems or issues were identified. The presentation of these reports is the first item on the agenda, thereby helping the committee set the goals for the upcoming year.

In the course of the presentation, the committee is reminded of a number of changes that it knew about during the prior year, but it also learns of several new areas. The committee was familiar with the issuance of new regulations that will impact plan operations.

It was also familiar with the fact that its external plan administrator was acquired and the plan operations will be shifting to a new platform. The committee was not aware that the payroll system underwent some changes and that new controls were added and some controls were removed. During the presentations, the committee members took turns drilling deeper into the information in the reports and what was being presented.

In the area of the regulatory changes, they asked:

- How will the new regulations affect plan operations?
- Will it affect some or all plan participants?
- How will this affect costs?
- Are controls being installed to reduce the risk of noncompliance?
- Will the plan need to be amended?
- When are the amendments due, and who is responsible for getting them done?

Because the regulations had limited impact and didn't require a plan amendment, the committee decided to ask for an update at the meeting after the new plan procedures for the regulations were instituted. The committee specifically asked that the report address the testing and controls being used to ensure compliance with the new regulations.

Regarding the change to the new administrative platform, the plan committee members asked:

- When will the transition take place?
- What controls are in place to ensure that the data, elections, transaction and plan rules (or terms) are properly mapped?
- What reporting will be provided during the process?
- What resources will be needed from the company to assist with the transition?
- What guarantees are in place related to the accuracy and completeness of the transition?

After learning that this transition will be occurring for all clients on the plan administrator's platform, that extensive testing and reconciliations will be performed, and that the administrator is guaranteeing 100% accuracy on the transition, the plan committee decides on its initial approach. It asks for a report on the results of the testing, including copies of the summary test data with reconciliations and test results. The chair asks that the year following the transition, the company's Internal Audit team test a sample of participant accounts to review participants' elections, contributions, and account balances before and after the transition.

Finally, for the payroll control changes, the plan committee wanted to know:
- Are the areas being changed areas that impact plan operations?
- What testing will be performed to ensure the accuracy of the change?
- Will the new controls replace the controls being removed?
- What risks will not be controlled or mitigated after the transition that are controlled before?
- What testing will be done by Payroll?

After learning that both Payroll and Internal Audit will be performing extensive testing, including assessing the new control environment, the plan committee made a decision. It decided that following the completion of the testing, it would like both Payroll and Internal Audit to present the results of the testing so it can decide if any other review or assessment of the area is needed.

Sue feels that the plan committee has taken the necessary steps to protect the plan participants, and is doing so without incurring unnecessary additional costs. She is looking to all the experts in the various areas for their support, but she and the other committee members aren't blindly relying on them. They know they are being held accountable, and will need to prove what they've represented to the committee at a meeting in the near future.

Quick Hits

1. At least annually, the plan committee should self-assess its performance on how it is governing the plan. Periodically, the committee should have its performance assessed by a third party.

2. The plan committee should identify areas that should be assessed each year (as part of its goal-setting process).
   a. The area(s) to be assessed should be based on risks, compliance, review efficiencies, or other priorities and considerations.
   b. When selecting areas to review, the committee should consider the environmental factors listed on pages 305-306.
   c. The committee should cycle between having the periodic assessments be self-assessments, performed by company (independent) resources such as Internal Audit, and external vendors for an independent and different perspective.

Oversight

"Boards don't need to hear how busy the CEO is – they need to hear about results."[389]
Jim Brown

"Coaches who can outline plays on a black board are a dime a dozen. The ones who win get inside their players and motivate."
Vince Lombardi

Introduction

If the plan committee had just one governance principle to adhere to, it would be oversight. Oversight is the primary role of the plan committee; oversight defines the function and purpose of the committee. All other governance principles are subsumed into its oversight responsibility. The committee is responsible for overseeing risk management, compliance, clear performance measures, succession, and so on.

Far too often, however, the plan committee becomes a passenger on the plan's journey, and it neither sets the destination nor plots the course. It defers to the "experts," the vendors, the attorneys, and the consultants who drive the agenda, set the goals, and control the discussion leading to decisions. To fulfill its oversight role, the plan committee must leave the passenger seat and take control as the captain. Rather than deferring to the "experts," oversight demands that the committee use them as tools of the plan committee that serve at its pleasure.[390]

---

[389] <u>The Imperfect Board Member</u> *supra* at 85.
[390] And the committee's pleasure is always based on fulfilling its fiduciary duties to the plan participants.

What is Oversight?

At its essence, oversight is the responsibility to oversee an area. It means holding entities and groups accountable.[391] This means defining in advance what is expected, and checking on whether what is promised is done, timely and correctly. It involves *managing* the vendors, groups, and individuals that work on the plan. But it goes beyond this managerial role and encompasses key leadership attributes.

Oversight lets the plan committee ensure that the plan's various vendors and individuals working on the plan are focused on the larger *mission* and underlying goals of the plan. For example, if having low cost is part of the mission, do part of the activities of the vendors and individuals include actions to identify new cost reductions or improve efficiency?

But oversight also gives the plan committee the duty to *motivate* everyone working on the plan. The committee can push everyone beyond bare expectation. Don't just be compliance, but change compliance into a tool to be more efficient. Don't just try to avoid risk. Analyze it to take advantage and capitalize on risks that others overestimate and avoid due to an overabundance of caution.

Oversight, therefore, encompasses *overseeing and leading* with these three characteristics:

- *Managing* (toward accountability)
- Driving the *Mission*
- *Motivating* the Team

---

[391] To a large extent, the "roles, responsibility, and accountability" principle lays the foundation for who has what role and responsibility, and to whom are they accountable. Oversight builds on this foundation of information and has the committee implement it. But it goes beyond just managing.

How to Implement Good Oversight

The role of the plan committee is similar to that of a director for a movie. The committee members are not playing any of the roles, but they're providing guidance on what should be done and what is expected. They're also the judge of whether what is done is acceptable or if it will fall to the cutting-room floor.

The committee can provide direction and oversight, detail expectation and goals, and help establish criteria and plans. It can, and should, provide feedback on the work that is being done, especially if it is below expectations, late, or costs more than anticipated.

There are several tools that help with oversight, and they are part of the 12 governance principles. For illustration, here is how some of the governance principles serve as oversight tools:

- Clear Roles, Responsibilities, and Accountability – Start with a clear set of roles, responsibilities, and accountabilities, and use them as the framework for what is expected from vendors and staff. They should be clear about who is reporting to whom. The plan committee will want to be sure that it gets its reports, but also that each managing individual or entity is providing oversight and getting the reports they're expecting. When gaps in the roles, responsibilities, and accountabilities are identified (for example, it isn't clear who is responsible for a certain action), force that it be resolved and that the documentation is updated.
- Rigid Accountability – Everyone needs to expect that they will be held accountable, and the plan committee needs to actually hold all the vendors and staff accountable. This can involve placing deadlines, milestones, or report presentations on the agenda for a future meeting, or when items are expected to be circulated to the committee members.
- Use Company Management Tools – Companies will use various tools to help their management team and boards oversee the company and projects. Leverage these tools

and the familiarity that plan committee members will have for these tools. For example, be mindful of whether they're used to seeing status reported on a dashboard, through the use of "traffic lights," or via another tool.

- Have Vendors and Staff Work with the Committee's Schedule - To effectively oversee the plan, the plan committee needs to have useful information far enough in advance of the scheduled meetings so the members can digest and understand it. Don't let vendors or staff spring presentations and reports at the last minute unless there is truly an unexpected crisis.

- Have Agenda Items Tied to the Plan's Mission or Goals – If someone wants to present something to the plan committee, and it doesn't relate to the plan's mission or any of the plan's current goals, that agenda item should be questioned and perhaps removed.[392] The plan committee's time is valuable, and the mission and goals are what it needs to focus on. Stay on task. Cut irrelevant items.

- Limit Presenter Time – On the agenda the amount of time each part of the meeting should take should be identified. This helps prioritize the topics and lets the committee spend more time on more important topics. (For example, a status update on an ongoing project might be three minutes, while a final report on a vendor change might be 30 minutes.) It is also helpful to have the presenters identified with their role, and what is expected of them during the meeting. (Is the presentation strictly informational, or are they providing a recommendation?)

- Before the meeting, each plan committee member should receive a copy of the draft agenda (so they can comment on it and request any changes) and a summary of the progress toward the various goals.

---

[392] This will generally apply to non-committee members. For example, vendors may want to add an item to the agenda because it advances *their* goal of selling more work, a new fund or a product. In general, committee members should be allowed to explore items that may be outside the current goals or missions if they believe it is in the best interest of the plan participants.

Challenges in Overseeing Oneself

It isn't uncommon for the individual who is responsible for the administration of the retirement plan to also be a member of the plan committee, or one of the primary advisors to the committee. For example, the Director of Benefits or the VP-HR might be charged with administering the plans on a day-to-day basis, and handling the vast majority of interactions with the vendors, legal counsel and others. This creates a situation where the person handling the plan administration is overseeing (at least in part), their own work. (It also creates the risk of conflicts of interest.)

From a practical perspective it makes sense to have the individual with the most experience and current knowledge of the plan's operation involved with the committee (either as a member or an advisor). Nevertheless, the committee still needs to exercise its oversight responsibilities. Some best practices in this regard include:

- Make an extra effort to have the committee take the lead in setting goals. In addition, identify areas where the member who is acting in dual roles might be making decisions that could be fiduciary decisions. In these situations, be sure the committee has given the individual clear criteria to use when making these decisions. This helps insure that it is the committee, and not the individual, that is acting as a fiduciary.
- Have the individual step out of their committee role when reporting on the work being done in their area. In some situations, I've seen the individual move from their seat so they're presenting to the committee, rather than sitting alongside the other committee members.
- Acknowledge at the beginning of these discussions the areas of potential conflict (such as incentive pay opportunities), and decide how to address any conflicts.

Quick Hits

1. Incorporate into all of the plan committee's activities its core function of oversight. View oversight as consisting of the three key components:
    a. *Managing* (toward accountability)
    b. Driving the *mission*
    c. *Motivating* the team

   Use the tools on pages 312-313 to help provide focus to the committee's oversight.

2. Consider incorporating the best practices from page 314 if any committee member is potentially in the position of overseeing themself or their team.

Documents and Documentation

*"Documentation is a love letter that you
write to your future self."*
Damian Conway

Introduction

I despise the chore of collecting documents and creating documentation. It seems to distract one from the immediate needs of the plan and future planning. What can the collection of documents have to do with good plan governance? How can such mundane activities support the elevated role of the plan committee as an oversight body?

Despite my dislike for collecting documents and the whole exercise of documentation, this is a vitally important and exceptionally easy exercise for the plan committee to take to advance its goal of good governance. The goal is to collect documents that support the existence of good governance, and emphasize the collection of *documentation of activity* that is critical to good governance.

Focus on Documents and Documentation that Support Plan Governance

Focusing on a select number of key governance documents and documentation activities accomplishes several goals:

- It requires that there be *evidence of activity* necessary to support good governance. For example, requiring that performance standards be measured and documented regularly (*e.g.,* annually) forces the activity of evaluating performance to occur with some regularity.
- It creates an *early warning system* that notifies the plan committee of activities that are not occurring or areas that

have not been properly addressed. For example, the plan committee might require that the investment policy statement be updated by the investment advisor annually, that plan committee minutes be published, and that Legal provides a report on plan compliance. If these documents are not provided, it is a warning to the committee that the IPS hasn't been adequately reviewed, the committee hasn't been holding meetings, or Legal has not addressed all the compliance issues.

Delegating Responsibility for Documents and Documentation, and Keeping the Plan Committee Apprised

As noted earlier, collecting documents and documentation is not the role of the plan committee. However, like most activity, the plan committee can and should delegate the responsibility for annually (or more frequently) collecting the necessary documents and documentation. Like any delegation, the committee should be clear on *who* owns this duty, *what* needs to be done, *what* is the format, *when* it is expected, *where* it will be stored, and *how* it should be presented.

In my experience, it has been easiest to have one or two individuals or groups responsible for collecting the plan documents and documentation. In several cases, the investment advisor has taken on this role and even established a web-portal that contained all the documents to support the plan committee. In other cases, the corporate accounting or financial reporting team collected these documents to facilitate the annual external plan audit.

The documents and documentation that need to be collected are those documents that:

- Are required to operate the plan and establish its governance structure
- Are required to establish compliance
- Help manage and minimize risk
- Support the avoidance of conflicts

- Support the establishment and oversight of performance measures
- Expand transparency and accountability
- Support the fulfillment of the plan committee's fiduciary duties
- Improve knowledge and skills

For illustration, the following are *some* of the documents and documentation that would support the list provided. (The documents described in the following bullets correspond to the item in the prior bulleted list.)

- Plan document and amendments, governance charter, trust document
- Plan compliance tests, governmental filings, 404(c) legal opinion, Form ADV
- Risk assessments, investment risk analysis, legal risk evaluation
- Vendor contracts with performance measures, performance reports from vendors, performance reviews done of vendors
- Plan committee goals and objectives, meeting agendas and meeting minutes; participant communications
- Cost analysis, investment analysis, diversification studies, participant investment studies
- Training and orientation material for new members, legislative and regulatory updates, investment training, and the like

In addition to collecting the documents and documentation, the plan committee should provide instructions on the format in which the documents and documentation will be collected and presented to the committee. *The manner in which the information is presented to the plan committee is critical and will dictate whether the information is actionable by the committee.* The individuals or groups responsible for collecting the documents or documentation must know or understand the subsequent facts or events that can trigger the need for the document or documentation to be updated. The following is an example of some of the documents from the list presented, and what the individual or group gathering the information should consider.

Document	Last Update	Events Triggering Need to Update	Develop-ments	Risks
Plan Doc	2012	Legislative or regulatory change; plan operational change; vendor change	Law change in 2014; vendor change in 2016	Plan not current with law or vendor operations; update required
404(c) Opinion	2013	Change in investment funds or information available to participants	Investments changed in 2014	Unclear if new investments satisfy 404(c); update required
Form ADV	2016	Required annually	NA	Form ADV required for 2017
Vendor Contract	2007	Vendor change, change in contract terms; generally review every 3-6 years	Last contract over 6 years old	Review contract for competitive pricing and service level, addition of performance measures, etc.

The plan committee doesn't receive the detailed list with all the document and documentation requirements. Rather, the committee receives an exception report, showing only those areas where there are problems or issues with the documents or documentation.

As part of the plan committee's oversight role, it will periodically ask for feedback and a critical review of what is being collected on the document and documentation list from its partners (*e.g.*, Legal, Finance, vendors, HR, investment advisors, and so forth). The review will look for items where documents or documentation is being collected that are not important to the good governance of the plan. If they do not help with the plan's governance (compliance, controls, risk management, vendor management, and the like), there is no longer a need to collect those documents or that documentation. However, if there are areas that are key to supporting the good governance of the plan that are not being collected and overseen, one would hope that the plan committee's partners will highlight those absences so they can be included for the future.

When It Should Be Collected

Practically, some of the documents and documentation will be collected in conjunction with meetings of the plan committee. In other cases, they will only be collected once a year to complete the oversight function being performed by the plan committee.

I find that, at a minimum, the documents and documentation need to be collected at least once per year. In general, it is helpful to collect the documents in anticipation of the meeting at which the plan committee assesses its progress against the goals it established for the past year, and is looking forward to establishing new goals. (This is usually the first or last meeting of the year.) Collecting the documents at this time also gathers the documents that might be required as part of the annual ERISA financial audit.

Where It Will Be Stored

I've seen the documents and documentation needed to support good governance stored in three-ring binders and locked away in the corporate secretary's safe. Secure, but inaccessible and ultimately unable to support and improve good governance.

The best approach for *where to store* the documents and documentation is one that is readily accessible, such as on a web-portal that is available to all of the plan committee members and the extended support staff for the committee. The web-portal is for informational purposes only; it is not where working copies are stored, or where individuals are drafting documents.

Because the web-portal is to support the plan committee's oversight role, it only contains the final version of documents. In addition, the documents stored on the web-portal should be read only. Neither committee members nor staff should be able to change these documents.

How It Should Be Presented

The information from the earlier table highlighting Risks and Events Triggering the Need to Update (or the exception report), can be on a spreadsheet or a dashboard. Different committees will have different preferences on the actual presentation of the information. It should be in a manner that is most comfortable for the plan committee. The form of how it is presented is, in my opinion, not as important as the fact that it is timely presented to the plan committee.

Often, staff will want to resolve all issues so there are not exceptions on the report or issues for the committee to consider. This can take time, and it is counter to the goals of transparency and the committee's oversight role. They don't need to be shielded from any problems; they need to be made aware of them so they can plan and govern effectively.

Epilogue

*"We are all in the gutter, but some of us are
looking at the stars."*
Oscar Wilde

"The enemy of a good plan is the dream of a perfect plan."[393]
Carl von Clausewitz

What defines successful plan committees and outstanding plan committee members? There's obviously a lot of work that goes into it, and being successful involves a multitude of facets and skills. There are, however, several elements that are always present in successful committees and members (and absent from those committees and members that are not successful).

The elements are enthusiasm for the role, a passion for the plan participants (your employees, co-workers, and their families), and a drive to gain new experience and new knowledge. Another element is ownership of the role. Successful committees see that they are *the* governing body, and they own the responsibility for the plan, and the participants' success.

Begin today to blaze the path forward for your plan and your participants. Start by setting goals that will improve the plan—simple, attainable goals that over time progressively take the plan to excellence. Work as a team. Be sure that everyone is clear on their roles; hold everyone accountable. Build on the team's expertise and strength but allow everyone to identify their weaknesses and, while they are working at improving and growing, support the team with experts.

---

[393] This quote has also been "often cited" by John C. Bogle, the founder of the Vanguard Group. *See, The Dream of a Perfect Plan,* Money Matters Conference, Boston Globe (Boston, Mass. Oct. 16, 1999), *available at* www.vanguard.com/bogle_site/lib/sp19991016.html.

Most of all, you will be successful if you keep the 12 principles in mind as you navigate plan decisions. And always approach each decision thinking of the plan participants with *undivided loyalty*.

About the Author

Charlie Yovino is the principal for Global HR GRC LLC,® and writes about, and serves as an expert witness, on HR governance, risk management, and compliance (GRC). Prior to creating Global HR GRC, ® Charlie led the Atlanta Global HR Services (GHRS) practice for PwC and was a national resource for HR and benefit plan GRC, focusing on financial management, risk management and controls, transaction effectiveness, and HR operational excellence.

Included among the variety of special projects on which Charlie has consulted are:

- Design and administrative considerations for all types of qualified and nonqualified retirement plans, including preparation of administrative manuals and quality controls
- Compliance, controls, risk management and governance reviews covering all plan and benefit types (including qualified retirement plans, nonqualified plans, COBRA, HIPAA, ACA, cafeteria plans, and others), which in the aggregate benefit approximately three million participants
- Developing strategy and implementation roadmap for global HR compliance organization
- Evaluate global benefit plan governance, compliance and risk management and propose strategy to improve GRC
- Training of plan committee members and employee benefits and Internal Audit personnel
- Work-flow and staffing studies of employee benefits departments
- Plan spin-offs, mergers, and terminations
- Due diligence reviews and golden parachute calculations
- Total benefit program design and implementation following corporate spin-offs
- Implementing benefits-based tax strategies, such as 404(k) dividend deductions
- Project management of complex benefit program

implementations, including open enrollment, benefit outsourcing, vendor transitions, and global GRC reviews involving seven-to-32 countries
- Benefit plan vendor searches and reviews

Charlie frequently speaks and writes on HR issues. The following is a sampling of his work:

Governance
- Presenter before The Governance Center at The Conference Board's Global Benefits and Compensation Roundtable on "Global De-Risking of DB Plans" (July 2014), and served as an advisor for the organizing committee on presentations
- Authored "All together now: An effective approach to global HR and benefit plan governance," HR Innovations (April 2015)
- "Improve and streamline global performance: The power of governance risk and compliance to corral chaos," HR Innovations (Winter 2014)
- Presented at the NCPERS Public Safety Employees Pension & Benefits Conference in 2008 on *"Pitfalls and Practicalities of Pension Plan Governance"*
- Co-presented a Webinar in 2008 sponsored by PwC and the National Association of State Retirement Administrators (NASRA) on *"Public Pension Plan Governance"*
- Co-authored a Whitepaper for PwC on *Plan Governance* (republished in HR Innovations, CFO Direct, and Financial Executives International)

Risk Management and Controls
- Served as a subject matter specialist on the re-write of Internal Control – Integrated Framework prepared by the Committee of Sponsoring Organizations of the Treadway Commission (COSO) (released May 2013)
- Speaker at Institute of Internal Audit (IIA) Atlanta, Boston, Las Vegas, and San Jose local chapters on "Internal Audit of HR"
- Speaker at the 2010 Profit Sharing/401(k) Council of

America National Conference on *"Risk Intelligent 401(k) Management"*

- Extensively quoted in <u>Bloomberg BNA's Human Resources Report</u> (as part of a *Workforce Strategies* white paper on managing benefit plan risks)

Compliance

- Chaired a webinar for the National Association of College and University Business Officers (NACUBO) on *"New Compliance and Audit Requirements for Section 403(b) Plans"* (2009)
- Panelist at University of Georgia's School of Law Working in the Public Interest Conference on *Issues Post-Obergefell v. Hodges* (February 2016)
- Co-presenter at webinar, *"Affordable Care Act (ACA) Employer Reporting with PwC and Workday"* (Oct. 2015)
- Contributing editor for the Thompson Publishing Group's book, <u>HR and Benefits Guide to Mergers & Acquisitions</u>
- Other articles published in sources such as: <u>The Monthly Digest of Tax Articles</u>, <u>The Journal of Compensation and Benefits</u>, <u>The Journal of Taxation of Exempt Organizations</u>, <u>Contingencies</u>, <u>The National Psychologist</u> and <u>SHRM On-Line</u>. He is often quoted in the benefits press including: <u>The Wall Street Journal</u>, <u>Business Insurance</u>, and <u>Human Resource Executive Online</u>

Prior to joining PwC, Charlie was a tax/ERISA associate with a Washington, DC law firm, and served as a Senior Reviewer in the Employee Plans Technical and Actuarial Division in the National Office of the IRS.

Charlie received his B.A. (cum laude) in history (with honors) from Hofstra University, a J.D. from American University, and a Masters of Law in Taxation from Georgetown University Law Center.

Charlie can be contacted at charles.yovino@gmail.com.

For updates on <u>Undivided Loyalty</u>, retirement plan governance, volume book discounts, and other books, please visit charlesyovino.com.

I need your help!

Remember the section on periodic assessments and getting feedback? Well, ***your feedback is critical to me!*** Providing a review at Amazon, or wherever you purchased the book, will provide that feedback and also help other potential readers.

Also, if you would like to continue on this journey and receive periodic updates, opportunities to participate in surveys, and receive benchmarking information related to plan governance, and an opportunity to have a dialogue, please go to charlesyovino.com and sign-up for periodic updates. (Don't worry, your e-mail address won't be sold or shared, and there will be only around one e-mail per month.)

Of course, if you would like to contact me directly with any questions, you can e-mail me at charles.yovino@gmail.com, or through my website, charlesyovino.com.